HMAS DIAMANTINA

Australia's last River Class frigate, 1945-1980

From war ship to oceanographic research vessel - between 1945 and 1980, Diamantina gave outstanding service to the Australian nation - in war; in making the peace; then in the Cold War years, by undertaking important oceanographic and scientific research in the Indian and Pacific Oceans.

Most of HMAS *Diamantina*'s crew, October 1945. (AWM 097608).

HMAS DIAMANTINA

Australia's last River Class frigate, 1945-1980

Peter Nunan

SLOUCH HAT PUBLICATIONS
McCrae, Australia

OTHER BOOKS ON AUSTRALIAN MILITARY HISTORY PUBLISHED OR DISTRIBUTED BY SLOUCH HAT PUBLICATIONS

AS ROUGH AS BAGS: The history of the 6th Battalion, 1914-1919 (R Austin, 1992)*
AUSTRALIAN ILLUSTRATED ENCYCLOPEDIA OF THE BOXER UPRISING 1899-1901, THE (J Corfield, 2001)
AUSTRALIAN ILLUSTRATED ENCYCLOPEDIA OF THE ZULU & BOER WARS, THE (R Austin, 1999)
BLACK AND GOLD: The history of the 29th Battalion, 1915-1918 (R Austin, 1997)
BODY SNATCHERS, THE: The history of the 3rd Field Ambulance, 1914-1918 (S & R Austin, 1995)*
BOLD, STEADY, FAITHFUL: The history of the 6th Bn, Royal Melbourne Regt, 1854-1993 (R Austin, 1993)
BUSHVELDT CARBINEERS & THE PIETERSBURG LIGHT HORSE, THE: (W Woolmore, 2002)
COBBERS IN KHAKI: The history of the 8th Battalion, 1914-1919 (R Austin, 1997, 2004)
FORWARD UNDETERRED: The history of the 23rd Battalion, 1915-1919 (R Austin, 1998)
FROM LAW TO WAR; Brig-Gen Lachlan Wilson of the Light Horse (R Likeman, 2004)
IN THE ANZAC SPIRIT: 4RAR/NZ (Anzac) South Vietnam 1968-1969 (B Avery, 2002)
KOKODA TO THE SEA: A history of the 1942 campaign in Papua (F Sublet, 2000)
KURRAH: An Australian POW in Changi, Thailand & Japan, 1942-1945 (FW Power, 1991)
LET ENEMIES BEWARE: The history of the 2/15th Battalion, 1940-1945 (R Austin, 1995)*
MAYGAR'S BOYS: Biographical history of the 8th Light Horse Regt, 1914-19 (C Simpson, 1998)
MEN OF THE NINTH: A history of the 9th Field Ambulance 1916-1994 (R Likeman, 2003)
MY CORPS CAVALRY: The history of the 13th Light Horse Regiment, 1915-1918 (D Hunter, 1999)
OUR DEAR OLD BATTALION: The story of the 7th Battalion, 1914-19 (R Austin, 2004)
OUR SECRET WAR: 4RAR Defending Malaysia Against Indonesian Confrontation, 1964-1966 (B Avery, 2001)
SILENT FEET: The history of Z Special Operations, 1942-1945 (GB Courtney, 1993, 2001)
SOLDIER'S SOLDIER, A: The life of Lt-Gen Sir Carl Jess (R Austin, 2001)
WE TOO WERE ANZACS: 6RAR/NZ (Anzac) Sth Vietnam 1969-70 [B Avery, 2004]
WHITE GURKHAS, THE: The 2nd Inf Bde at the Second Battle of Krithia, Gallipoli (R Austin, 1989, 2000)
* denotes out of print

A catalogue listing details of these and other Australian military history books is obtainable from:

SLOUCH HAT PUBLICATIONS, PO Box 174, Rosebud, 3939. Phone (61) 03 5986 6437, Fax (61) 03 5986 6312
Email: slouchat@surf.net.au Web site: www.slouch-hat.com.au

National Library of Australia.
Cataloguing-in-publication entry.

Nunan, Peter, 1938- .
HMAS Diamantina: Australia's last River class frigate, 1945-1980

Includes Index.
ISBN 0 9579752 7 9.

1. Diamantina (Frigate) - History. 2. World War, 1939-1945 - Naval Operations, Australian. 3. World War, 1939-1945 - Campaigns - Bougainville Island. 4. Research vessels - Australia - History.
I. Title.

940.545994

Cover painting by Phil Belbin
Typography & design by Double Jay Graphic Design
Printed by Impact Printing Pty Ltd, Brunswick, Victoria

CONTENTS

Foreword   6

Introduction   8

1   The Beginning   9

2   Fitout and Commission   17

3   Sydney and Workup   20

4   Bougainville   23

5   Making the Peace   30

6   1946   50

7   Second Commission 1959-1969   54

8   1970-1979   104

9   *Diamantina* Comes Home   150

Appendix 1 HMAS *Diamantina* - List of Commanding Officers   154
Appendix 2 HMAS *Diamantina* - Commissioning Ship's   154
            Company 1945
Appendix 3 Christenings in HMAS *Diamantina's* Bell   156
Appendix 4 The Name Lives On   157

Index   158

A Foreword
from
His Excellency Major General Michael Jeffery, AC, CVO, MC (Retd)
Governor-General of the Commonwealth of Australia
for the 60th Anniversary of HMAS *Diamantina*

HMAS *Diamantina* paid off on 29 February 1980; the last of the wartime frigates still in service with the Royal Australian Navy she had steamed 615,755 miles since first commissioning. But as one chapter of her life closed, so another began when the Queensland Maritime Museum Association permanently dry berthed her as an exhibit in the old graving dock at Brisbane.

Diamantina's vice-regal connections should not go unmentioned and are not limited to my experiences. Indeed she was named after the river bearing the name of the wife of the first Governor of Queensland. The ships' first commission story (1945-6), covers her construction in Maryborough, Queensland; the provision of gunfire support to the Army's Bougainville campaign as senior ship in "Savige's Navy"; participation in the surrenders of Bougainville, Nauru and Ocean Islands (the last two signed on board), and post-war cruises in New Guinea.

The second commission, carrying out civilian and naval oceanographic research, saw *Diamantina* based in Fremantle (later at HMAS *Stirling*) from 1959 to 1979. As well as research cruises in the Indian, Pacific and Southern Oceans, the ship carried out training, relief and 'show the flag' duties.

The ship's story has been written to coincide with the 60th anniversary of its commissioning which occurs on 27 April 2005. This event will be commemorated both at the Museum's South Brisbane Dry Dock – home of *Diamantina* – and in Western Australia, the base for her second commission. *Diamantina,* as the sole naval presence in Western Australia, constituted the "Western Australian Navy", and was affectionately known as the "Grey Ghost of the West Coast", sporting an unofficial black swan emblem.

My personal recollections include a very happy passage on *Diamantina* in 1960 to the north west coast of Western Australia where my SAS platoon was tasked to build coastal helicopter pads to support Army survey operations. On one occasion, whilst fishing from a small rubber boat with a soldier companion, a huge sea crocodile boarded our craft. We speedily exited and in answer to my question as to who was going to raise the anchor to get our boat plus crocodile back to shore, the young soldier rightly replied, "You're the officer Sir!"

We both survived; the crocodile did not.

A Maritime Museums of Australia Project Support Scheme Grant allowed the detailed research for the book to be undertaken. Sources including National Archives material, Navy Logs and Reports of Proceedings, as well as the interesting accounts and photographs of crew members. These are wonderful personal stories that add colour and life to the official record.

I believe that in the coming years there will be a greater focus on the South West Pacific campaign and its place in the defence of Australia from 1942 to 1945. Although we are now removed by several decades from the events of World War Two, I see this book as a contemporary reminder of the sterling service given by hundreds of Australian sailors who served their nation faithfully as officers and crew of a very fine ship.

I commend Maritime Museums of Australia for funding this project and Slouch Hat Publications for publishing an excellent work, which will contribute to a greater appreciation and understanding of the *Diamantina's* role in our national affairs, during both war and peace.

Michael Jeffery

Diamantina is Australia's largest World War II survivor and the last of over 200 River class and variant frigates the Allies built during that conflict.

In two commissions between 1945 and 1980, *Diamantina* gave outstanding service to the nation - in war, in making the peace, during the Cold War, and in oceanographic research.

Built in a long gone shipyard in a small Queensland city, crewed over her long life by thousands of men from all states and territories, based for most of her second commission in Western Australia, and operating in the Indian and Pacific Oceans to as far away as The Gulf, Hong Kong, and the Southern Ocean, *Diamantina* embodies much of the Navy's story in the latter part of the twentieth century.

It is a proud story for all Australians.

A Maritime Museums of Australia Project Support Scheme Grant financed this book's research. The Royal Australian Navy and the National Archives of Australia were generous in their assistance as were members of the oceanographic community in Australia and the United States. Former crew members from 1945 to 1980 generously shared their memories in words and pictures.

To all of these go my heartfelt thanks.

Peter Nunan

CHAPTER 1

THE BEGINNING

'Keel laid Corvette Number 4 HMAS *Diamantina* 12th. April 1943' was the entire text of The Principal Overseer, Maryborough's SECRET message of 21 April to the Assistant Chief of the Navy Board, Naval Officer in Charge, Brisbane, and The Principal Overseer, Queensland. A more detailed month's end report stated an average of 82 men had worked on the ship's hull. As well it listed expected dates of launch, sea trials, and delivery as January, July, and September 1944.

This planned 17 months construction time was optimistic and had stretched to 24 months and 15 days before the last of Australia's wartime built frigates was commissioned on 27 April 1945. In fact, only Mort's Dock's *Gascoyne*, which was completed in 16 months and 8 days, beat *Diamantina*'s proposed building time. The other four's time to delivery ranged from *Burdekin*'s 20 months and 20 days to *Lachlan*'s 22 months 23 days.

Burdekin's hull was still two months from launch on Walker's No.1 Slip when *Diamantina*'s keel was laid on No.2. HMAS *Gladstone*, the yard's last corvette/Australian Minesweeper, had vacated the fitting-out berth in March.

It was a busy time and Walkers' 1,200 men, three-quarters of them in the shipyard and its shops, were working 56 hours a week. Shift changes saw bicycles pour out the gate and through the town up to eight abreast. One resident later recalled when the tide of workers was in full flow there was "...no hope of crossing the road, although a cow once did with dire results."

Working conditions were basic with high noise levels and the air thick with rust and dust. Steel splinters and welder's flash caused eye problems. Amenities were few with buckets of water sometimes the only washing facilities. But there was also light relief as *Diamantina* grew. One retired worker recalls helping a driller working on frames aft when a lighting failure plunged them into darkness. Work continued with the driller, feeling his drill heating up, urging his helper to increase the water flow. The puzzled helper was complying and wondering at the driller's complaint. Then the lights were restored and the reason became apparent. The water had indeed kept flowing - not onto the drill, but into the tradesman's boot.

During the ship's fitting-out a boilermaker knelt on a sugarbag as he caulked a watertight door at the galley. A wayward rivet set the bag on fire. When a quick thinking mate threw the smouldering bag into the river not only did the caulker not thank him, but immediately followed it overboard. His wallet was in the bag. Both survived their immersion.

An electrician returned from unauthorised honeymoon leave to face an unexpected problem. During his absence the Low Pressure Room hatch had been installed. The switchboard he was working on should have been first put in place for the essential reason it would not fit through the hatch. A sympathetic friend carefully cut it in two; they manoeuvred the pieces down; then welded them together in place.

The monthly report for January 1944 - the initial launch date - amended the launch, trials, and delivery months to March, September, and November. Two months later, launch was put back another month to April. The May report rescheduled trials to December and delivery to January 1945. The ship was finally commissioned on 27 April 1945.

The delays had two main causes. The first was the late delivery from Sydney of the steam generators. This, in turn, held up installation of the main engines. A more important factor was the nationwide shortage of electricians. In a 23 May letter, Walkers informed the Navy that even wages of £6.17.1 ($13.71) for a 44-hour week with 12 hours overtime and a generous living-away-from-home allowance of £2.2.0 was not successful in attracting the tradesmen. There were none to be had.

Another letter in early 1945 restated the problem, *With the exception of electrical work the vessel could be completed in three to four weeks*. This crisis had been forcibly brought home to the Low Pressure Room switchboard electrician when he had tried to enlist. His interview went well, until the recruiting officer heard his trade. Immediately he terminated the interview and told the man to "...get back to Walkers at once or go under escort."

Launching

On the morning of 6 April 1944, the Thursday of Easter Week, *Diamantina*, in the Maryborough *Chronicle's* words, *...slid gracefully down the slipways into the water. It was a perfect launching...to a burst of cheering by the crowd of workmen and spectators.*

Diamantina takes to the Mary River - 6 April 1944. (Walkers)

The newspaper's Easter Saturday report, under the heading, 'Proud Moment for Walkers', detailed the proceedings. Following items from Walkers' band and the National Anthem, Mr. H. Goldsmith, the firm's General Manager, introduced Mrs. W. J. Riordan, wife of the Member of the House of Representatives for the north-western seat of Kennedy, to the large crowd. Mr. Riordan, who was also Chairman of Committees and Deputy Speaker, was absent on Government business in Cairns.

Mrs. Riordan accepted a bouquet and scissors from Mr. A. Horsburgh, Walkers' Deputy Chairman of Directors. Rev. A. Taylor led the crowd in prayer and a hymn. Then, ...*while the yard resounded to the hammering of workmen knocking away the chocks,* Mrs. Riordan spoke the words: "I name this His Majesty's Australian Ship, *Diamantina.* I congratulate the workmen who have so faithfully and skilfully constructed her. May she prove a valuable addition to the Royal Australian Navy, and may God's protecting care be on all who voyage on her." In quick succession she cut the string, the bottle smashed, and the frigate took to the water where she was taken in hand and berthed at the fitting out wharf.

The official party, which also included the local member of State Parliament and representatives of the Navy Minister and Board, adjourned to the directors' room for refreshments and more speeches. There the deputy chairman's hopes for the ship in part paralleled Mrs. Riordan's, "...May she prove a valuable addition to the Royal Australian Navy." He then went on with what turned out to be prophetic words for the vessel that was to become the RAN's longest serving, and the world's last survivor of the River class frigates: "...The workmanship of Walkers Ltd. will stand the test of all weather and will prove the *Diamantina* equal to all the world's best of its class of warship."

River Class Frigates

In 1940, as U-Boats ranged further into the Atlantic from their recently acquired French bases, the need for more ocean-going escort vessels became acute. The Flower class corvettes, built to a whale-catcher design as coastal escorts, were too small for the increased weapons, crew, and range needed.

So, that year, 27 'Twin Screw Corvettes' were ordered. The type was also designated 'New Corvettes', and 'Twin Screw Long Endurance'. Designed to have better sea-keeping ability, and be more spacious, powerful, and heavily armed, these vessels differed so greatly from the Flowers that the designation, 'Frigate', incorrectly resurrected by the Canadians for them, was adopted by the Admiralty; 57 River Class were built in Britain, 8 in Australia, and 70 in Canada. The United States adapted the design to produce 74 Tacoma class vessels. The Canadian vessels were named after locations and towns, while the British and Australian ships followed the class title and bore the names of rivers.

The ships were a simple design so they could be rapidly built in small shipyards. The old-fashioned low-pressure steam reciprocating engines were also chosen for ease of construction, and also because the many reserve and ex-merchant navy personnel who would operate them were familiar with the type. These four-cylinder, triple expansion, reliable, rugged engines, the culmination of 160 years of development, produced a top speed of 20 knots. They are regarded as the finest of their type to serve with the Royal Australian Navy.

The ships, costing below £500,000, had an initial range of 7,500 nautical miles at a speed of 10 knots. The range of later vessels exceeded 9,000 miles.

Crew conditions were markedly better than on the 'Flowers'. As well as the excellent sea-keeping qualities there was sheltered access to boiler and engine rooms, more space, upper deck shelters for gun and depth charge crews, and drying rooms.

Armament reflected the anti-submarine mission. Four throwers and two rails for depth charges were mounted aft, and a Hedgehog for firing contact-fused bombs ahead of the ship was on the foredeck. Two single four-inch guns were mounted and 20mm Oerlikon guns provided anti-aircraft and close-range surface fire.

HMS *Rother* went down the ways on 20 November 1941 and sisters followed rapidly. Average building time was 14 months, with the record being 8 months and 17 days.

As with all ship types, experience with the early vessels led to constant modification. HMAS *Gascoyne*, the first of 22 Rivers ordered by the Royal Australian Navy for the Pacific War, was launched on 20 February 1943 - 15 months after *Rother*. So it is not surprising that experience and the Pacific's different war meant the Australian Rivers differed from the Royal Navy's vessels in detail - especially in armament, radar types, and ventilation. The Pacific Theatre was rather different from the Atlantic.

Anti-aircraft defence was improved in succeeding ships with high-angle low-angle mounts for the four-inch guns, and some of the 20 mm. Oerlikons and 40 mm. Bofors installed with power mountings. The four inch guns had a range of 19,500 yards and a ceiling of 30,000 feet.

Following *Gascoyne*'s commissioning on 18 November 1943, after 15 months and 8 days' construction time, came *Barcoo, Burdekin, Hawkesbury, Lachlan*, and *Diamantina* - which on 27 April 1945, was the last to be commissioned during the war. *Macquarie* and *Barwon* followed in December 1945.

Of the remaining 14 ordered, *Condamine, Shoalhaven, Murchison,* and *Culgoa* were completed to the modified Bay class design in 1946 and 1947. The other 10, including *Balmain* and *Williamstown*, named for their building sites rather than rivers, were cancelled in April 1944.

The ranks of the Australian 'Rivers' and 'Bays', products of dockyards in Sydney, Melbourne, Newcastle, Brisbane, and Maryborough, began to be thinned when the distinguished veterans of the Korean War, *Murchison* and *Shoalhaven*, were scrapped in September 1961 and January 1962 respectively. The others followed them into oblivion - except for *Diamantina*. Today, in the old South Brisbane Dry Dock, at the Queensland Maritime Museum, Australia's largest World War II relic, and the world's last River class frigate lives on into the new millennium to honour its Second World War sisters and their crews, and to educate and inspire its visitors.

Diamantina, Bowen and River

The Royal Australian Navy's River Class's names ranged from West Australia's *Gascoyne* through Tasmania's *Macquarie*, Victoria's *Barwon*, New South Wales's *Hawkesbury* and *Lachlan*, to Queensland's *Barcoo, Burdekin*, and *Diamantina*.

The name, Diamantina, brings together so many Australian threads. The river is typical of so many of ours - flowing only after rare heavy rains through its 150,000 sq. km. basin and dropping less than 300 metres over a 900 km course from north-west of Longreach towards Lake Eyre in one of the world's largest inland drainage basins. It is only in occasional floods that the Diamantina joins the Georgina to form the Warburton and actually reach Lake Eyre. In its course the river divides to form part of Queensland's Channel Country. Most of the time the bed is dry sand between waterholes. Combo Waterhole on Dagworth Station 150 km north of Wintons is the most famous. Here, during the shearers' strike of 1894, occurred the events immortalised in *Waltzing Matilda*. Banjo Paterson wrote the words soon afterwards during a visit to the area.

Like Australia itself the river's name has changed. McKinlay first put it on the map as Mueller's Creek in 1862. Landsborough later renamed it Diamantina after Lady Diamantina Bowen, wife of Queensland's first Governor. Diamantina, Countess Roma, of a noble Ionian Islands family of Italian origin married Sir George Bowen in Corfu.

Three years later, on 10 December 1859, the slender, graceful 27-year-old daughter of the former Prince President of the Ionian Senate landed in Brisbane as the wife of the new colony's first Governor. When she left eight years later, the name of the first Greek lady to live in Australia was firmly lodged in Queenslanders' hearts and on the map. In Brisbane Countess and Roma Streets, and a statue in West End commemorate her. The town of Roma bears her family name, as the river has her given name.

The Bowens' later vice-regal postings included New Zealand, Victoria, Hong Kong, and Mauritius - all places visited by the ship that was later to carry the name of the lady who had made her debut into society at a ball in Athens on board the Royal Navy's then largest ship, HMS *Albion*.

Diamantina, in its second commission, adopted Diamantina Candiano Roma's family shield that incorporates a heraldic eagle, a ducal coronet, and a martello tower. However, one source asserts, her family's Latin motto, *Respice finem* ('Look upon the end') was replaced by that of Philip II Duke of Pomerania (1573-1618) - *Hic regit, ille tuetur* (Literally, 'This rules, that protects', and generally rendered as 'He who rules also protects').

Walkers and Shipbuilding

HMAS *Diamantina* was the twenty-fifth of 69 ships built by Walkers at Maryborough in three periods between 1877 and 1974. The title of R. S. Maynard's 1946 company history, *Sugar, Ships and Locomotives*, captures the variety of Walkers' products since the firm's founding in 1864. Today Walkers makes and repairs equipment for the sugar, railway, mining, and general engineering industries. For Australia's railways alone, the firm has produced a variety of rolling stock and over 700 locomotives ranging through the steam, diesel, and electric eras.

The shipyard was established in 1877 to fill a Queensland Government order for three 350 tons self-propelled barges, *Nautilus*, *Dugong*, and *Schnapper*, for the Brisbane River. Two steam bucket dredges, *Saurian* and *Maryborough*, and five more self-propelled 350 tons barges for the Brisbane River, *Bonito*, *Stingaree*, *Pumba*, *Bream*, and *Dolphin* followed.

Another Government order saw the completion in 1880 of the stern-wheeled paddle steamer *Pioneer* from parts prefabricated in Britain. *Pioneer* then ran the mails between Gladstone and Rockhampton via the narrow channel separating Curtis Island from the mainland. The timber carrier, *Pacific*, and the paddle tug, *Sea Horse*, were handed over in 1884.

Sugar barges, lighters, and buoys, as well as gold and tin dredge pontoons were other products of this first 10-year shipbuilding phase. Then, from 1888 to 1918 the shipyard area was used to produce structural girders and boilers for stationary engines and locomotives.

With the Australian Government's 1917 decision to build ships at home for its new Commonwealth Shipping Line, Walkers were contracted to produce four 330 ft (100 m) 6,600 deadweight tons E class freighters. Two side by side building berths were constructed in 1919 to accommodate vessels of up to 350 ft (107 m) length and 55 ft (17 m) beam. The 350 wooden slipway piles were driven through 30 ft (9 m) of silt to solid rock. Then work began on the 'Billy Hughes' ships, *Echuca* and *Echunga*.

However, after these vessels were delivered in 1922 and 1923 the other orders were cancelled and the yards went silent until a Queensland Government contract for a 200 ft (61 m) steam bucket dredge renewed activity in 1925. But this was the last order and when *Platypus II* with her Walkers' built machinery and boilers was completed in 1928 the shipyard closed again.

The Second World War's outbreak on 3 September 1939, triggered the shipyard's reopening for what was its final and biggest phase. An Australian Government approach to the company to construct warships set off a period of intense activity. Silt and undergrowth were cleared from the slipways. Material was assembled, including an electric crane from interstate that served in 1942 as the model for another the company built itself.

Workers, too, were gathered. To the company's boilermakers were added men of the 30 other trades needed to build the ships. No time was wasted. Maryborough's first Australian Minesweeper's keel was laid in April 1940. HMAS *Maryborough* was launched exactly six months later on 17 October. During her construction the yard's workforce expanded 600%.

Maryborough entered service on 12 June 1941, nine months after her launching. It was not a bad performance for a company whose last ship had been completed 13 years before, and whose only previous experience in warship construction had been the provision of gun supports on two of the Brisbane River barges of the previous century.

Seven other Australian Minesweepers, *Toowoomba, Rockhampton, Cairns, Tamworth, Bowen*, and *Gladstone*, slid down Walkers' ways between 26 March 1941 and 26 November 1942. With *Tamworth* outfitting and *Bowen* about to make way for *Gladstone* on No. 2 Slip, a new keel was laid on No. 1 Slip in mid-1942. HMAS *Burdekin*, Walkers' first River class frigate, was 301.5 ft (91.5 m) overall, over 60% longer and twice the tonnage of an Australian Minesweeper. *Burdekin*, the first of three Walkers' built Rivers, was launched on 30 June 1943. *Diamantina* followed on 6 March 1944, and *Shoalhaven*, the last of Maryborough's wartime ships, took to the water on 14 December 1944.

At its peak Walkers employed 1,200 men working 56-hour weeks. Shipbuilding was not the only war work. Ships were also overhauled and repaired while other engineering products included anti-aircraft gun bases and four 1000-ton presses for producing shell cases.

But 90% of the firm's war effort was concentrated on building and outfitting ships. All Walkers' seven Australian Minesweepers and three frigates were also engined and fitted out by the company. Maryborough's ship furniture of metal and Queensland red cedar and tulipwood was reputed to be the best supplied to Australian warships. And the company's products were not restricted to its own ships. In fact none of the over 70 Australian built minesweepers and frigates were completed without some Walkers products ranging from steam and diesel engines through propeller shafts, pumps, watertight doors, winches, to valves and fittings.

With peace and the delivery of *Shoalhaven* shipyard output turned to a mixture of merchant and warships. The yard's location, 30 km upstream from the Mary River's mouth inhibited vessel size, but 43 varied ships were launched between the war's end and final closure in 1974. Seven coastal freighters, four dredges, a gravel barge, three survey vessels, one lighthouse tender, a seismic exploration and two oil rig supply vessels made up the merchant total. As well, 10 patrol boats, 8 heavy landing craft, 3 tugs, 2 general-purpose vessels, and a boom defence ship were built for the Defence Department.

The post war period saw many changes. As diesel power replaced steam the company's last steam propulsion engine went into HMAS *Kimbla* in 1955. Welding completely replaced riveting in 1966. A $670,000 modernisation programme, begun in 1963, was aimed at facilitating production and reducing costs. It made possible construction of ships up to 350 ft (107 m) long, 55 ft (17 m) wide and with a launch weight of 2,500 tons at the same time as smaller vessels. With assembly line construction, the 10 patrol boats were launched at an average interval of seven weeks.

Speaking after *Diamantina's* launching on 6 April 1944, the Commanding Officer of Maryborough's RAAF station identified himself as *...a Melbournite posted from South Australia to Maryborough...* He went on to state he *...was surprised to find it was such a big town and such an important industrial city...* It still is, and Maryborough and Walkers paid tribute to the shipyard's importance in the rise of the firm and the city, when they sponsored the memorial to the wartime shipbuilders and crews unveiled on 14 August 1993.

Diamantina's First Captain

Diamantina and her captain receive the usual footnote sketches in the second volume of the Royal Australian Navy's World War II history: HMAS *Diamantina*, frigate (1945), two 4-in. guns, 20 kts; and LCDR M. G. Rose, RANVR. RN 1940-44; commd. *Diamantina* 1945. Of Sydney; b. Reading, England, 22 Sep. 1902.

Accountant Maurice George Rose, whose first voyage was in 1919, had a long war. In an April 1980 letter to a shipmate, Rose referred to an imminent four-month European trip in which *...one of my objects is to re-visit the area between Narvik and Harstad where I operated in 1940 before Dunkirk.* Rose joined the Royal Australian Navy Volunteer Reserve as a lieutenant in 1934. In mid-1939, before the outbreak of war, he completed the anti-submarine course at HMAS *Rushcutter* in Sydney. Mobilised on 30 October that year, the mature-aged lieutenant had a short stint as Gunnery Officer on the surveying vessel, HMAS *Moresby* before sailing from Sydney on 10 January 1940 as a passenger on the Second AIF's first convoy to serve on loan to the Royal Navy.

Six weeks on the ex-Norwegian whale catcher HMS *Buttermere* ended when he went ashore at Harstad as *... an absolutely lone bird living in a Norwegian village [Evenskjar] where I commanded a flotilla of diesel fishing craft for the purpose of disembarking allied troops.* These included *...the Scots Guards with their chest plainly marked 'Officers' Mess silver'.*

Evacuated in June, Rose joined, as First Lieutenant, the corvette HMS *Erica* building at Harland and Wolff in Belfast. The ship was commissioned in July 1940. Promotion to Acting Lieutenant Commander with seniority from 4 October aroused in the 38 year old thoughts of his own command. So Rose wrote to the Admiralty informing them that, if this happened, he would like not a trawler, but a new corvette from Harland and Wolff, all his officers to be Australian Reservists, and named a friend who he desired as his First Lieutenant, Rose also requested that his anti-submarine ratings be Australians.

My Lords of the Admiralty had, surprisingly, granted every wish but one, when Rose commissioned HMS *Alisma* on 30 January 1941. His friend was not First Lieutenant - he was unavailable, already commanding a trawler. The new captain's specific request for a Harland and Wolff ship had come after a study of vessels from various yards convinced him of the superiority of that company's craft.

A year's unrelenting grind on North Atlantic convoys was followed by a February 1942 refit. Then it was back to the convoys. Christmas 1942, Rose's fourth away from home and his third at sea, was celebrated as a stormy westbound crossing in which U-boats had claimed four of the convoy was ending. One sinking, the destroyer, HMS *Firedrake*, had resulted in the loss of more than 200 from a ship's company of just over 230.

At this grim time, two days out of Argentia, Newfoundland, Christmas Day dawned fine and calm. The day further improved when a merchant ship signalled *Alisma* to close for provisions. Smartly there passed to the corvette a sack of potatoes, two of oranges and apples, one of 10,000 cigarettes, and a final transfer of enough pork for the whole ship's company together with a turkey. The stokers' mess won the toss for the turkey. Then the crew settled down to ...*truly a day of peace on earth and goodwill towards men.*

Two round trips later it was a different story. Late in March 1943 *Alisma* was part of the escort group that joined the eastbound convoy HX231. It was Rose's last voyage in command of the corvette. The crossing went down as a pivotal battle of the North Atlantic struggle. By dusk 31 March, Escort Group B7 (Cdr. [later Vice-Admiral] Peter Grettons) had marshalled the convoy into formation. The 61 ships in 13 columns covered an area six nautical miles wide and two miles deep.

Grettons tells the crossing's story in his 1974 book, *Crisis Convoy*; 21 U-Boats were directed onto the convoy and 17 initiated attacks between 4 and 7 April. The total result of all this effort was the loss of only six ships, three in the convoy and three others who had become detached. As well, two submarines were sunk and four others severely damaged.

The Escort Commander, with his destroyer refitting, was embarked on the River class frigate, *Tay*. He draws pen pictures of his force of one old destroyer, the frigate and four corvettes. His portrait of *Alisma*; The Alisma (K185) *was commanded by an Australian, Lieutenant-Commander M.G. Rose, RANVR and the remaining officers also came from 'down under', though the ship's company was from the United Kingdom. This unusual combination worked very well. The Australians had the advantage of a longer and more thorough training in anti-submarine warfare than had their British opposite numbers and the A/S standards of the* Alisma *were high. Rose, an accountant in private life, had been in command for some time and had escorted many convoys.*

There was another Australian captain in the escort - Lieutenant Harold Chesterman, RNR, commanded *Snowflake*. At dusk on 4 April the first submarine attacks sank one ship and damaged another that sank two days later. Early on the 5th *Alisma* detected and attacked a U-Boat with 10 depth charges. Post-war analysis revealed U564 was so damaged it had to return to base.

Torpedo damage to a tanker in the middle of the convoy about noon that day presaged a busy night for *Alisma*. Between 8.30 and 10 pm, three contacts each received 10 depth charges. Then came hours of silent vigil until at 3.10 am, 6 April, radar detected a surfaced submarine 2,000 yards away. Star shell forced the boat to dive and asdic tracked it until a pattern of depth charges was dropped. Rose's claim of damage to the enemy was not endorsed by the Admiralty on the grounds of 'insufficient evidence'. Grettons, writing years later and with the advantage of consulting evidence on both sides, credits *Alisma* with sinking U635 ...*at 0315*... and goes on, *It would certainly be a well-earned reward for a great night's work.*

HX231's hectic three days finally ended with a last fruitless U-Boat attack on 7 April. This action gained Rose his second Mentioned in Despatches. The 9 November citation notes the Commanding Officer's *initiative and dash*, and goes on, *This officer has commanded his Australian-manned [sic.] corvette with distinction since January 1941.*

Events had overtaken the citation writer. Late in April Rose had handed command of *Alisma* to his First Lieutenant to stand by and, in May, commission the new River class frigate, *Fal*. Nine months after that, in Freetown, Sierra Leone, he again relinquished command. This time it was to return to Australia for leave and three months of courses in Sydney before again standing by and commissioning a new River class frigate.

Rose arrived in Maryborough in October 1944. There the Commanding Officer, whose critical eye had been developed three long years before at Harland and Wolff's in far away Belfast, oversaw *Diamantina*'s completion. He later wrote, *I soon realised she was being constructed with first rate skill.*

CHAPTER 2

FITOUT AND COMMISSION

Diamantina (K377) shared the fitting out berth with her elder sister *Burdekin* until K376 was commissioned on 27 June 1944. Exactly 10 months later *Diamantina* joined the fleet.

Before *Burdekin*'s departure the ships had unwelcome visitors who considerably embarrassed the local defence force. Six Z Force trainees in three canoes tested their skills and dockyard security in an unconventional mock attack. Transported from their Fraser Island base on the unit's 9.75 m ketch, the three canoes were dropped at the Mary River mouth and entered the heads at 9.30 pm. The raiders reached their targets around 2 am. West Australian RAAF sergeants Jack Sue and his cousin Peter Wong quickly attached inert limpet mines below *Diamantina*'s waterline before passing downriver and across Hervey Bay to return to the island.

Captains Robinson and Lennard of the AIF, and Scots RAF officers Flt.Lt. Bird and PO Robertson went one better. After placing their mines on *Burdekin* they boarded the ship to chalk crosses on the gun mounts and even the captain's door. This extra activity meant they did not clear the river by dawn and were forced to hole up for the day before returning to camp the next night. It was a small price to pay for such a successful exercise.

The division of the labour force among the two fitting out frigates and *Shoalhaven* building on the slip contributed to *Diamantina*'s long fitting out time. Up to *Burdekin*'s completion fewer than 200 men worked on *Diamantina*. The peak of 306 was reached in August and then declined as *Shoalhaven* progressed. In the month before her commissioning *Diamantina*'s workforce sank to a low 149.

As construction progressed key crewmembers began to arrive. LCDR Rose had turned over command of his Royal Navy River class frigate *Fal* in Freetown in February 1944 and returned to Sydney for leave and three months of courses at HMAS *Rushcutter* to prepare him for his new command of a familiar ship type in a different ocean and war. In October a long train trip brought him to Maryborough and *Diamantina*.

Rose's dockside office was a short walk from his home, the Carlton Hotel, where he and his officers were quartered for six months. The ratings, as they arrived, were accommodated in former army barracks.

The most junior officer, Sub-Lt. Ian Parkin, was only 16 months out of school when he joined two months before commissioning. He recalls this as a comparatively easy time for deck officers. His main jobs as assistant to the navigator were correcting piles of charts and getting to know the ship and its crew.

Specialist officers and ratings were busier. The Engineer Officer, LCDR Ken Bull and his petty officers in particular had their hands full. Off duty, life in Maryborough was good. Ken Bull, in those days of strict petrol rationing, fulfilled a long held dream and bought a pony and sulky. He and 'Roslyn' became well known around the town. Mrs. Bull, on a visit before commissioning, came to realise her junior position to her husband in Maryborough society when the hotel maid, after deferentially addressing Ken, called to her as, "You at the back."

The whole crew enjoyed generous hospitality in public functions and invitations to peoples' homes. One 18-year-old radar operator was particularly fortunate - his uncle was president of the local RSL. Ken Bull was a popular guest at dinners with his invariable compliment to his hostess that "The memory of the dinner will linger long," followed with an offer to dry the dishes.

On 27 February 1945 at 7.30 am, *Diamantina* steamed downriver for shipyard trials in Hervey Bay. Then followed two months of tests and trials by Walkers' men and Navy engineers before commissioning.

The ship's Commissioning Ball at the Town Hall on Tuesday 24 April, the eve of Anzac Day, was the first of the season. The Maryborough *Chronicle* reported it as setting *...an excellent standard for the balls to follow.* The Mayor and Mayoress joined the ship's officers and the local army commander in the official party. Over 500 guests enjoyed dancing and a buffet supper up to and past the official 1 am close. The *...over 100 Jack Tars from all states of the Commonwealth* enjoyed not only the night but also the profits from the 3/6 (35 cents) paid by each dancer and 2/- by gallery spectators. The money was used to establish the ship's canteen.

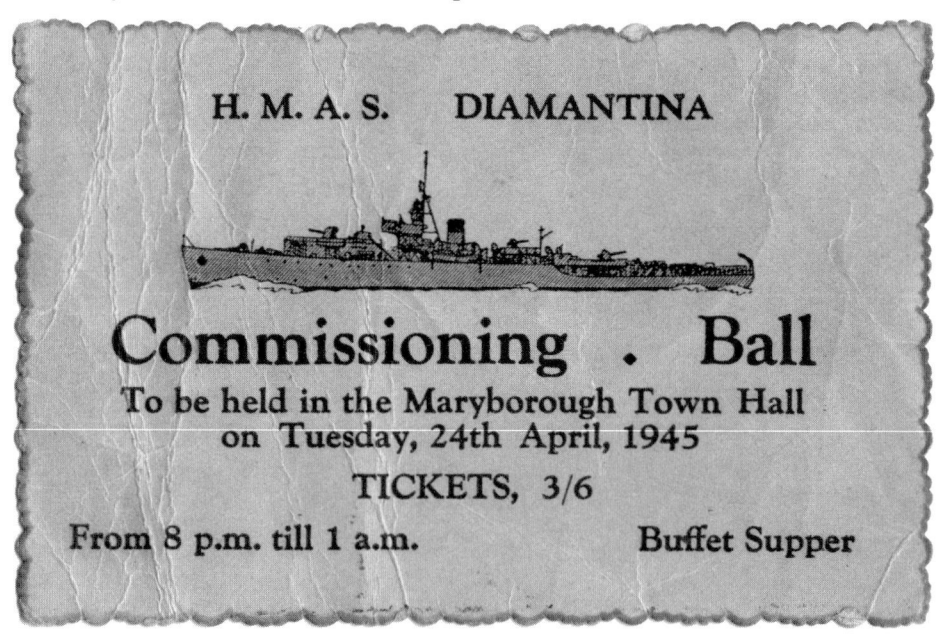

Commissioning Ball ticket (Queensland Maritime Museum collection)

LCDR Rose the next morning, at the head of his ship's company, led his first wartime Anzac Day march in Australia and laid a wreath at the Cenotaph. Then, after handing over to his First Lieutenant, he drove to the saluting base to take his place beside Wing Commander Winter-Irving, the local RAAF commander, as his crew led the march past.

At the subsequent citizens' service in the Town Hall, Rose seconded the loyalty motion. Then, at the Diggers' lunch, the captain spoke again. This time, however, his theme was not the usual one of servicemen or the fallen but rather "...our womenfolk...[who]...had carried the responsibility of caring for our children and our homes while we had been overseas, yet they were not awarded any decorations."

In the afternoon the new frigate was open to the people of the town that built her. Later Rose recalled that while over half the town had inspected the vessel the paintwork had remained completely unblemished. The busy Anzac Day ended with the crew boarding the ship to take up their quarters.

Next morning, with a local river pilot guiding and a minimum of ammunition, stores, and fuel embarked, *Diamantina* moved downriver to clear the bar at the peak of high water spring tide with a scant 30 cm clearance. Acceptance trials occupied a full day. Then, with the ship anchored close to Fraser Island, Rose signed a receipt and the builders left.

Z Force raided again that night. The ship's watch detected their canoes' approach well before the commandoes boarded to *...whoop and yahoo through the upper mess decks*. One canoe didn't make it and was swept past the ship and a line thrown from the stern to be cast up miles away in mangroves. Somehow the ship's crew, after their disturbed sleep, felt not a shred of sympathy when they heard the two raiders had to make a long hot portage through the mangroves back to their camp.

At 8.a.m.the next morning, Friday, 27 April 1945, anchored at Tyroom Roads, with the officers and men fallen in on the quarterdeck the White Ensign was hoisted and LCDR Rose commissioned HMAS *Diamantina*. Late in the morning the ship sailed for Sydney. The ship's log first entries laconically record the events:

> 0800 Ship commissioned
> 0815 Hands turned to daily routine
> 0905 Alarm bells tested
> 1059 Commenced heaving in anchor.
> 1103 Anchor aweigh.

Trials in Hervey Bay, April 1945, with Hedgehog uncovered on the foredeck (Walkers)

CHAPTER 3

SYDNEY AND WORKUP

At 3.50 pm, 27 April 1945, the Breaksea Spit light buoy off Fraser Island's northern tip was half a mile to starboard; 10 minutes later course was set south-east for Sydney, and *Diamantina* met the open sea for the first time into a Force 4/5 south-easter.

The new ship's company, drawn from all states of the Commonwealth, began the process of working up into a crew. For many young men like Sub-Lt. Parkin and 18-year-old Radar Operator Murray McFarlane this was their first ship. All the officers, from the captain down, were reservists. But there was also a good leavening of experience. One of Parkin's jobs was assistant to the Supply Officer and he found in the crew records that many had served with distinction on RN and RAN ships in all theatres. The reservist captain, for example, had crammed a lot of experience into four years' service in the stormy North Atlantic before he left HMS *Fal* in February 1944 to stand by and commission *Diamantina*.

But Rose's North Atlantic experience counted for nothing on the short and lively run on a not so pacific Pacific to Sydney. The light ship, drawing only 9 feet 9 inches forward and 11 feet 9.5 inches aft combined with the south-easter to give the crew a rough passage. The captain blamed the long good time ashore in Maryborough for the severe sea-sickness that afflicted many in the lower deck and five of the eight officers - including himself.

Still the two days of choppy seas and delays caused by a faulty engine room valve were behind them when the gleaming blue frigate, dressed overall, and with its crew smartly lining the sides, approached the boom inside Sydney Heads. LCDR Rose's previous commands had been in another navy on the other side of the world. Now he was bringing his smart new Australian ship into his home city.

As *Diamantina* passed through the anti-submarine boom a dirty offal barge pushed by an equally disreputable looking tug was exiting. Its course caused *Diamantina* to take hasty avoiding action. Rose promptly used the loud hailer to voice his opinion of the tug's errant ways. A moment later there emerged from the smaller vessel's wheelhouse a squat man whose shabby dress matched his craft and in no way approached that of the crew of the smart ship towering above him. Not in the least abashed he fixed his gaze on the frigate's bridge and delivered a loud sustained torrent of obscenity. Nowhere in it, the poker-faced frigate's crew noted, was, "Welcome to Sydney." After this, tying up at Kurraba oiling jetty at 4.10 p.m. was an anticlimax.

25 days of constant work fixed defects, completed the electrical installations and installed LORAN. The ship passed inclining tests, was degaussed, and the magnetic compasses were adjusted. V-E celebrations were a welcome diversion as *Diamantina* continued her preparations for the Pacific war.

On Anzac Day LCDR. W.J. Nethertons had reported favourably on the ship's gun trials in Hervey Bay. He enumerated the weapons:

> 4" gun Mk.XVI* on Mk.XX mounting in B position—centreline
> forward signal deck.
> 4" gun Mk.XVI* on Mk.XX mounting in X position on upper deck aft.
> 40 mm. Bofors Mk.1 on Mk.IIIA mount on starboard side quarterdeck.

40 mm. Bofors Mk.1 on Mk.IIIA mount on port side quarterdeck.
20 mm. Oerlikon Mk.IV (Mk.VIIA) starboard wing of bridge.
    "   "   "   "   port   "   "   "
Twin 20 mm. Oerlikons Mk.IV (power Mk.Vc mounting) stbd. side fcsl deck abreast ER casing.
    "   (Mk.IV, II)   port   "
Twin .303 Bren (Mk.V twin) stbd. side lower bridge.
      "   "   "   port   "   "
.303 Vickers (.303 Vickers) stbd. side upper deck abreast 4" gun shelter fwd.
    "   "   "   port   "   "   "   "
3x .455 Thompson SMG in rack on mess deck.
3x.303 SMLE rifles on rack in lobby fwd.of ward room.
1x.303 Linethrowing.
1x Schermuly in Gunner's store.

Depth charges
Rails 2 sets capacity 12 charges at stern.
Throwers 2xMk.IV 25'9" from stern angled 90 degrees from centre line.
    "   "   35'9"   "   "   95   "   "   "
Depth charge stowage: in rails 24; on throwers 4; elsewhere on upper deck 30; in depth charge magazine 52.
Hedgehog on forward deck.

In Sydney the gun mounts for the port and starboard twin Oerlikons and the port and starboard Bofors were replaced and both 4" guns and their mountings tested. An additional Bofors was mounted on the forward gun shelter. On 17 and 18 May, trials of all weapons were carried out. (Murray McFarlane, No. 1 on the starboard twin Brens, wrote, in a letter of 19 July 2000, the Vickers machineguns were not used in action. Most likely they were landed when the Bofors was installed.)

On 24 May, to avoid a looming Sydney industrial dispute delaying the fitting of the anti-submarine gear, the ship was fully ammunitioned, the gear loaded, and, at 4.30 pm, *Diamantina* sailed for Brisbane. A pleasant two-day transit was followed by three days at a wharf before the vessel entered the South Brisbane Dry Dock on 29 May. It was the frigate's first time out of the water since her launch on 6 April 1944.

In the dock the Type 144Q anti-submarine dome was fitted and the hull cleaned and painted. An unpleasant surprise, *...the amazing amount of corrosion which has taken place on the shell plates below the waterline of this new vessel* was reported in the Base Engineer's letter of 1 June to the Navy Office in Melbourne. A later letter from the Chief of Construction sheeted home the cause to either galvanic action from mill scale or zinc plate corrosion and recommended Walkers' future vessels *...be well wire brushed and cleaned and painted before launching.* Zinc plates were added before *Diamantina* left the dock on 2 June.

Day and night 4" and anti-aircraft gunnery shoots in Moreton Bay that showed up a defect in the forward 4" mounting preceded the return to Sydney. The run south was a fast one through rain and early heavy weather that caused many to regret their pork chop breakfasts alongside at Pinkenba before the ship slipped at 7.15 a.m. on 9 June. In the moderate seas the following morning *Diamantina* romped along, covering 149 nautical miles from 6 am to noon - 26 between 10 and 11. She tied up at Garden Island at 3.04 pm.

With the forward 4" gun and mounting replaced the frigate sailed at 6.32 am on 14 June for two days gunnery trials off Point Perpendicular, Jervis Bay. The 4" guns' targets were towed by HMS *Guardian* while the anti-aircraft crews peppered drogues trailing behind Vultee Vengeance aircraft. At 2.15 pm on 15 June, a louder explosion punctuated the gunfire. The log records its cause as ...*one depth charge accidentally dropped overboard.*

At 5.25 pm on 16 June, *Diamantina* began taking on a capacity load of fuel at Kurraba oil wharf. The ship sailed at 7.02 am the next day. Seven weeks of working up were over. She was off to war.

It was an idyllic passage off the coast to Curtis Channel and then via Hillsborough Channel and the Whitsunday Passage. Telegraphist Stanley Lane noted in his diary *the beautiful weather, pale blue sea, and the intensely green islands.*

After berthing at Cairns at 3.22 pm on 21 June, the crew enjoyed leave while four and a half tons of naval workshop machinery went aboard. The next day at 8.20 a.m. they sailed for Madang. The Great Barrier Reef transit via Graftons Passage led to a calm deep blue Coral Sea with skimming flying fish. The New Guinea coast was raised at 10 am on 23 June. *Diamantina* rounded the island's eastern tip, passed through China Strait, crossed the entrance to Milne Bay, and then tracked north-west to anchor at Madang on 25 June at 10.57 am.

Here, *just a place* in Lane's diary entry, was Australian naval headquarters. Mail came aboard and the crew caught a five-foot shark. The captain reported ashore to receive orders and new American charts of the ship's area of operations - Bougainville. More high explosive 4" ammunition came aboard and 11 ratings joined for passage.

They sailed for Torokina, Bougainville, at 5.05 pm 26 June. In a brief stop at Langemak an American oiler topped up the fuel and one passage rating landed. Then, as the ship traced its course for Torokina, the crew learned the reason for taking on the high explosive ammunition - the ship's likely assignment was bombardment duty.

LCDR Rose used his new American charts to con his ship into Torokina harbour and dropped anchor at 10.25 am on 29 June. The passage ratings disembarked. *Diamantina* had arrived in her theatre of war. But when Rose transferred his anchorage's latitude and longitude to the frigate's Admiralty chart the captain was forcibly made aware of a local hazard just as dangerous as enemy action - his ship's position, according to the old chart, was five nautical miles inland.

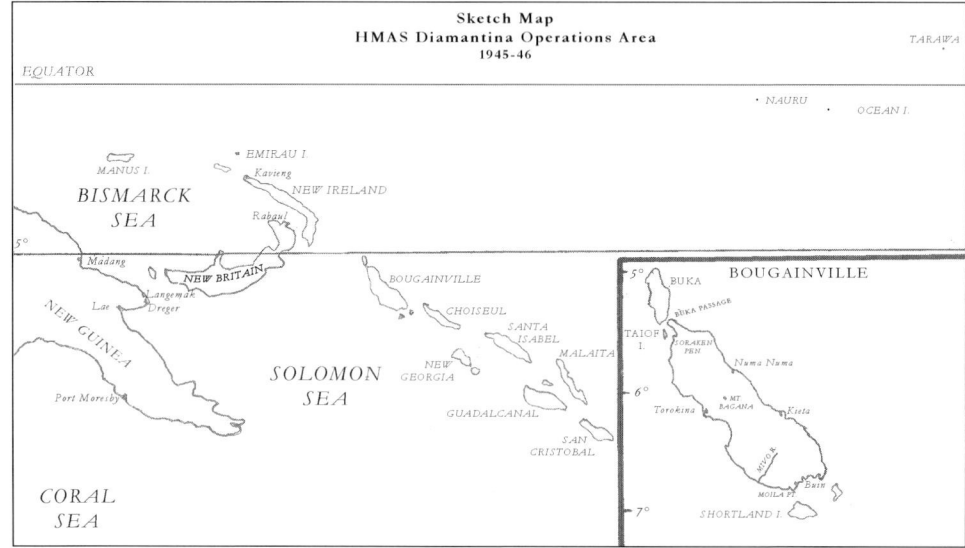

Sketch Map
HMAS Diamantina Operations Area
1945-46

CHAPTER 4

THE BOUGAINVILLE CAMPAIGN

The 1 November 1943 American landing at Torokina was part of their western Pacific advance. The difficult Torokina site was chosen on the quite correct assumption that the Japanese defence there would be light. By the time the enemy was able to mount a counter attack, an airfield was in operation, the perimeter was secure, and the attack was repulsed.

The US Pacific advance then moved on, cutting off the Japanese in north and south Bougainville from their main forces. Pursuing a policy of letting such isolated garrisons 'wither on the vine', the US forces left them alone.

When on 12 December 1944, the Australian II Corps replaced the last of the American XIV Corps, the Torokina perimeter was only 15 miles by 7 (24 x 11 km). The opposing forces had adopted a tacit policy of 'live and let live,' with the Americans setting up a comfortable base and the isolated enemy, cut off from resupply, and with one-third not fit to fight and another third occupied in gardening and fishing, devoting most of their energy to the struggle to stay alive.

This all changed when the Australians launched attacks on the Japanese to the south, east, and north of Torokina. This Bougainville campaign was not popular. Many Australians agreed with Macarthur that the cut off enemy should be left to 'wither on the vine' as the war drew to its close. Peter Charlton includes Bougainville in his 1983 book, *The Unnecessary War*. On the other hand, the Australian Army commander, General Blamey, argued the Army, while keeping casualties to a minimum, should free Australian territory and liberate the local people.

So, the Australians went on the attack in Bougainville and the Japanese were stung into resistance. The Americans had estimated the island's enemy strength at 12,000. Australian intelligence put the figure at 25,000. In fact, the enemy numbered almost 40,000 including elite marines. There were some fierce clashes.

When, after the dropping of the atomic bombs, Tokyo ordered its forces to cease fire on 15 August, the eight months Bougainville campaign's casualty lists were not light. About 9,800 Japanese had died of illness and 8,500 in action. Australia's losses were 516 killed and 1,572 wounded.

The Role

Diamantina became senior ship of the eight RAN vessels supporting II Australian Corps's Bougainville campaign. In addition to the brand new frigate, the corvettes *Kiama*, *Lithgow*, *Dubbo*, four Motor Launches, ML 427, 428, 808, and 816, and army landing barges made up 'Savige's Private Navy.' Although contact with major Japanese naval forces was unlikely, the ships faced hazards from enemy artillery and reefs in the sketchily charted waters. The danger from enemy land fire had been made very apparent a month before the frigate's arrival when, on 26 May in a late afternoon action at Choiseul Bay, two hits from enemy artillery killed two sailors on the corvette, HMAS *Colac*, and flooded the engine room. Two other sailors were wounded, and the vessel had to be towed to Sydney for repairs.

But it was the navigational hazard *Diamantina* faced first. At Madang LCDR Rose had been informed of his ship's first duty. It was to carry the Governor-General, the

Duke of Gloucester, King George VI's brother, to visit the troops in north Bougainville. So the first order of the Naval Officer in Charge North Solomons at Torokina to Rose, was to survey a safe route through the poorly charted waters north to Freddies Beach so that when the Governor-General boarded a few days later the ship could proceed with confidence.

So, on 1 July, using army maps made from air photographs, the frigate felt its way northwards to the beach within earshot of Australian artillery. The 23 Brigade rear troops quickly took advantage of *Diamantina's* surprise arrival, and when the vessel came to anchor again at Torokina at 5.45 pm, eight stretcher cases and five walking wounded soldiers were landed from the sickbay and wardroom. The troops were in hospital days earlier than usual and after a much more comfortable trip. One mud-spattered Digger on waking up in the ship's cool, clean, white sickbay with an overhead fan gently stirring the air had to be convinced he was not in heaven.

Rose had already renewed an earlier request for a medical officer. To his former point that the well equipped sickbay and the 160 crew merited a doctor he added the powerful argument that neither the other seven ships nor the 90 officers and men at the short lived (5 Mar-20 Oct.) shore establishment, HMAS *Lusair*, included a medical officer in their complements. His submission got results and 25-year-old Surgeon-Lieutenant L.R. (Bob) Finlay-Jones later joined the ship.

Torokina was a well-developed base. HMAS *Lusair* ('Porpoise' in the local language) was only a small part of the American-built sprawling complex that included three movie theatres, a number of ovals, and even an ice cream and a soft drink factory. A newspaper, *The Torokina Times*, appeared regularly and the broadcasting station, 9AC, included Russ Tyson, a popular post-war ABC personality among its staff. Programmes included the best of American shows together with Australian mainland race broadcasts, local quizzes, and amateur hours. Mail deliveries were regular.

On 4 July the Governor-General's personal flag was delivered to the ship as the crew applied last minute polish for their distinguished guest. HMNZS W276 was ready to carry the vice-regal party from Beach 4's pontoon wharf to the frigate. A double dose of bad news greeted Rose as he stepped ashore at 9.00 am the next day to attend the Duke's pre-embarkation military review. The Prime Minister, John Curtin, had died and the Governor-General was already on a plane for Canberra.

Disappointed, Rose returned to his ship. There the bo'sun's mate informed the crew, recovering from days of hard spit and polish. Pacing through the mess decks, the mate piped his call intonsing, 'The-Duke-of-Gloucester-will-not-be-joining-the-ship-for-his-tour-of-the-islands.' His progress through the ship was followed by heart-felt cries of, "F*** the Duke of Gloucester."

But the show went on with lesser stars. With Lieutenant-General Sturdee, General Officer Commanding First Australian Army, Lieutenant-General Savige, General Officer Commanding Second Australian Corps, Commander Fowler, Naval Officer in Charge at *Lusair*, and other luminaries embarked the ship sailed north to anchor off Saposa Island at 5.40 pm. War correspondent, Timothy Ryan of the Melbourne *Sun* and a photographer were also on board.

Next day the captain went ashore to drive with Brigadier Potts, commander of 23 Brigade, to the artillery position at the tip of Soraken Peninsula. The jeep ride was not a comfortable one as they bounced along rutted tracks past fenced off Japanese gardens and over the hard sand of beaches before diving into the jungle again. But Rose had it easy compared to the 50 ratings who also made the trip. Dressed in anti-malarial rig of long pants and long-sleeved shirts and with freshly whitened caps and blackened shoes the party was met at the beach by a wiry lightly dressed Digger guide. Setting a cracking pace he led them for several miles through the jungle. Mud quickly covered the shoes and sweat stained the clothes as the sailors struggled to keep up with their fit guide. The trek ended at the 25-pounder battery which treated the matelots to a 20 round shoot.

Then came the trek back, which included the unwelcome addition of the afternoon downpour. The guide nonchalantly donned his ground sheet and stayed comfortable under it and his slouch hat. The quickly soaked sailors endured the extra discomfort of their cap whitener running down their faces. The mud-spattered weary excursionists reboarded their clean dry ship with a deep appreciation of the other service's hardships.

That evening Rose was ashore again as the absent Duke's programme proceeded. This time it was a dinner with the generals on Saposa followed by a movie *in a beautiful open air tropical setting*. His lower deck fellow visitors to the artillery gratefully retired to their hammocks.

The next day it was down to business. 'This is for the boys in Singapore' was chalked on the first four inch round *Diamantina* fired on the enemy. It was sent on its way at 12.23 pm, 7 July 1945. The ship was west of Madehas Island and the target was Japanese artillery positions eight miles (c.15km.) away out of sight on Sohana Island. A Royal New Zealand Air Force Corsair aircraft directed the 103 high-explosive shells on to the gun emplacements, camp, and a jetty. The spotter reported a number of hits on the emplacements and camp, and near misses on the jetty.

No._____

H.M.A.S. "LUSAIR".
5th. July, 1945.

COMMANDING OFFICER,
   H.M.A.S. "DIAMANTINA".

        Being in all respects ready and having embarked the General
Officer Commanding, Ist. Aust Army and General Officer Commanding, 2
Aust Corps and party proceed to SAPOSA about I500L 5th. July.

        Carry out bombardment on the 6th. and 7th. July at targets in
Buka area as arranged with Army authorities and return to Torokina
before dark on the 7th. July.

        Signal requirements in Tac R aircraft. Set watch on New Guinea
intercept and 2990 Kcs.(N.O.I.C. Torokina). Report your R/T call sign
before sailing. Tac R frequency will be communicated. Avoiding action
is to be taken in the event of encountering enemy fire other than close
range weapons. You are not to enter areas where you cannot manoeuvre at
full speed and caution is to be exercised in navigation in Buka area.

        You are not to bombard targets which can be reached by A.M.S.
or shore guns.

                                        LIEUTENANT COMMANDER R.A.N.
                                        NAVAL OFFICER-IN-CHARGE,
                                        TOROKINA.

First bombardment order (RAN, QMM collection)

The sailors had been keyed up before their first action. And pre-bombardment tension had not been confined to the lower decks. On the bridge the two generals and their attendant officers volubly enjoying their elevated position, distracted *Diamantina's* officers as they conned the ship near a minefield and into its firing position. Rose abruptly changed the atmosphere by ordering the officer of the watch to clear the bridge. Quiet concentration on the job ensued as the ejected generals led the way down the ladder. Later, elation at the bombardment's success swept the ship.

Next morning, after a grandstand view of a squadron of RNZAF Corsairs strafing and dive-bombing enemy positions on Bonis Peninsula, *Diamantina* took aboard eight stretcher cases and one walking wounded soldier for the return to Torokina. At 4.16 pm, they, the generals, and their entourage landed.

The disembarkation occasioned another Army-Navy incident. As the motorboat headed for the shore one of the generals produced a pipe. The boat coxswain's direct, "Hey, Sport, no smoking on the motorboat," made up in clarity for what it lacked in military courtesy. The pipe went back in the pocket. The coxswain was later counselled on the inappropriateness of addressing Australia's second most senior Army officer as "Sport."

After two lazy days of reading and writing mail, surfing, fishing, football, and movies at the base cinemas, at 8.16 am, 11 July, the frigate left again for Saposa with the corvette HMAS *Lithgow* and Motor Launch 816 in line astern. At anchor that night the sentries redoubled their vigilance as Japanese in canoes raided the army ashore. The next day the motor launch and *Diamantina's* motorboat sounded a channel between Taiof Island and the mainland for future bombardment positions. A Japanese battery gave away its position and hastened the survey when its 75-mm. rounds straddled the motor launch.

Meanwhile on the ship, anchored about one and a half miles south-west of Saposa, Stoker 'Snowy' Kilburn was following his usual hobby at 12.20 pm, when he pulled in a six-foot (1.8m.) shark. But this fish story ended up in the Captain's Report of Proceedings, Australian newspapers, and Ripley's 'Believe It Or Not'. When the catch was cut open on deck, feathers and a metal capsule were found in the stomach. Inside the capsule was a 7 July message to their headquarters from the Saposa detachment of 42 Australian Landing Craft Company. The message was only a few days late when *Diamantina* completed the pigeon-shark-ship-radio communications link. (Jack Woodman, commander of one of the barges, detailed procedures in a 1999 letter. Each barge would collect 12 pigeons from the loft on Saposa before setting out. Two birds would separately carry each message. Darkness, bad weather, over water flights, and hawks were especial hazards. Possibly a hawk had forced the pigeon down to become the shark's lunch. 'Smoky Joe', the volcano that dominated central Bougainville, always had hawks soaring around it.)

On 13 July, *Lithgow* swept the newly surveyed channel for mines before the

Snowy Kilburn (r.) with the message shark. (R. Hilbig)

small flotilla returned to anchor at Torokina under the now familiar plume from the volcano, Mount Bagana (Smoky Joe).

In *Diamantina's* absence CDR A. Fowler, Naval Officer in Charge at Torokina, had reorganised the Bougainville Naval Force. South Bougainville Force, the corvettes *Kiama* and *Dubbo*, and the motor launches, 427 and 428 were assigned to be based on Treasury Island with HMAS *San Michele* in logistic support. North Bougainville Force was set up with Rose as senior officer and the corvette *Lithgow* and the motor launches 808 and 816 joining forces with *Diamantina*. Both forces were tasked with supporting the army in bombardment, surveying, minesweeping, barge control, and escort duties.

While the crew relaxed, the captain attended a briefing at II Corps headquarters on the coming bombardments. When the ship again sailed for Saposa at 7.59 am on 17 July an Army Bombardment Officer, Captain Ward of 4 Field Regiment, and signallers were aboard en route to Taiof Island. On passage the close range weapons were test fired. Using the newly surveyed and swept channel the vessel moved to anchor off Taiof Island before firing 46 high explosive rounds from each 4" gun on enemy camps and two gun positions on Sohana. The Bombardment Liaison Officer radioed that about 80 of the 92 shells in this second operation fell in the target area. Enemy return fire was, thankfully, not up to this standard. Five minutes after the anchor was weighed, about eight shells of 105-mm. calibre or larger fell on the port quarter. The nearest was 400 yards (c.400m) off.

After spending the afternoon off Saposa the ship sailed north about 5 pm, for the other side of Buka Passage. As this involved sailing around enemy-held Buka and across the route of Japanese supply barges and submarines from Rabaul the ship was carefully blacked out and radar and Asdic watches at peak concentration.

At 4.30 am, 19 July, a distinct medium sized object not showing an Identification Friend or Foe signal registered on the radar screen. No friendly craft was reported in

Forward 4 inch gun crew deafened and sweat-soaked after the 8 August Bonis Peninsula bombardment.
(L to R) Back: PO Trevor Cathierwood, AB Charlie Howe.Front: ABs Ray Bulfin, 'Curly' Taylor, Bob Rabbage, Ron Hird, Jack Anderson, Jim Robb. (Jim Robb)

the area. Radar operators Murray McFarlane and Norman Theakstone did well to pick it out from the background of Buka Island. Then, switching from the 286 set to the 272, they tracked it for over 10 minutes before it suddenly disappeared. The ship closed up to submarine action stations. Murray and Norm heard Rose urging the Asdic operators on as he ordered, "Stand by to ram." However, an intensive Asdic search found nothing and *Diamantina* moved on. (The ship had two radars - a 286 calibrated in miles for long range detection, especially for aircraft, and a 272 measuring in yards for gunnery. At night on more relaxed occasions the captain on the open bridge put them to another use. The operators were instructed to report any heavy rain clouds at close range so the captain could call his steward for his raingear.)

8.55 am, saw the ship stopped in a dead calm sea five miles off Buka Passage's eastern end to begin a morning of shelling. The targets were six inch gun positions at Haheila and nearby Sorum and other installations on northern Bougainville and southern Buka. The spotting Corsair reported excellent results from the 174 rounds fired. One whole salvo, at a range of 18,000 yards (16,500m), dropped its 10 shells in an area 10 x 15 yards (9 m x 14 m); 50 minutes after *Diamantina* opened fire, enemy retaliation shots fell to starboard. Rose moved his ship further out as a single larger round dropped closer. However, neither the ship nor spotter aircraft was hit.

The bombardment ended at 12.40 pm. In the afternoon the frigate retraced its course northwards closing to within 200 yards of the beach on two occasions near Cape Putputan to rake huts with Bofors, Oerlikon, and machinegun fire.

Then, from Buka's northern tip course was set for Manus Island where the port anchor was dropped in Seeadler Harbour at 7.43 am, on 21 July. *Diamantina* was a very small presence among the more than 50 ships in the busy US Navy base's harbour. As well as US aircraft carriers and other ships there were vessels of the British Pacific Fleet train. On 5 August the battleship HMS *Duke of York* made a majestic entrance.

The frigate loaded 250 rounds of four inch and 18,208 rounds of 40 mm ammunition. The boilers were cleaned. The anti-aircraft gun crews enjoyed a refresher course ashore at the American gunnery school on Los Negros. Their fire regularly cut

AB Joe Campbell at bridge wing Oerlikon. (J. Spotswood)

the towlines connecting the drogue targets to the towing aircraft. The honing of their skills was not the only plus. The men appreciated the Americans' relaxed approach to discipline and the 'five star' food - ham chicken, ice cream, and iced tea. Finally the ship was repainted converting its dockyard dark blue to Seventh Fleet grey.

It was not all work. There was swimming and both Rugby League and Australian football matches against other crews. Tours of the giant base where some intersections even had men directing the traffic, and visits to battle sites and Manus Island villages were interspersed with buying sprees at the Post Exchange and movies.

The supply department took the opportunity to replenish the ship's depleted clothing stocks. When the American storeman filling in the form asked *Diamantina's* stores assistant where he was from he got the geographically if not nautically truthful answer, "Melbourne." That was the last the ship heard of the matter. Presumably the clothing was debited to a HMAS *Melbourne*.

At 1.56 pm on 5 August, after fuelling from the American tanker, *Edward Sinclair*, *Diamantina* sailed for Torokina and its *own little war and navy*. The day after arrival the ship was bombarding again. On 8 August off Taiof she fired 148 rounds of 4" high explosive shells on Japanese naval and air headquarters on the Bonis Peninsula - reputedly the last RAN shots of the war.

Ordered back to Torokina immediately after, the vessel loaded stores before sailing at dusk for the *very pretty and charming* harbour on the northern end of Choiseul Island where, only weeks before, Japanese fire had put *Colac* out of the war. Rose's orders were to harass enemy barge traffic and carry out bombardment and anti-submarine patrols. His ship, *Lithgow*, and motor launches 808, 818,and 820 were to be based in this former enemy occupied harbour. However, with Japanese capitulation believed imminent, Operation Baker Six was terminated and *Diamantina* recalled to Torokina from where she was ordered to Lae.

There on the morning of 14 August the ship loaded 310 rounds of four-inch ammunition. This was not without incident. When Rose queried why the party was ceasing work in the middle of the day the officer in charge replied his men were working tropical routine (early start and finish to avoid midday heat). After Rose's acerbic reminder, "There's a war on!" work was resumed. Some weeks later, after the Japanese surrender, *Diamantina* passed the ammunition vessel at sea. It was with some trepidation the frigate's signalman reported the other vessel's signal, "What price your f****** war now?"

With the ammunition loaded *Diamantina* sailed for Madang with a two-hour fuelling stop at an American oiler at Langemak. It was 6.52 am, 15 August when the ship tied up. Two hours later a crewmember was in the dentist's chair ashore waiting for an extraction when the public address system announced Japan's surrender. Back at Torokina English singing star, Gracie Fields, was resting before an evening performance. At midday a general summoned her to what she later recalled as "a clearing packed with servicemen." The general then announced the Japanese capitulation. He went on, "I have England's Gracie Fields here. I am going to ask her to sing The Lord's Prayer." Fields wrote in her memoirs: *There was a movement as of a great sea - every man had taken off his cap...I started to sing, 'Our Father which art in Heaven...' The hushed thousands of men in front of me seemed even to have stopped breathing. Each note and word of the prayer carried across the utter stillness of the rows of bent heads till it was lost in the jungle behind them. It was the most privileged and cherished moment of my life.*

The senior ship of 'Savige's Private Navy' was far away from the moving scene at its base at Torokina. In Madang that night on *Diamantina* there was an extra beer issue - three bottles per man - and *a makeshift concert got under way* on the forecastle.

CHAPTER 5

MAKING THE PEACE

During *Diamantina*'s hot quiet two weeks at Madang over 10,000 rounds of 40mm. ammunition were loaded. The usual shark fishing haul included one female tiger carrying 48 young. Little mail caught up with the ship. Some of the crew attended a local sing-sing celebrating the end of the war. Early in the stay a Martin Mariner flying boat alighted near the ship. The men cheered the young women disembarking. It was Gracie Fields and her party. That afternoon the crew sat for two hours on coconut logs waiting for the pouring rain to stop to allow the concert to begin.

On 19 August, a chaplain from shore conducted the ship's first full church service. The next Sunday, in almost unbearable heat, the captain led prayers. On Monday 27 August, *Diamantina* joined HMAS *Vendetta* in fuelling from the oil barge, *Rocklea*. The barge was another product of Queensland's wartime shipbuilding industry being the first vessel launched at Evans Deakin's shipyard, established early in the war downstream from Brisbane's Story Bridge.

Rumours of orders to Rabaul were proved wrong when the frigate sailed on 30 August at 1.56 pm for Torokina. The voyage back began in choppy seas that settled into a long swell. An uneventful passage was drawing to a close when, about 5.am on 1 September, during Sub-Lt. Parkin's watch, the ship suddenly heeled, shuddered, and began to vibrate. In record time the captain was on the bridge. An examination of the chart revealed no nearby reefs or shoals. Reduced speed moderated the vibration.

Inspection at Torokina identified a damaged starboard propeller and shaft with no damage forward. From this the captain deduced his vessel had struck an 'underwater

Australian Rules football team - Torokina 1945. (J. Spotswood)

object.' Although some crewmembers on the quarterdeck at the time of the incident asserted it was a whale, it went into the captain's report as a log.

The large quantities of mail waiting at Torokina raised the crew's spirits. On the next day, Sunday, *Diamantina* was the venue for a church service conducted by an army chaplain. The congregation included personnel from other ships, nurses, the army, and HMAS *Lusair*. Later the ship fuelled, with the freighter *River Burdekin*, from the Dutch tanker, *Cleodora*.

Again on 4 and 5 September, *Diamantina* visited *Cleodora* to take on other fuels. The Liberty ship *James Ives* also refuelled. The restricted conditions and high winds and seas made manoeuvring difficult and the frigate's bows dented a side plate of the tanker.

Diamantina sailed south in the afternoon of 6 September, to anchor in Gazelle Harbour at 6 pm, near the Australian Army's southern force's headquarters. ML 816 tied up alongside. On board the frigate was the Naval Officer in Charge Solomons, CDR A. Fowler, Army officers, correspondents, photographers, and interpreters.

The ships again got underway at 4 am, 7 September for Moila Point, Bougainville's southern tip. Here the larger vessel hove to six miles east of the point off the minefield with guns manned while the motor launch proceeded to Buin. Its mission was to return with Lieutenant General Masatane Kanda, the commander of 17 Japanese Army.

When the launch reappeared, it was accompanied by two Japanese barges. From one of these a Japanese Navy lieutenant boarded *Diamantina*. In fluent English he stated that Kanda had orders from his superiors in Rabaul to surrender the next day. The envoy returned to Buin. ML816 retired to Gazelle Harbour, and *Diamantina* anchored off the mouth of the Mivo River - the dividing line between the opposing forces.

Next morning, 8 September, the motor launch again escorted the barges to the frigate. The Japanese surrender party transferred at 8 am. Accompanying Kanda were his Chief of Staff, Major General Makata, Vice Admiral Baron Samejima, commander of the region's Japanese Navy forces, and Commander Ikegama and Lieutenant Commander Shinkawa. Sick Berth Attendant A.L. Dowling later wrote the general *was a sick old man, and appeared to be stunned by the defeat.* Commander Fowler met them and received the two senior officers' swords. As well, two carefully packaged boxes, 'presents for General Savige', were warily accepted, given a stethoscope examination by the doctor, and isolated on deck. (Lieutenant General Masatane Kanda's career had included service on the General Staff and in Korea and China before his appointment in December 1942 to command the 6th Division on Bougainville. A very capable field commander, he succeeded General Hyakutake as commander of 17 Army on 17 February 1945. His sword is now in the Australian War Memorial.)

The Japanese were escorted to the sick bay from which all drugs and instruments had been removed. LCDR. Rose later discovered some crewmembers had made an unauthorised addition to the bulkhead - a newspaper photograph of a Japanese with sword upraised about to behead a European.

Diamantina sailed at 8.10 am direct for Torokina. The Commonwealth Battle Ensign streamed from the masthead with the Senior Officer's flag on the port yardarm. At the mainmast flew the large ensign. A RNZAF Corsair squadron provided an air escort. Below the Japanese kept the Sick Berth Attendant busy complying with their repeated requests for black tea.

```
HMAS DIAMNTINA                                    NOIC TOROKINA


     I WISH TO EXPRESS MY APPRECIATION OF THE KINDNESS AND ATTENTION

     TO MYSLEF AND STAFF OFFICERS ON THE RECENT SURRENDER OPERATION.

     THE SIGNING OF THE SURRENDER TERMS BY LIEUTENANT GENERAL KANDA

     MARKS THE TERMINATION OF THE BOUGAINVILLE OPERATIONS AND IS THERE

     FORE OUR V/P DAY.    IT GAVE ME PROFOUND SATISFACTION TO BE AT THIS

     TIME IN THE SENIOR SHIP OF THE BOUGAINVILLE NAVAL FORCES.    YOUR

     SHIP HAS CONTRIBUTED LARGELY TO THIS SUCCESSFUL CONCLUSION.    THE

     SHIP AND SHIP'S COMPANY WAS ALL THAT COULD BE DESIRED AND REFLECTS

     GREAT CREDIT ON ALL THOSE RESPONSIBLE.    THE DISPLAY OF SKILLFUL

     SEAMANSHIP SHOWN ON BERTHING ON THE PONTOON WAS A PLEASURE TO WATCH.

     I WISH YOU ALL THE BEST OF LUCK IN THE FORTHCOMING OPERATION.

                                       // 090216Z SEPTEMBER 45

     DIAMANTINA HAS BY HAND

     XXX ORIGINATOR ..NOIC

     LOG        ......... PLAIN LANGUAGE       R....0220    LKS   9.9.45.
```

NOIC's message. (RAN, QMM collection)

At 11.45 am, Rose skilfully brought his ship alongside the crowded Torokina wharf to land his passengers into the custody of II Australian Corps. The captain then, as protocol demanded, took up position beside the gangway to return the surrender party's salutes. Rose was astonished when not one of them observed the etiquette.

The Torokina Times, 'The Official Newspaper of the Australian armed forces on Bougainville' reported the surrender in its 8 and 9 September six page mimeographed issues. The coverage showed a true Australian sense of proportion. Of the two issues' total of 12 pages, four carried radio news from the rest of the world, two pages were devoted to local entertainment and the Bougainville University, and two covered local sport including cricket, soccer, Australian Rules, Rugby League, and the 'Solomon Islands Surf Club Championships.' This left only four pages for the surrender.

The Torokina Times reported that as *Diamantina* steamed south on Thursday 6 September two Japanese envoys delivered a message to General Savige at Torokina from General Kanda.They then spent the night in II Corp's VIP hut, which formerly had housed the Governor-General and stage and screen stars. Early Friday morning,

Flight Lieutenant Barry Davis of 5 Tactical Reconnaissance Squadron dropped General Savige's reply on to a marked area at Kanda's headquarters.

So, the next morning, the party boarded *Diamantina*. Kanda was first on the quarterdeck where he stood to attention but made no move to salute Commander Fowler, the greeting officer. Vice-Admiral Samejima, the next on deck, saluted smartly. Both officers were in dress uniform and surrendered their swords to the Naval Officer in Charge.

For disembarkation at Torokina's No. 4 Beach the swords were returned. The Japanese were driven through grimly silent Australians and New Zealanders to II Corps headquarters. There, at 12.15 pm, in the Battle Room, the General and the Admiral laid their swords on the table in front of General Savige and formally surrendered their forces.

It was appropriate that, flanking General Savige, were representatives of the other forces in the Bougainville campaign, the RAAF, RNZAF, RAN, and Lt. Col. J.P. Coursey, United States Marine Corps. The marines' landing at Torokina on 1 November 1943 had begun the struggle for the island.

The surrender documents were read in English and Japanese and then signed. General Savige then bluntly told Kanda how seriously he viewed his delay in surrendering. He went on to make it clear any further failure to quickly carry out orders would not be tolerated. Kanda promised full cooperation. (Savige had previously ordered Kanda to meet HMAS *Lithgow* at the rendezvous six miles off Moila Point at 8 a.m. on 20 August. Instead of the General, a staff officer, Captain Takenada, and a civilian interpreter had attended. Takenada delivered to the Australians the message that his commander refused to surrender until directed to do so by his superiors. The young, self-assured officer apparently had expected to speak directly to General Savige on the ship and made his displeasure apparent when additional demands were presented to him. The situation came to a head when the Japanese refused to travel to Torokina on *Lithgow*. Sub-Lieutenant Marshall drew his revolver and forced the envoy to sit and comply. The next day when the captain and interpreter were returned at the rendezvous, shots were fired in the vicinity of the corvette. Feelings were high on both sides.)

A Japanese urgent request for food and medical supplies was passed to II Corps staff officers for action. Another submission received short shrift. Admiral Samejima put to Savige that his superior was not Kanda but the Naval Commander in Rabaul. *The Australian ...peremptorily ordered Samejima to place himself and all his men under the orders of General Kanda... Samejima just looked sour.*

There were two other additions to the proceedings. The two tastefully wrapped and tied wooden boxes were carefully opened at a safe distance from Corps Headquarters. Each contained a magnificent 30cm high willow pattern blue vase - presents for 'Your Excellency,' General Savige, from the General and Admiral.

After the surrender Kanda asked to pay tribute to the Australian dead of Bougainville. Permission was granted. So, in the small open garden, under the Australian flag, the Japanese faced General Savige in two rows with the senior officers in front. Kanda then led them in removing their caps and deeply bowing, *standing rock still and silent for a minute.*

In response, the Australian addressed the Japanese, "Thank you for this tribute from a leader of troops who have fought so tenaciously." He went on to "...hope that the blood shed by both sides would cement a better understanding and contribute to goodwill in the future."

Flight Lieutenant McNally of 10 Communications Unit soon after took off to deliver the document at the end of twelve-and-a-half hours of flying time to Mascot in Sydney. The Japanese had lunch and were then driven to the wharf to join motor launches for their return to Buin.

Diamantina remained at Torokina to prepare for another task. The next morning, 9 September, a party attended a church service ashore. Then, at 4.23 pm, the ship sailed for, in LCDR Rose's words, "...the highlight of *Diamantina*'s active service." Rose, appointed Senior Officer of the Nauru Occupation Force, was in charge of a three-ship convoy. During the operation two more surrenders were to be signed - this time on his ship's quarterdeck.

On board the warship was Brigadier J.R. Stevenson representing both the Australian Government and the United States Theatre Commander. The Brigadier, whose 11th Brigade *Diamantina* had supported in earlier bombardments, was well qualified for his new role - in civilian life he was the New South Wales Parliament's Usher of the Black Rod. With Stevenson's staff, print and radio correspondents, movie and still photographers, an official war artist, and military police, made up a total of 17 passengers.

In formation with the frigate were the cargo ships, *River Burdekin*, and *River Glenelg*. These were loaded with supplies, civilian officials, and 200 soldiers of the North Queensland 31/51 Battalion AIF under the command of Lt. Col. J. Kelly, DSO - Acting Governor designate of Nauru and Ocean Island. Kelly was to hold this office until he handed over to Mr. Matthew 'Mark' Ridgeway on 1 November (Ridgeway served as Administrator of Nauru 1945-49). Ambulance, engineer, and transport troops were also aboard.

At a stately 10 knots the three ships sailed through idyllic weather for two days. Just before dark on 10 September already high spirits on the frigate were raised further when a Navy Board order cancelling blackout restrictions was received. Full navigation lights came on for the first time in six years as cool night air flowed below decks through open deadlights.

Diamantina increased speed at 1 pm on September 12, to push ahead of the transports. At 7 am the next day Rose had the crew at Action Stations as the ship closed Nauru at 16 knots. When there was no response to the ship's light signals the captain ordered the International Code flag signal, 'Send boat with representative.' This brought LCDR Kishimoto and a Nauruan-Chinese interpreter, Ma Nai Fai, on board at 7.33 am.

Interested observers of these proceedings were the passengers and crew of HMS *Kia Kia*, an 85-tons ketch carrying the British Resident Commissioner of the Gilbert and Ellice Islands, Colonel V. Fox-Strangways. The ketch's passage from Tarawa had been faster than planned and she had arrived off Nauru for her arranged rendezvous with the frigate an hour early with *Diamantina* nowhere in sight. When five Japanese barges put out and converged on his small vessel *Kia Kia*'s captain, not liking the odds and wary of their intent, withdrew seawards. When the current brought the ketch in again the Japanese advanced again and *Kia Kia*, armed only with two light machine guns, withdrew again. With the whole procedure recurring one more time the situation was becoming farcical when *Diamantina*'s arrival put an end to the advances and retreats. Later it became clear this was the Japanese first attempt at surrendering.

Half an hour after boarding the frigate the envoy was on his way ashore with his instructions. Rose turned to rejoin his transports. By 1 pm, the River class frigate and *River Glenelg* lay off the west of the island in waters too deep to anchor. *River Burdekin* was secured to a Japanese buoy 300 yards offshore. However, by the morning of the 14th, *River Burdekin* had joined the other two. The buoy had parted from its moorings and *Diamantina* had used its close range weapons to dispose of it as a danger to navigation.

The commander's sword lies on the table, others to the rear, as the Ocean Island surrender is signed. LCDR Rose is in white beside Brigadier Stevenson. Sir Albert Ellis is the bearded civilian. Translator PO L.S. Marquis RAAF stands behind LCDR Suzuki. 11 Brigade's Captain G. Renwick stands at the end of the table. (J. Spotswood)

At 2.45 pm, on 12 September the surrender party was accorded honours as they ascended *Diamantina*'s gangway. Boatswains' pipes shrilled and sentries presented arms as the six naval officers were greeted and escorted to the table on the quarterdeck where, at the second demand, they reluctantly surrendered their swords, Captain Hisayuki Soeda to Brigadier Stevenson, and the other five to Captain George Renwick of 11 Brigade.

At 3 pm, Brigadier Stevenson began reading the terms of surrender with, at his invitation, LCDR Rose at his right hand. Pilot Officer L S. Marquis, RAAF, repeated the terms in Japanese. Captain Soeda signed on behalf of the Japanese force on Nauru and Ocean Island, with his adjutant following as witness. Brigadier Stevenson then signed twice - first 'as representative of the United States Theatre Commander..' and second '...as representative of the Commonwealth of Australia as Territorial Authority in respect of Nauru Island.'

Stevenson's two signatures followed two weeks of political activity. Both the Australian and British governments regarded the prompt resumption of phosphate production as 'of urgent importance.' A 27 August cable from the Australian Legation in Washington had informed the Prime Minister ...*the British Chiefs of Staff would be most grateful if the United States Chiefs of Staff could arrange that the Japanese surrender in these islands [Nauru and Ocean] be made as follows:*

(a) At Nauru to an Australian commander;
(b) At Ocean Island to an Australian commander acting on behalf of the United Kingdom.

Two days later Mr. Chifley told the House of Representatives, "In view of our special interest in Nauru and Ocean Island we offered the Australian army and navy for the surrender."

A cable next day from the Washington Legation gave the Prime Minister the United States Chiefs of Staff's reply. They did not want to disturb General Order 1 that the Japanese surrender at Nauru and Ocean Island should be to the Commander in Chief of the US Pacific Fleet. However CIC US Pacific Fleet had placed these islands' surrender on a low priority. So, to expedite the surrender, they had no objection to Australian forces and shipping being used, provided the Australian commander reported to CIC US Pacific Fleet and accepted the surrender in his name. Whether the CIC sent a representative was up to him.

A final cable from the British Dominion Affairs Office to the Department of External Affairs in Canberra on 31 August sealed the matter by agreeing to defer to US wishes and having Australia accept in the name of the Commander in Chief of the United States Pacific Fleet. So Stevenson signed twice at each surrender: first as the US Theatre Commander's representative; and, second, at Nauru as Australian representative, and at Ocean Island as the United Kingdom representative. His NSW Parliament experience helped him skilfully negotiate the procedural maze.

Representatives of the major stakeholders were among the dignitaries at the surrender. They included Colonel Fox-Strangways the Commissioner of the Gilbert and Ellice Islands, Sir Albert Ellis, the New Zealand representative on the British Phosphate Commission, and Commander Phipps of the Royal New Zealand Navy. However there was no United States representative.

Sir Albert's attendance was the result of some high level cables. The first was sent by the New Zealand Prime Minister to his Australian counterpart on 4 September requesting the pioneer of the islands' phosphate industries attend ...*because of his special association with the islands and the Commission* (Sir Albert had discovered the phosphate deposits 45 years earlier). In view of Sir Albert's age a companion, Mr. Bissett, the New Zealand manager of the Phosphate Commission, accompanied him. They and Commander Phipps landed at Torokina the day before the convoy sailed. Other Phosphate Commission staff, civil administrators, and stores reached Torokina from Melbourne on m.v. *Trienza* just before the convoy sailed. *Trienza* later landed them on Nauru.

After the surrender the Japanese commander returned ashore leaving officers to arrange details of the Australian occupation. The Allied dignitaries relaxed with refreshments in the wardroom where Soeda's sword with its sharkskin handle was a centre of attention.

At 4 pm, an armed reconnaissance party of a petty officer and 10 ratings under *Diamantina*'s First Lieutenant landed to a rapturous welcome from the Nauruans. The Japanese occupation, which had begun on 26 August 1942, was over. The sailors assessed the harbour's capability and distributed tropical chocolate to the pumpkin-rind chewing children. A nearby Japanese officer, imperiously waving some Nauruan ladies off a bench with his fly whisk so he could sit down, was made forcefully aware of the new order when the petty officer waved him off with his Thompson submachine gun before inviting the ladies to resume their seats.

The Australian force began landing at 7 am on 14 September. Japanese working parties, small craft, and vehicles helped land supplies and equipment. At 2 pm a guard of two officers and 30 seamen from *Diamantina* took part with 17 Platoon of D Company and a detachment of Gilbert and Ellice Islands police in the ceremonial hoisting of the Union Flag in front of the occupation force's camp on the golf course. As the flag was slowly hoisted, a pair of white terns fluttered in a tree nearby. Some saw them as an emblem of future peace. Hurrying to complete the discharge of material in the good weather the freighter crews did not attend and even worked through the night. Two hours after the flag raising *Kia Kia* departed. It was an unforgettable scene as its crew and passengers lined the rigging, singing .

Conditions ashore seared into the memories of the servicemen. The island's 5,200 residents, including 3,200 Japanese and 500 Korean labourers were subsisting mainly on pumpkins and fish among the debris of shelling and bombing dating back four years. Sir Albert Ellis summed it up in, *Nauru was the world record pumpkin patch*; 300 of the former enemy had died and 130 were in hospital. The last supply shipment had come in a submarine in September 1944, and there was a strictly enforced rationing system. This allocated the highest scale to the Japanese with Nauruans next and Koreans and Chinese on the lowest level. Each pumpkin had identification carved on its skin when it was about a week old. The death penalty had been enforced on some food thieves, even Japanese. Coconut trees had been distributed among Japanese, Nauruans, and Chinese in the ratio of 3:2:1. The occupiers heard reports of cannibalism.

Appalling levels of sanitation exacerbated the situation. Human and vegetable waste fertilised the many fuel drums containing pumpkin vines. Heaps of rotting pumpkins added to the odour. One diary recorded ...*stench from the island was unpleasantly noticeable 200 yards out to sea*. Australian hygiene squads co-opted garrison members into setting fire to the drums and spreading disinfectant. By the time *Diamantina* returned on passage to Ocean Island there had been a marked improvement and Nauru was on its way to again meriting its alternate name of Pleasant Island.

There were other horrors. The remaining Nauruans (two thirds of the population had been deported) reported incidents of torture, rape and killings. The Australian administrator, medical officer, his assistant, and two Phosphate Commission staff had disappeared on 22 February 1943, the day after the first American bombing of the island. Evidence pointed to them being killed in reprisal.

Pilot Officer L. Marquis, the interpreter, saw another side of the invaders. Invited after the surrender by a young Japanese officer to their headquarters he rode there in a motorcycle sidecar to pass a convivial hour of tea, rice cakes, and conversation while concerned authorities searched for him.

The occupation proceeded smoothly with the troops setting up their tents south of the phosphate loader until 3 p.m. on 15 September when, in a tragic accident, Pte. D. Sheffer was fatally wounded by the accidental discharge of his own weapon.

The BPC survey party set up camp with the navy officers on the tennis court site and quickly set to work. The powerhouse diesels were found to be in need of overhaul while the BPC launch *Tern*, which the Japanese had used to attend the surrender was repossessed. Assessment of damage to other machinery was begun.

The landing of Japanese-American interpreters disconcerted the Nauruans; they were uneasy at seeing armed persons of obvious Japanese appearance in Allied uniforms.

By late Sunday 16 September, all cargo had been discharged and the shore radio station was operational. At 4 pm, Lt. L. Lever took up duties as Port Director, Nauru. The 500 Korean labourers remained on the island to help in rehabilitation. So too did some Japanese including those accused of war crimes. The remaining 2,500 assembled for embarkation. As they boarded the barges for transport to *River Glenelg* and *River Burdekin* a group of Chinese attacked them with sticks. The Australian troops fixed bayonets. Their point made, the Chinese left.

The Japanese climbed cargo nets onto the ships while their possessions, including pandanus mat wrapped parcels and urns with the ashes of dead comrades were winched aboard. With its passengers in the 'tween decks, *River Glenelg* sailed for Torokina in the early afternoon. *Diamantina* followed at 6 pm, after circling the island to inspect the formidable defences, which included ten 150mm British naval guns from Singapore and many smaller artillery pieces integrated in outer and inner fortification lines incorporating an extensive tunnel system. Six Japanese died on passage and were buried at sea. The unavailability of road transport at Torokina meant an eight-mile (13 km) march to the camps. A further eight died on the road. There were few tears from the captors.

Cruising to Torokina at 14 knots, *Diamantina* detoured for a three-hour loop north of the Equator to ...*give all crew members the satisfaction of 'Crossing the Line'*. Even so, the warship's arrival at 9 am, 19 September, preceded *River Glenelg*'s. *River Burdekin* came into port the next day and its passengers also marched to their camp on the Torokina River's east bank.

The frigate's crew's next three days were pleasantly occupied with mail, a sailing race, and a ship's concert organised by the stokers. Then, with Brigadier Stevenson and his staff back aboard, the vessel sailed again at 7.40 pm on 22 September - this time for Ocean Island.

In a one-hour stop at Nauru, *Diamantina* landed mail and embarked Lt. Col. Kelly. The ship then got under way at 9 am, 25 September for Tarawa in the Gilbert Islands. This most enjoyable three-day visit had its genesis in a conversation at the Nauru surrender between LCDR Rose and the Resident Commissioner. Colonel Fox-Strangways had asked the captain to bring his ship to the island as, during the previous six years, the intensely loyal islanders had seen many Japanese and United States ships but not one British vessel. Rose suggested the colonel make a formal request through channels. It did not take long - three days after *Diamantina* returned from the Nauru mission, orders to Tarawa arrived.

So the ship's third and fourth (and the captain's 28th and 29th) Line Crossings occurred on the indirect route to the Ocean Island surrender.

Arrival at Tarawa was delayed by the sighting at 9 am, 26 September, of a derelict American landing barge about 40 miles (65 km) offshore. It was taken in tow, but, as this severely reduced the ship's speed, the decision was taken to sink this hazard to navigation. The starboard Bofors quickly accounted for it and the frigate anchored off Betio Island at 2 pm.

The US Marines' desperate battle for Tarawa had stripped the island of trees and it glared white in the hot sun. A flotilla of canoes greeted the ship. One came alongside with an urgent request - a cricket match against the ship's team.

The initial American reception was cool. This warmed considerably with the realisation that the White Ensign denoted not a British, but an Australian ship. Then generous American hospitality engulfed the crew as they were entertained at canteens, guided over battle sites, and visited the memorials to the dead of the costly battle for the island of less than one square mile; 1,000 Americans and most of the 4,000 defenders had died.

A simple cross erected by the Americans was visited by LCDR. Rose, Colonel Fox-Strangways, and Brigadier Stevenson. Its inscription read, *In memory of 22 British subjects murdered by the Japanese at Betio on 15th October 1942. Standing unarmed to their posts, they matched brutality with gallantry and met death with fortitude.* It commemorated the New Zealand radio operators and Coast Watchers, retired sea captain, trader, hospital dispenser, and missionary killed in retribution after the first heavy American air attack.

One rating particularly enjoyed his time ashore. His three-months leave stoppage had been overturned by the King's amnesty. His pleasure at getting off the ship was increased when he discovered the going barter rate was one case of American beer for a bottle of Australian.

The cricket match across the lagoon at the mission and village on Buariki Island, was played the day after arrival. Warm relations with the Gilbertese were cemented in a most enjoyable game won by *Diamantina*.

The toss - Buariki, Tarawa. (AWM 097585)

More local hospitality on Buariki the next morning was returned that afternoon when the crew entertained the cricket team, police, and friends on board. The large, happy crowd particularly enjoyed training and elevating the power operated Oerlikon guns. The day ended with the visitors' impromptu choral performance on A deck enthralling the crew.

There was another pleasant surprise before the ship sailed at 10 am on 29 September. The supply officer had taken the opportunity the large American base presented to requisition four tons of meat. He struggled to control his expression when the apologetic response came that, since only three tons of beef were available, "...Would you accept the final ton in poultry and ham?"

Ocean Island was raised in the early morning of 30 September. *Kia Kia* lay two miles offshore. Japanese officers boarded for instructions and had returned ashore by 9 am. An hour later an armed party followed them for a two-hour reconnaissance. Later in the day *Maureen* arrived with labourers and stores from Tarawa as *Diamantina* slowly steamed around the island. As at Nauru, sea depth made anchoring a safe distance offshore impossible.

River Burdekin, carrying 140 troops, the occupation force and guard for the garrison and the remaining 600 Nauru Japanese, was the last to arrive at 6 am on 1 October. She also carried stores for the Australian force and the Commission. Two barges trailed behind the ship.

At 9 am that day, Brigadier Stevenson and many other of the Nauru surrender participants repeated the now familiar ceremony. This time, one mile off the island, the Japanese signatory, LCDR Nahoomi Suzuki, smartly turned out in dark green uniform, polished leggings, and white gloves, surrendered his sword without hesitation. Another difference was Stevenson's second signature, this time as *...representative of the Government of the United Kingdom of Great Britain as territorial Authority in respect of Ocean Island.* Thus, on the quarterdeck of HMAS *Diamantina*, World War II's last Pacific surrender was signed.

Sir Albert Ellis wrote, in 1946, of the ceremony, *It could not have been more impressive on a battleship: not as much so, I think, for on a large vessel the human element would have appeared in diminutive proportions. I trust the snappy little warship with her courteous commander and officers may have many years of useful service ahead.*

Within an hour the Australian troops began landing. They found formidable fortifications that included electric wires that, they were later told, had been tested by forcing islanders to run to their deaths against them. At 1 pm, the Union flag was hoisted before a guard drawn from the occupying force, the Gilbert and Ellice Islands police, and *Diamantina* on the same spot it had been first raised in 1901.

The island was a smaller version of Nauru but markedly cleaner and healthier. The 513 Japanese naval personnel were the sole occupants. (Suzuki had a simple explanation for the absence of Banabans, Gilbertese, and Europeans. Most had been sent to Truk. The remaining 150 young men had risen against the Japanese and been killed in the fighting. On 2 December suspicions were confirmed. Kabunare emerged from hiding in a cave to tell of the Japanese massacre of his companions the day after Tokyo surrendered. The sole survivor later testified at the War Crimes Trial in Rabaul. There Suzuki and LCDR Nakayama, found guilty of the murder of the Europeans on Nauru, were among those found guilty and executed).

The last supplies had arrived in August 1944 - over a year before - so food was strictly rationed. Hospital patients were the only personnel allowed rice and, even on their meagre individual allotment of 430 grams per day there was only 30 days supply left. A healthy man's ration was 2 kg of pumpkin OR one and a half kg. of sweet potato, supplemented by whatever fish could be caught, salt produced near the harbour, and alcoholic palm toddy.

LCDR Rose noted the lowest rating in the isolated garrison was petty officer. He mused in his report on ...*how the petty officers relished taking turns as Cooks of Messes and Captains of the Heads [toilet cleaners]*.

Both Nauru and Ocean Island produced fine hauls of souvenirs, which the army distributed from a central pool. *Diamantina*'s captain received Nauru's second best sword and a Japanese bow and arrows from Ocean Island's commander - a noted archer. Not everybody adhered to the system, however. *Diamantina*'s libertymen had only been a short time on Ocean Island when they were recalled. A sword, pair of binoculars, and the Japanese copy of the surrender had disappeared from the commander's house. An extensive search did not recover the document and another copy went ashore.

This document is still missing, but, 48 years after it was signed on *Diamantina*'s quarterdeck, and 13 years after the ship was decommissioned, a copy of the Nauru surrender sold in London. In the Aeolian Hall, Bloomfield Place, on 9 July 1993, Sothebys sold the surrender order, the instrument of surrender, and a collection of contemporary snapshots and press clippings. Lot 378's hammer price was £3,500 (in excess of $A8,000). The relics with the three corrected misspellings of 'Diamantina' on the instrument of surrender are now in the Forbes Magazine collection at 60 Fifth Avenue, New York. The vendor's name was not made public.

With the Japanese garrison embarked on *River Burdekin*, *Diamantina* sailed for Torokina at 6 pm, 2 October. After a four-hour stop at Nauru the frigate reached its destination at 9.17 am, 6 October, where Brigadier Stevenson and his party disembarked. The crew welcomed mail. However, the general good feeling was diluted when a heavy swell during fuelling drove the frigate into the side of the tanker, *Cleodora*. *Diamantina* came away with a dented port bridge wing and both whaler falls crushed.

At noon the next day, two weeks before HMAS *Lusair* decommissioned, *Diamantina* left Torokina for Madang by way of Jacquinot Bay on New Britain. Off New Guinea the frigate encountered the cruiser *Apollo* heading north and the aircraft carrier *Formidable* speeding south with returning prisoners of war. At Jacquinot Bay the ship entertained a party of Australian nurses en route to Rabaul.

Madang was reached at 7 am on 10 October. During the 18-day stay the boilers were cleaned, the ship painted a lighter peacetime grey, and the captain was drafted onto a Board of Inquiry into a fire on a small ship that had caused the death of a petty officer.

But it was not all work. Shark fishing, regular mail, and 13 sporting events filled the time before the ship cast off on 28 October. *Diamantina* won most of the cricket and football matches against *Bunbury, Cowra, Dubbo, Kanimbla*, and *Manoora*.

Arrival at war-shattered Rabaul the next day saw Rose put to work again on a Board of Inquiry - this time as President - into the grounding of a motor launch at Jacquinot Bay.

Sailing from Rabaul at 9.13 am on 2 November, *Diamantina* was towing a landing craft. The barge was to be filled at the Emirau Islands with materials abandoned by the Americans. This would be brought to Rabaul to enlarge the RAN's shore establishment. Emirau already had an indirect connection with *Diamantina*. Captain Fish of *River Burdekin* had been landed there with the other merchantmen survivors from the raiders *Komet* and *Orion* in December 1940.

Diamantina had a surprise awaiting her at Emirau. The small band of soldiers that met the ship at Hamburg Harbour was living proof the Americans had not abandoned the material. So the anticipated plunder ended up as a much smaller haul - one 30 cwt truck, 400 superficial feet of timber, and 500 feet of two-inch galvanised pipe did not go anywhere near filling the order.

With the lightly loaded barge trailing behind, the frigate moved to New Hanover's north coast for its next task. The specialised crew of the barge located and destroyed three Japanese mines before the vessels sailed for Rabaul on 9 November. One of the exploded mines was reported by the inhabitants of a storybook beautiful tropical island. While the party destroyed the mine *Diamantina*'s doctor treated the wounds of a small boy injured in the explosion of ammunition found on a beach.

Immediately on arrival at Simpson Harbour the next morning Rose signalled a request to report ashore to the Naval Officer in Charge. Unhappy at the reply that he would be seen the next morning, the captain was shaving in his cabin when the leading signalman knocked to offer a message and his smiling congratulations. The Naval Board communication announced his promotion to Commander with seniority from VP Day - 15 August. The newly appointed Commander immediately sent his NOIC - an acting Commander - a second message 'inviting' him aboard to celebrate the promotion. During the visit, Rose delivered his report.

On 22 November, at 7.09 am, *Diamantina* again anchored in familiar Torokina Harbour. Ever since the war ended three months before, Rose's thoughts, like those of most of his crew, had focussed on demobilisation and return to family and civilian life. The Government had devised a discharge system based on points accrued according to age at enlistment, marital status, number of children, and length of service. Time at sea and overseas service merited double points. Rank was not considered.

The newly promoted commander had been 37 years old with a wife and two children when he began his six years' service that included almost five years abroad at sea. Consequently few men's score exceeded his of over 400 points. So it was no surprise that at 10 pm on 22 November, the evening of the ship's return to Torokina, LCDR Philip Jack Sullivan relieved CDR Rose as captain.

The next day, at 10 am, Rose addressed the 152 ratings and 8 officers for the last time before, two hours later, quietly leaving the ship to board *Westralia* for Brisbane. From there a train trip had *Diamantina*'s first captain at home in Sydney on 30 November, exactly six years and one month after he had left on mobilisation. In those long years Rose had risen to command three ships in two navies on two oceans. In the Atlantic, Rose had covered 83,969 and 24,756 nautical miles in command of HMS *Alisma* and *Fal*. Under him *Diamantina* had ploughed through 14,576 miles in the Pacific. All told, Rose had covered in command a distance equal to more than five times the earth's circumference.

There was another significant statistic. Fearing a too rapid loss of ratings at war's end, the Navy Board promoted a scheme inviting ratings to extend their service for a further two years. The take-up rate in the RAN as a whole was 3.5%. On *Diamantina* it was 5% - an indication of a happy ship.

Two hours after Rose's departure the anchor was aweigh and the ship sailed for Dreger Harbour. Here NOIC New Guinea embarked for Madang. Four days later the vessel left for Wewak where she anchored at 9.40 am, 1 December. Sunday 2 December, was a true day of rest. After a Catholic Church Parade, 'Hands to Bathe' was piped. The day ended with an army party aboard to enjoy a ship's concert ending at 11 pm.

4 December the ship sailed in another role; 100 soldiers of 6th Division were embarked for Madang on a passage that one Digger recalled 50 years later as "never to be forgotten". There were also two officers for Sydney. When the soldiers landed

on 5 December, their places were taken by four RAN officers and 52 ratings, 13 army other ranks, one RAAF officer and 12 ORs, and one distressed Norwegian seaman. The crowded ship sailed at 4.07 pm, for Sydney with a call at Langemak the next day to embark a rating for mainland detention.

The cramped conditions were made tolerable by the realisation they were on a fast run home. At 7.55 am, 13 December, *Diamantina* tied up alongside *Queenborough* in Sydney. The passengers disembarked with the hapless rating being escorted to detention. After the ship's conversion to peacetime colours was completed, the crew began 21 days' home leave. On 25 December the log recorded: *0910 Hands issued with Christmas beer.*

After eight packed months that included firing the last RAN shots of the war and taking part in three surrenders, the ship settled down to 'Peace on Earth; Goodwill to Men.

River Burdekin

S.S. *River Burdekin*, the first merchant ship built by Evans Deakin, slid down their ways downstream of Brisbane's Story Bridge on 6 March 1943 and, when its stern hit the water, stuck there. Brisbane's *Sunday Mail*, the next day carried a photo of the 'stuck up' vessel 'at a Queensland shipyard.' The upbeat article reported that after Mrs. Kim Beazley had named the ship, 'a slight defect' had stopped it on the ways. The report's focus then shifted to speech excerpts and the celebratory lunch at which the firm presented four-year-old John Beazley with a five-foot (1.5m) long model of a destroyer. As for the *River Burdekin*, 'the ship would soon be afloat, it was said.' However, 'Soon' was a relative term. The 24 March issue of the paper reported, '…it [the ship] had taken the water at the third attempt yesterday.' *River Burdekin* went into service on 12 December 1943.

After voyages around the Australian coast and to the Middle East, July 1945 found the ship in Melbourne. Here the holds were filled to capacity with vehicles, guns, small arms, and 1,000 tons of ammunition. Then the vessel sailed to Sydney where the 'tween decks were crammed with medical supplies, toiletries, cigarettes, chocolate, and 500 tons of beer. Two large landing barges were then secured on deck across number two hatch. Finally the fully laden freighter sailed for Torokina. On arrival *River Burdekin* anchored by the corvette *Bunbury,* and immediately hoisted the barges into the water before beginning the long process of emptying the holds.

The quiet dawn of 15 August at Torokina was followed by wild celebrations as news of Japan's surrender spread. The freighter still had all the ammunition and some of the beer aboard. The decision on which had priority in landing was an easy one for the dockworkers as they took the opportunity to toast the victory. Military police, sent to halt this diversion of the cargo, bowed to the inevitable. Little was unloaded from the ship that day in its original container.

In early September modifications were under way on the ship. Toilets and showers fed by the fire-fighting line were constructed on the port side abreast of two and four holds. A stairway led to number three hold's 'tween decks where bunks were installed. The crew deduced their vessel was to return troops to Australia and the bunks were for officers. They were finally proved right, but the first task of their ship and its similarly modified sister *River Glenelg* was to carry troops to occupy Nauru. From 2 p.m. on 9 September in a thunderous torrential storm the soldiers climbed aboard from barges in a heavy swell.

River Burdekin also carried the New Zealand members of the surrender party including Commander P. Phipps RNZN, and the discoverer of Nauru's phosphates deposits, 73-

year-old Sir Albert Ellis. Sir Albert was also the New Zealand Commissioner of the British Phosphate Commission. Mr. Mark Ridgeway, the Civil Administrator of Nauru and other civil and Phosphate Commission officials completed the party.

When *Diamantina* pushed ahead of the two merchant ships, their captains, 'rumoured… not the best of friends,' began a race to the island. *River Glenelg*, the faster, slowly drew ahead, but Captain W.W. Fish of *Burdekin* had a burning will to win.

In early December 1941 Fish's ship, *Komata*, was one of five delayed by storms off Nauru. Without warning the German raiders *Komet* and *Orion* appeared and ordered the crews ashore preparatory to sinking their ships and destroying the island's loading facilities. Refusing to obey, Fish made a run for it in his New Zealand ship. *Komata* had no chance and, after the chief officer had been killed beside the captain and the second officer mortally wounded, the ship went to the bottom and the survivors joined the other prisoners on the raiders before being put ashore on Emirau Island later that month.

Now the captain of the last allied merchant ship to leave Nauru wanted his new vessel to be the first to return.

While the captains raced, the troops enjoyed three days of *fair weather and glassy seas*. Cots in the 'tween decks, or, for many, bedding down on the open deck made for comfortable sleeping. Each morning, after the atebrin parade and a few light duties, the troops' time was their own. Meals were collected from the field kitchen forward on the starboard side and eaten on deck. There were unlimited saltwater showers, but drinking water was limited to two water bottles per man per day.

The men of 42 Australian Landing Craft Company spent their days preparing Barges Number 14 and 19 on No.2 Hatch for service in the landing. In the evening the five young Nauruans returning home from a war-lengthened stay in Geelong entertained with concerts of traditional and Australian songs learnt during their stay in Australia; *Waltzing Matilda* was a favourite with the troops. Battalion Headquarters produced a daily *Ocean Times* incorporating news collected from short wave broadcasts.

Using his local knowledge and seamanship skills to the full, Fish did arrive first, and, after being assured by *Diamantina* it was not mined, tied up to the Japanese-laid only mooring buoy. In waters too deep to anchor safely offshore and with the prewar buoys destroyed, *Diamantina* and *River Glenelg* had to steam slowly offshore. When the buoy came adrift *River Burdekin* joined them.

After unloading the Australian troops and cargo *River Burdekin* took on 1,600 Japanese prisoners up the gangway, two pilot ladders and two nets. The former enemy were crammed into 1, 2, 4, and 5, 'tween decks while the 40-man guard from the 31/51 Battalion occupied the No.3 'tween decks with its bunks.

The sailing orders to the merchant captains were coldly clear: *At Nauru Masters are to embark the maximum number of prisoners of war consistent with the safety of their vessels. A large degree of discomfort to the prisoners is to be accepte*d. The Japanese, under almost impossibly crowded conditions, kept their spaces spotless. Every morning under the eyes of the eight strategically placed guards armed with Owen guns, the prisoners stretched across the forward end of their areas and, on their hands and knees, *literally blew all the dust and dirt to the after end and then picked it up.* An army field kitchen and 44 gallon drums cooked their food. Each man had been issued with a dixie. At mealtime these were laid in rows in each area and the mess orderlies ladled the food into them. At an order the owners retrieved them and ate. After, small metal pipes filled with tobacco or part of a cigarette were shared. The saltwater showers were filled all day long. The prisoners' organisation and discipline under the crowded conditions impressed the Australians.

Two Japanese died during the voyage. The captain's refusal to stop meant their bodies were committed to the sea as the ship steamed on. The prisoners' resentment at this made the crew and guard happy to see the last of their passengers at Torokina. *River Glenelg* also had some tense times after the accidental discharge of an automatic weapon wounded two prisoners.

After the Ocean Island roundtrip, *River Burdekin* transported Australian troops to Rabaul. Her first return to her homeport came when she carried 800 happy Australian troops from Torokina to Brisbane. Postwar *River Burdekin* was in the coastal coal and iron ore trade until her sale on 11 August 1959 to Jakarta Lloyd for £70,000 sterling. Renamed *Djajadwitya* she last appeared in Lloyd's Register in 1971-72.

Sir Albert Ellis

Sir Albert Ellis's book, *Mid-Pacific Outposts*, completed in March 1946, only six months after the Ocean Island surrender, gives background and many details of both events.

Japan occupied Nauru and Ocean Island to deny phosphate to Australia and New Zealand and take it for itself. In 1914 the Japanese had attempted to occupy the islands, and, in the years before World War II they had bought over half of their phosphate production. Under occupation the islands served as bases and communications links. In the event, problems on the islands and shipping losses meant no phosphate ever reached Japan.

Australia saw the loss of the islands as a serious blow to our agricultural production. Jointly owned by the governments of Australia, New Zealand, and the United Kingdom, the British Phosphate Commission mined on them our major supplies of phosphate fertiliser. Rationing was introduced and supplies were arranged from the United States and other sources. But less than half of the country's usual consumption could be obtained. As it happened, the residue of previous applications of fertiliser and good rains helped maintain agricultural production, but at war's end, resumption of supplies was a high priority.

So, with only a few days' notice, the septuagenarian New Zealand member of the Board of the British Phosphate Commission flew out of Whenuapai airfield near Auckland at 3.30 am on 7 September 1945. With him was Mr. J. A. Bissett, the BPC's New Zealand manager, and CDR. P. Phipps, RNZN. Exactly 30 hours later the DC3 landed at Torokina.

There, with the nearby smoking volcano *much resembling our Ngaruahoe* looming over the camp, Sir Albert linked with a survey party of five of the BPC's most experienced island managers and engineers under the Commission's Chief Engineer, Mr. Bott. Their task was to assess damage and prepare for resumption of operations as soon as possible. The Nauru Administrator, Mr. Mark Ridgeway, his assistant, Mr. Cude, and five young Nauruans who had been studying at Geelong when the island was occupied were other party members. Mr. Bott had wasted no time and already had acquired surplus army equipment for transport to the island.

Less than nine hours after his arrival Sir Albert was an interested spectator at the Bougainville surrender. As New Zealand Corsair fighters circled overhead, military police on motorcycles escorted three vehicles carrying the Japanese and Australians from the wharf to Headquarters. In Gloucester House (prepared for the recent visit of the Governor-General) ...*a picturesque building constructed largely of native materials*, General Kanda drank tea while details were dealt with. Then, in the nearby Battle Room the surrender was signed. After more refreshments were served in Gloucester House the Japanese were driven away. That night Sir Albert was General Savige's guest at dinner. He noted the General's amusement at the wrapped vases gift and the early apprehension that they might be bombs.

The BPC party, CDR. Phipps, Messrs. Ridgeway and Cude sailed on *River Burdekin*. About 500 troops of 31/51 Battalion AIF were divided between the transports. The North Queensland battalions, depleted when many men were discharged to essential industries, had merged on 12 April 1943. After service in West New Guinea the troops had seen tough fighting in Bougainville since December 1944 including the costly battle at Portons Plantation.

At sea many of the troops slept on deck rather than in their 'tween decks accommodation. Sir Albert noted cards were an important part of their recreation. The senior officers and civilians including four doctors were crammed into the few cabins. Sir Albert gratefully accepted Captain Fish's offer of his settee. The pioneer was used to more space altogether. He wrote he had ...*travelled these mid-Pacific seas for well over 50 years...usually not seeing another ship from beginning to end of the voyage*. He found it 'singular' to look a mile abeam to see *River Glenelg* and ahead to *Diamantina*.

Sir Albert was moved by the surrenders and his return to the islands he had first landed on almost a half century before. But this courtly mature New Zealander was particularly affected by the troops. He remembered them as *young fellows of excellent type, mostly from Queensland...longing to be back home with their own people*. However he had one criticism, noting on their handling of their Owen guns, ...*they appeared to be rather careless with these deadly little weapons*.

Sir Albert summed up the soldiers he met as ...*big men in every sense of the term and a fine advertisement for Australia*. He also noted the *highest appreciation* of the Australians of the exploits of the New Zealand airmen who had *done such splendid work in the hard fighting on that mountainous and jungle-clad island [Bougainville]*. Sir Albert concluded, *Even the original Anzacs could not have co-operated more heartily and effectively than at Bougainville Island*.

Officers, October 1945. (L to R) Back: Lts J. Church (Asdic), W. Reid (Navigator), Sub-Lt I. Parkin (Capt's Secretary), Lts L. Finlay-Jones (Surgeon), W. McKendrick (Gunnery). Front: Lt C. Younger (First Lt.), LCDR M. Rose (Captain), LCDR K. Bull (Engineer). Absent: Lt. R. Burgess (Supply). (QMM collection)

First Commission Personalities

LCDR Philip Jack Sullivan, RANVR(S), was Diamantina's second captain. The (S) designated him as a professional seaman in the Navy Reserve, and, during his time in command of the frigate he impressed officers and crew alike with his seamanship. One summed it up with "He drove the old girl like a taxi." Another recalled Diamantina's last 1946 docking in Port Moresby, "We docked in a very high off-shore wind and experienced another example of the skipper's expert ship handling."

Sullivan's biographical note in the RAN's official World War II history is typically laconic: Lt-Cdr P.J. Sullivan, VRD, RANR. Comd HMAS Adele 1939-42, Castlemaine 1942-44, Goulburn 1945. Master mariner and law student; of Mosman, NSW; b. Sydney, 10 August 1897.

It makes no mention of his professional skill acquired during years at sea. Similarly it does not record his ability to maintain a happy, efficient ship. A private man, Sullivan was little seen off duty except for lengthy chess games outside his cabin with the coxswain, CPO 'Marie' Lloyd. But both officers and crew appreciated his confidence in them and relaxed yet effective discipline. One young sub-lieutenant officer of the watch, sweating on the accuracy of his plotting as Diamantina bore down towards a reef in a tricky passage off Kavieng, had a close up of the captain's coolness and skill. With his ship closing the reef at six knots Sullivan quietly waited for his officer's call when the bearing came on. Then the helmsman reported the vessel was not answering the wheel. With a quiet, "Well, now, that's a bit awkward," the captain coolly ordered the ship astern and manoeuvred it to safety on the engines.

Then Midshipman David Smith remembers Sullivan as ...a fair and quietly spoken man...a seaman and ship handler of considerable skill. Writing in 2002, Smith went on, ...On a personal note I was in his debt for the example quietly set at the beginning of my seagoing service. There was one more memory...The Navy knew its midshipmen as 'snotties' with one exception. He addressed me as 'Mister' in accordance with Merchant Service protocol thereby not diminishing what little authority a midshipman had.

The ratings too appreciated 'Spike' Sullivan's manner. One recalled overhearing his quiet admonition to an officer shouting at a hapless berthing party, "Don't swear at the men."

The captain of the port Bofors was grateful for Sullivan's reaction to a tense situation during firing. A decision had been taken to use the direct approach to disposing of ammunition from ashore. This had become a competition between the Bofors' crews. A problem with the ammunition had led to hand feeding and a crew shortage had meant the gun captain was feeding the rounds. The man passing them in the makeshift crew was not doing the job to the feeder's liking, and, without looking up from his task, the gun captain forcefully and loudly gave his opinion of the man's skill. In the ensuing unnatural silence he looked around to find the fill-in crewmember he had just blasted was the First Lieutenant. As the hapless seaman considered his position the captain, watching with others above, lifted his right arm, forefinger up, and pushed his cap peak up slightly. Then he started to laugh. The rest on the afterdeck joined in - with two exceptions. The unfortunate gun captain stayed out of the First Lieutenant's way the rest of the day. However, reporting on watch at midnight, he was appalled to find he was on the bridge. A pleasant, "Blasted anybody lately, Mac?" showed the incident was closed.

Sullivan's mobilisation card records him as five feet four inches with brown greying hair when he reported for duty on 21 October 1939. His Merchant Navy records begin with him joining Wyandra at Sydney on 8 August 1922 as Third Mate. Three years

LCDR P. J. Sullivan (QMM Collection)

later he was a Master. July 1929 was his last recorded Australian voyage before his merchant record resumes post war with interrupted periods of service as master and mate to as far as Singapore, until he left his last ship in Adelaide one month before his 65th birthday.

Appointment as Lieutenant RANVR began Sullivan's Navy career on 1 July 1932. He was transferred to RANR(S) the day before reporting for full time duty, and became Lieutenant Commander on 21 October 1940. Demobilised on 9 September 1946 Sullivan was reappointed RANVR and then promoted to Commander on 30 June 1947. Jack Sullivan transferred to the Retired List on 10 August 1955 and died on 16 October 1987.

LCDR Ken Bull Engineer 'Chiefy' Ken Bull combined a love of the sea and the bush. One of *Diamantina*'s younger officers remembers him as very proficient and a helpful and encouraging colleague with *a wonderful sense of humour.*

The captain, an accountant in civilian life, naturally took a particular interest in the ship's books. Noting that Bull's totals of fuel taken aboard were always in whole tons, Rose questioned this precision. The Engineer, who had to arrive at his figure by means of a very imprecise large dipstick, quickly found a way to satisfy his superior. To each whole tons total he added a decimal point and four random figures. There were no further questions.

Rose was also particular about his binoculars. These were kept in a box on his bridge chair that Walkers had made to his specifications. The eyepieces were precisely adjusted to his requirements and all others were forbidden to touch them. On more occasions than they cared to remember the junior officers felt the sharp side of their captain's tongue when he took his glasses out of the box to find the settings changed. The watch keepers each denied responsibility and eyed their fellow officers with resentful suspicion. Years later 'Chiefy' cheerfully admitted that he was the culprit. In the evenings he would frequently visit the watch keepers on the bridge. As he left it was a matter of seconds to flick open the box, tweak the settings, and close the lid. His defence was it kept the junior officers on their toes.

Lt. Charles Younger, the veteran reservist First Lieutenant, teamed with experienced, respected Petty Officer Jack May to create and maintain effective yet relaxed discipline.

'Chiefy' Bull beats petrol rationing in Maryborough. (K. Bull)

Lt. Bill McKendrick, the Gunnery Officer, was a former Bursar of Scotch College, Melbourne. A very approachable man, he, of all the officers, had the best rapport with the crew.

Lt. John Church, the anti-submarine and radar officer, came to *Diamantina* after spending most of the war, like his commanding officer, on a Flower class corvette in the Atlantic. As with the captain and the first lieutenant, this service gained him quick demobilisation at war's end.

Lt. Bill Franklin, the second Gunnery Officer, had known Bill McKendrick at Scotch College. After joining the RAN under the Yachtsmen's Scheme in December 1941 he trained in the United Kingdom before serving in MTB678 in the English Channel until granted home leave in January 1945. Following a gunnery course Franklin joined HMAS *Pirie* in June 1945, transferring to *Diamantina* three months later. He found *Diamantina ...a happy ship under a first class captain...who handled his ship with great skill in sometimes difficult conditions.*

Sub-Lt. Ian Parkin, the youngest officer, and the only one to serve on the ship throughout the first commission, (fewer than 30 ratings shared this distinction.) joined *Diamantina* just 16 months out of school. He was Assistant to the Supply and Navigation Officers as well as Captain's Secretary.

Lt. Bill Read was the Navigation Officer, while Lt. Ron Burgess was the Supply Officer.

Lt. J. S. Austin, DSC, RAN, succeeded Charles Younger as First Lieutenant in December 1945. Tall, athletic, and a good boxer, he was the only regular navy officer of the first commission. Austin was awarded the DSC 'for skill, determination and courage' while serving on *Shropshire* in the Leyte Gulf operations.

Coxswain Chief Petty Officer Frederick, 'Marie' Lloyd, was a father figure to the young sailors. With greying hair and wearing 'Bombay bloomers' shorts, he led the crew by force of personality and with his encouraging call of "Press on regardless." An enthusiastic chess player, he often filled off duty time in games against all comers, including officers and the second captain.

Leading Stoker Leslie 'Snowy' Kilburn, was the ship's shark fisherman, an accomplished musician on the saxophone, clarinet, piano, drums, mouth organ, and spoons, and *a great bloke and good mate.*

CHAPTER 6

1 9 4 6

1946 opened with *Diamantina* at No. 5 Buoy in Sydney Harbour. On 2 January the Queensland, South Australian, and Victorian crewmembers departed on 21 days leave and travel time. Two days later the ship moved to alongside the destroyer HMAS *Bataan* at Garden Island and the next day came another shift to outboard of HMAS *Quality*. There it stayed for the rest of a month of maintenance, remedying of defects, and completing the conversion to peacetime colours.

Maximum value was wrung out of the movies shown on the quarterdeck. *U-Boat Surrender* screened on 19 and 21 January, with half of *Going My Way* on the first occasion, and the whole feature two nights later. Bing Crosby and Ingrid Bergman entertained yet again in the Academy Award winner on 3 February.

The routine of life alongside was interrupted less pleasantly at 9.20 pm on 23 January when two police boarded to investigate the theft of typewriters.

Just after noon on 1 February, the frigate returned to sea when it got under way for Brisbane. There were many new faces aboard replacing men transferred or demobilised. Changes continued throughout the year so, when the Navy List appeared in July, Ian Parkin was the only original wardroom member of the eight officers.

At 10.30 am on 5 February the ship entered Cairncross Dry Dock with a Brisbane Harbour Board hopper dredge and HMAS *Maryborough* - a full house of Walkers' built ships. When she emerged on 18 February the frigate's underwater hull had been cleaned and covered in anti-fouling paint. As well, both propellers had been replaced and the port shaft renewed. A further entry on 23-4 February replaced the Asdic dome, damaged in the first docking.

After fuelling at the Shell wharf, *Diamantina* cast off at 7.50 am the next day for Dreger Harbour. Victory in a cricket match at St. Lucia oval against HMAS *Cowra* and a successful court appearance by the captain and another officer on behalf of a crewmember had capped a good port visit. Morale was dented a few days out when refrigeration failure resulted in the dumping of all meat and a straitened diet.

Cyclone generated rough seas and Force 6/7 winds between Frederick Reef and Jomard Passage gave the refit a severe test. Sullivan reported, *...the ship behaved splendidly.* He went on to note that, with its newly cleaned bottom, the vessel, on one boiler and at 114 revolutions per minute, maintained 12 knots.

A diversion had *Diamantina* arriving at Oro Bay at 12.13 pm on 1 March to assist the Air Sea Rescue launch, *Air Chief.* With the launch's engine broken down, the frigate took it in tow the next day, and both reached Dreger on 3 March. Here the Naval Officer in Charge, New Guinea, embarked and the ship was on its way to Milne Bay at 10 pm, 5 March. When Captain Stewart was diagnosed with a poisoned foot, course was reversed for Dreger to land him and embark Commanders Mathers and Cairns to deputise for the ill NOIC. After successful visits to Ladava and Modena, *Diamantina* returned the officers to Dreger and sailed for Rabaul. The frigate anchored in Simpson Harbour at 7.45 am on 13 March.

Nine days later the ship sailed again - this time for Kavieng with the General Officer Commanding the Australian New Guinea Administrative Unit, Major-General

Basil Morris, and his staff aboard. The General landed at Kavieng on 23 March, and at Namatani the next day. At the latter *Diamantina* dressed ship and flew the ANGAU flag to lend pomp to the occasion. The locals' gifts of fresh fruit and vegetables made a much-appreciated change from tinned supplies.

The day after returning the General to Rabaul on 25 March, the ship surveyed the approaches to Kokopo as part of its assessment as the site of the proposed new capital. The rest of the month was spent in harbour. Lazy days were filled with games (all lost), going to the horse races, and attending the War Crimes trials held in the Burns Philp warehouse. Some men visited the camp where Chinese were awaiting repatriation. Almost all enjoyed escaping the heat by swimming over the side under the watchful eye of an armed guard on the bridge wing.

The ship now had a public address system and music often wafted through the mess decks - mainly pop, but *The Skaters' Waltz* was a frequent choice. A greater entertainment asset, however, was a copy of the Humphrey Bogart, Lauren Bacall classic film, *The Big Sleep*. It was a pre-release version for the American Forces and the film had not yet been released in Australia. This meant *Diamantina* could obtain two other films from other ships and shore bases for the loan of Bogey and Bacall. When no loans were possible the crew enjoyed its treasure again and again until some knew the dialogue almost by heart.

The languid time ended abruptly on 3 April with a 4.15 am hasty slipping to race at full speed to rendezvous with HMAS *Quiberon*. At 12.45 pm, *Diamantina*'s doctor transferred to the destroyer by breeches buoy. 'Marie' Lloyd kept his

4 RACE 1055 Hours

A.M.F. Cup

No.	NAME	OWNER	JOCKEY	Barrier No.
1	ACK WILLIE 37/52 Inf Bn Wishful Thinking— Heading South		Weight............	
2	SNOWDROP HQ RAE 11 Div Drip—Snowflower		Weight............	
3	SHADY LADY HQ 11 Bde Mistake—Dark Girl		Weight............	
4	ZERO AAOD Spitfire—Skies		Weight............	
5	CURVACIOUS 29/46 Inf Bn Lamour—Sarong		Weight............	
6	FLASH PIR Lightning—Night		Weight............	
7	DUNTROON 22 Inf Bn Getus—Here		Weight............	
8	OVERSEAS 31/51 Inf Bn Youth—Points		Weight............	
9	GOOD DRUM HQ 4 Bde Chifley—Parliament		Weight	
10	CHAOS 8 MD Movement—Control		Weight.	

1............ 2 3

TOTE·

Starters in the main race, Rabaul Army Race Club's final meeting, 20 April 1946. (QMM collection)

word and steered a straight course to ensure his chess opponent did not receive an unscheduled ducking. While the doctors conferred, *Diamantina* returned to Rabaul. With the decision taken to monitor developments and wait for a more stable operating room ashore, *Diamantina*'s medical officer settled down on the destroyer as guest of the wardroom. The operation was successfully carried out at the US hospital a few days later.

For the week after the return from the *Quiberon* dash, the forecastle and quarterdeck were chipped and red leaded. This task was not the most popular job for the crew - so Japanese prisoners carried it out.

On 12 April the ship put to sea again - this time, first to Kavieng to embark Major Shand of ANGAU and then to search for marooned airmen or sailors on the islands east and north of New Ireland. The motorboat was dropped off south of Kavieng to pick up the Major and a rendezvous was arranged to the north. After an idyllic passage to the port, the boat set out in the afternoon with its passenger into increasing wind, rain, and seas. With everyone bailing, they at last glimpsed the ship through the squalls. The big bridge signal lamps were flashing at them - as the Morse-illiterate boat crew thought, to guide them home. It was only after they had boarded and been summoned to the captain's cabin to be greeted with rum and congratulations the sailors found they had just traversed a minefield and the flashings had been a warning.

A six-day cruise to Nuguria, Namatanai, Tench, Emirau (visited the previous year for building materials), and Tingwon Islands found no castaways but produced some memorable moments. As a party prepared to land from the ship anchored outside the reef at Nuguria an outrigger war canoe with 30 paddlers approached. The warriors exchanged their paddles for spears and an old man parlayed with the ANGAU party before the canoe led the motorboat through the reef. It was the beginning of a memorable visit. The Nugurians had been completely ignorant of the war's end. This was balanced, however by an equivalent indifference to who won. Still, *Diamantina* was welcome and a feast capped the visit.

On Tench Island the visitors met a German missionary resident there since World War I. The courteous old man, completely content in his isolation, treated one crewman to *some of the best rum-cured pipe tobacco I have ever smoked.*

Two days of leisure followed the return to Rabaul. On 22 April the ship sailed west for three days in Massava Bay where a mooring buoy for ships to fuel and water was placed before return to Simpson Harbour. The next duty was a local one. On 3 May, *Diamantina* pumped out the bombed Japanese tanker, *Naruto*. The next day the frigate ran her aground on a bank off Hot Sulphur Creek. The grounding was accompanied by an earth tremor as a snapped hawser lashed the deck.

Captain Stewart, NOIC New Guinea, fully recovered from his poisoned foot, was aboard when the frigate sailed at 9 pm, 8 May for Manus Island. There Admiral Sir Louis Hamilton, KCB, DSO, RN, the First Naval Member and Chief of the Australian Naval Staff, joined the ship with his entourage. *Diamantina* then slipped to take its distinguished passenger on a tour of Dreger, Rabaul, Milne Bay, and Port Moresby where Sir Louis disembarked on 18 May.

After only five hours alongside the ship was under way again. Soon after transiting the China Straits the frigate came to anchor in Bartle Bay. At 1.48 pm on 20 May a colour party of an officer and 19 ratings accompanied the NOIC ashore where he presented the ensign flown by HMAS *Arunta* during action against Japanese land force nearby to the Anglican church at Dogura high above the bay.

The NOIC disembarked at Dreger the next day and *Diamantina* was occupied in local duties including ammunition disposal until the end of the month. When the ship sailed at 1.58 pm on 30 May the frigate was bound for Sydney with the Air Sea rescue launch 912, *Air Foam*, in tow. But only seven hours into the voyage the tow parted, forcing a return to Dreger. The two vessels resumed their voyage the next day. It was slow going, broken by a call at Port Moresby the night of 4/5 June to discharge tyres and tubes from Dreger. Then the two vessels headed south.

As the launch crew were not able to cook or even make hot drinks, the ships anchored overnight on 9/10 June in Challenger Bay on Palm Island, so the launch crew could come aboard the frigate for showers, hot food, and a rest. Then, at 4 am, in continuing rough weather, the tow resumed.

Four days later *Diamantina* entered Sydney Harbour with the launch secured on her starboard quarter. At 9 pm, she tied up at No.6 Buoy. *Diamantina*'s successor on Walkers' building slipway, *Shoalhaven*, had commissioned on 2 May. After trials she sailed to New Guinea to relieve her elder sister in the First Frigate Flotilla.

So, in Sydney, *Diamantina* unloaded her ammunition, took on 20 tons of Squid antisubmarine equipment, and, at 8.05 am on 22 June, sailed for Melbourne. The combination of rough seas and a light ship caused a run for overnight shelter in Jervis Bay before the voyage resumed at 7.36 the next morning. At 8.25 am, 25 June, the ship secured alongside Nelson Pier, Williamstown. There she prepared to go into Reserve.

As crew numbers diminished, two-inch rocket flare projectors were fitted to the forward four-inch gun mounting. Other fittings were carefully 'mothballed'. On 17 July the crew, except for a Care and Maintenance Party and the Engine Room Branch, were discharged ashore for leave, dispersal, or demobilisation. That day's log tersely recorded: *1201 Barometer and Wet and Dry Bulbs [thermometers] returned to store. Further readings not possible*. The remaining crew now ate ashore. The ship's accounts were closed. On 25 July LCDR Sullivan relinquished command and left for HMAS *Rushcutter* to be demobilised.

Although the mess decks were silent there was still dockyard activity. At night watchmen did rounds on *Diamantina* and her fellow Queensland Rivers, *Barcoo*, and *Burdekin*. On the morning of 2 August, the silent ship was moved alongside her Walkers' elder sister *Burdekin* at Inner East Nelson Pier. A week later, on 9 August, *Diamantina* paid off to E Reserve.

Care and maintenance went on. In a tragic accident on Boxing Day AB W. Bromley was killed on board. As his death occurred within the time frame, Bromley's became *Diamantina*'s only name on the Australian War Memorial's World War II Roll of Honour.

Time passed. In January 1947 *Burdekin*'s keys were placed in *Diamantina*'s care. As the months rolled into years the Hedgehog was removed, the forward four-inch gun was moved onto the forecastle deck and Squid mortars took its place. Periodically the ship was moved and entered dry dock as part of ongoing maintenance.

Diamantina might be needed again.

CHAPTER 7

SECOND COMMISSION 1959-1969

1959

At 11 am on 22 June 1959, HMAS *Diamantina* was commissioned for the second time into the Royal Australian Navy. LCDR B.D. Gordon assumed command in a ceremony that included Protestant and Roman Catholic chaplains blessing the ship alongside the Cruiser Wharf at Garden Island in Sydney.

The ship's company, which had been living on HMAS *Fremantle* alongside, moved into their messes on 25 June. *Fremantle*, a World War II Australian Minesweeper, smaller and slower than *Diamantina*, had been the Navy's presence in Western Australia, training National Servicemen and Reservists from March 1953 until it sailed for Sydney on 3 May 1959. LCDR Gordon and a number of her crew transferred to *Diamantina* as did her canteen before she paid off to Reserve the day after the frigate recommissioned. *Fremantle* was sold out of service on 6 June 1961.

At Williamstown in E Class Reserve, *Diamantina* had undergone a refit between July 1946 and February 1947. In March that year two triple-barrelled Squid anti-submarine mortars were fitted forward of the bridge. As well, in the same month, the Asdic dome was removed. Then *Diamantina* and her elder Walkers' built sister, *Burdekin*, were moved to Geelong's W Buoy at the north end of Corio Bay. The years then passed in a routine of maintenance, moves, and dockings until the ship was returned to service after a refit at Garden Island to prepare her for oceanographic research.

On 23 June, *Diamantina* slipped at 8.50 am and moved under her own power to No.4 Buoy to load ammunition and swing the compass. Six days later came gun functioning and sea trials. The full power trial was abandoned when bearings in the port engine overheated. The last day of June saw the ship sail at 7.55 pm for five days working up in the Jervis Bay area. Back in Sydney on 6 July, *Diamantina* embarked dockyard and CSIRO personnel for sea and oceanographic trials. In spite of the recurrence of the overheating in the engine, a speed of 18 knots was recorded. The next day Rear Admiral D.H. Harris, Flag Officer in Command Eastern Australia, and Mr. J. Gorton, Minister for the Navy, carried out a two hour morning inspection.

After this period of intense working up, *Diamantina* sailed from Sydney at noon on 11 July. That evening between 5.25 and 8.10 pm the first oceanographic research readings were made east of Ulladulla in 2,300 fathoms. The scientists on this historic occasion at 35 degrees 8 minutes South, 151 degrees 28 minutes East were D.J. Rochford, J. Stanifort, and H. Jitts.

In Melbourne on 13 July a spare bearing was fitted to the troublesome port engine while the ship was open to visitors. At 10 am next day, the voyage to Fremantle was resumed. Eight hours later the anchor went down in Apollo Bay for more work on the recalcitrant bearing. South of Kangaroo Island and Eucla five and a half hour deep oceanographic probes were made on 16 and 18 July. Off Eucla a break in the wire sent five Nansen water-sampling bottles to the bottom.

More work to fix the recurring bearing problem went on at Albany's No.1 Berth from 9.30 am to 5 pm on Monday 20 July. Then, with twenty 13 to 18-year-old cadets from the Training Ship *Vancouver* aboard, the ship sailed on the last leg to Fremantle.

F377 soon after recommissioning with 4 inch gun on fore deck bandstand. (RAN)

All but two of the cadets under the command of LT J.L. Wilkinson were from Albany High School. Cadets and crew handled with aplomb the rough weather 'turning the corner' round Cape Leeuwin. Action Stations on the morning of 21 July was followed with a gunnery shoot.

Diamantina arrived at Fremantle for the first time at 8.40 pm 21 July 1959, tying up at No. 4 Berth North Wharf. Next morning West Australian members of the crew departed on three weeks' leave. The remainder settled into a self-maintenance period. An early task was decorating life-raft paddles with Western Australia's black swan emblem.

Late on 27 July the *Vancouver* cadets returned to Albany - by train. Other cadet units succeeded them on the ship. Three officers and 41 cadets from T.S. *Bedford* and *Cresswell* embarked on 7 August for two days' training alongside. They were followed, on Monday 17 August, by the same number of officers and cadets from T.S. *Cunningham* at Scotch College for a cruise to Geraldton.

A morning departure from Fremantle on 20 August was followed by an afternoon 4-inch and 40/60 mm. shoot. The next day the ship tied up at Geraldton's No. 3 Wharf for three busy days of the Geraldton Sunshine Festival. In the afternoon over 1,000 visitors toured the ship which was dressed overall. The following day, Saturday 22 August, an armed guard and three unarmed platoons joined the cadets and the Naval Reserve Band in a march to the Recreation Ground. The Naval Officer in Charge, Western Australia, Commodore J.C. Morrow, took the salute. That evening the Commodore hosted a cocktail party aboard. On Sunday afternoon another 1,000 visitors boarded the ship and watched a diving display before the cadets and the band departed for Perth by bus.

At 10 am, Monday, 24 August, with Lt Neville Smethurst and 13 other ranks of the Special Air Service embarked, *Diamantina* sailed to end a very successful 'show the flag' visit. After taking on fuel at Onslow, course was set for Derby. En route bathythermograph readings were taken and a Royal Guard practised on the quarterdeck. At Derby on 29 August, SAS stores were unloaded. Until 13 September the ship surveyed with the SAS in the remote extreme north-west from Admiralty Gulf to Prince Frederick Harbour. The troopers, as well, built eight helicopter landing pads about 50 miles (80 km) apart for an Army survey team to use the next year.

The ship's motor cutter, equipped with an echo sounder, Type 625 radio, and radar reflector mast, was busy leading the ship and exploring uncharted waters on its own. Crocodiles were plentiful. On a trip up the Hunter and Roe Rivers the cutter crew shot 15.

Close observation aided navigation. The captain's report noted discoloured water and whirlpools in one area were ...*always a good indication of deep water.* A deep passage into Doubtful Bay was discovered by following a humpback whale and her calf.

On 10 September an Army chartered Cessna aircraft was a welcome visitor when it dropped the first mail received in 14 days. This period of stimulating activity ended when Lt. Smethurst and his party landed at Derby on 14 September. Then *Diamantina* sailed for three days of fisheries surveillance at Rowley Shoals. Two big Chinese trawlers and a small Indonesian fishing boat were the only sightings.

Another task that was to become familiar in later years followed the sailing from Onslow at 7.20 am on 20 September. In the Monte Bello Islands that afternoon and the next day LCDR A.A. Andrews, LT A. Watson, and a staff Atomic Biological and Chemical Warfare instructor made a radiation survey of the atomic test site. While they worked, Commodore Morrow, Mr. F. Sampson, the Mayor of Fremantle, and the crew enjoyed an afternoon's fishing. The Monte Bello's visit ended with the Commodore and the Mayor as guests of the wardroom at a mess dinner ...*which resulted in all participants being radioactive at breakfast the following morning.*

The visit to Carnarvon from 9 am, 24 September to 1 pm the next day provided the last highlight of the first cruise. The crew were guests at the Picnic Races ...*a most enjoyable, and, in isolated cases, a most profitable afternoon.* At 8 am, 27 September, the ship tied up at Fremantle's No.4 Wharf, and Commodore Morrow and Mr. Sampson disembarked.

On 3 October the Royal Guard's hours of practice paid off with a nearly faultless display of drill at the Showground. Two days later six CSIRO scientists under Mr. D. Rochford joined the ship. Then, at 10.30 am on 11 October, *Diamantina* sailed on an extended oceanographic cruise. Departure had been delayed for four days awaiting the arrival of essential instruments from Japan. Before securing to Onslow jetty at 10.10 am, 15 October, to take on 100 tons of furnace oil, *Diamantina* had carried out a foreign fishing vessel survey, bathythermographic dips, and plankton tows. The echo sounder had run continuously. During the six hour stay the CSIRO team disembarked before the ship sailed for Christmas Island; 34 oceanographic dips to a maximum depth of 18,720 feet had been carried out by the time the ship secured to C Buoy, Flying Fish Cove at 10.10 am, 22 October. The captain's Report of Proceedings detailed the work carried out at 2 am, 6 am, 2 pm, and 6 pm daily. The two o'clock stations involved dipping the bathythermograph to 900 feet, then collecting phytoplankton by towing the Hardy Indicator at 12 knots for 30 minutes.

For four to five hours from 6 o'clock the oceanographic winch lowered Nansen bottles to collect water samples at depths of 1,000m and between 3,000 and 6,000m. The starboard bathythermographic davit and winch collected from depths of 25, 50, and 100m, as well as at the surface. The oxygen, salt, nitrate, phosphate, and carbon dioxide content of each sample were measured in varying combinations.

Pigmentation was also recorded. When water sampling was completed, the ship streamed a Clarke-Bumpus net at two knots to a depth of 270m for 30 minutes to collect zooplankton.

Some stations stretched to 9 hours when the messenger weight, which took up to 50 minutes to travel down the wire on the deepest stations, failed to trip the sampling bottles forcing a repetition of the dip. On the morning of 21 October, the wire's lack of flexibility caused it to break consigning 3,000m and five Nansen bottles to the bottom.

Ten hours after reaching Christmas Island on the first of what was to be many visits, the ship sailed for Cocos Is. Early in the evening of 24 October the routine of oceanographic stations was interrupted. The log entry reads: *1645 course and speed various for carrying out an appendix operation.* Surgeon Lieutenant Mulholland's skill on his unstable operating table was apparent to all when M.E. 2 D.M. Woolstencroft was discharged from the sick list on 2 November. The morning after the operation *Diamantina* came to single anchor in Port Refuge, Cocos Islands. A soccer match and cocktail party were highlights of a pleasant two days before the ship sailed.

After a call at Onslow on 3 November, the cruise ended at 10A Berth, Fremantle at 7.12 am, 19 November. In 40 days at sea, 133 stations had been occupied over a distance of 8,269 nautical miles. In the cruise's second half, the watch on deck had performed all deck duties, thus freeing the scientists for laboratory work as well as allowing stations to occur at any hour, day or night.

The ship settled down to a period of self-refit and long leave. Its first year's tasks foreshadowed the range of those in the years ahead - RAN training, 'show the flag' to Western Australian towns, monitoring the Monte Bello's atomic test sites, surveillance, and oceanographic research.

Early in December there was a ceremony on the 15-year- old recommissioned ship. Chief Petty Officer C.G.F. (Charlie) Seymour, a 33 year Navy veteran, received a clasp for his Long Service and Good Conduct Medal. Charlie Seymour, of Fremantle, was not looking forward to his retirement in 1961. Nobody at the ceremony dreamed that when *Diamantina* finally steamed out of her new home-port, the time since her first commissioning would exceed Charlie's length of service by two years.

Diamantina's Badge

Two weeks before *Diamantina* recommissioned, Commander N.H.S.White of the Navy Office in Melbourne wrote on 8 June 1959 to the captain, LCDR Gordon, then on HMAS *Fremantle*. After telling Gordon *The Honours, Badges, and Nomenclature Committee are scratching their heads like mad about a design for the badge*, White lightly touched on some rejected ideas. These included designs incorporating such outback symbols as windmills and even camels. An inspired suggestion to Gordon was that he find and send a copy of Diamantina Bowen's Roma-Candiano family crest - *as in the case of* Gascoyne *we may be able to make an effective ship's badge out of it.*

On 9 July, Gordon, by then on *Diamantina*, sent a copy of the family crest with a further request for a motto - *...some suitable Latin phrase which would include oceanographic and survey duties.* Three weeks later Mr. N. Constantino of the Italian Embassy sent Gordon the Candiano family motto, *Hic regit; ille tuetur.* He attached a translation by 'a professor of Sydney University', *The one rules (or reigns); the other protects (or defends).* The Navy Office refined this to *Whoever rules, protects.*

The Naval Board considered and then approved both badge and motto on 30 December 1960. In January 1997 the Ships' Names, Badges, and Honours Committee revisited the matter. The new minehunter MHC05 was to become the second ship to bear the name, *Diamantina*. It would adopt *Diamantina* I's badge. But, after considering the new ship's tasks and modern tastes and sensibilities, the Committee decided its motto would be in English rather than in Latin, and would be rendered as *Whoever leads, protects*.

Why oceanography?

(Requests to Australian, British, New Zealand, and United States authorities for details of *Diamantina*'s defence related operations have proved fruitless. The following has been compiled from other sources.)

George Humphrey, chief of the Commonwealth Scientific and Industrial Research Organisation (CSIRO) Division of Fisheries and Oceanography, was pleasantly surprised when the RAN made *Diamantina* and her sister, *Gascoyne*, available for oceanographic research in mid-1959. The small division's scientists, used to basic leased fishing boats, had gratefully accepted use of HMAS *Queenborough* and *Quickmatch* in 1958 for International Geophysical Year observations in the Coral and Tasman Seas.

From 1959 *Diamantina* in the Indian Ocean and *Gascoyne* in the Pacific were godsends to the researchers. In her final configuration, *Diamantina* had two fully equipped laboratories and two four-berth air-conditioned cabins for the scientists with attached shower and toilet. The senior 'boffin' had a single cabin.

Why such generosity from a perpetually cash-strapped Navy? Oceans cover over 70% of the globe and most of the world's trade flows over their surfaces. Until the late 1950s most international passengers crossed them by ship. Countries like Australia with a seaboard also use ships for internal transport. Oceans are also an important food source and, increasingly, minerals like oil and gas are extracted from the sea-bed. The oceans' water masses also influence the world's weather.

Organised study of this major part of our environment - oceanography, had its origin in the three- year world voyage of HMS *Challenger* in the early 1870s. Subsequent studies were small scale and fragmented until survival stimulated research.

Twice in the 20th century German submarines came within a hairsbreadth of defeating Britain in war. As well, in the Second World War, United States submarines devastated Japanese merchant and naval shipping. Both sides in both wars carried out intensive oceanographic research to gain an edge in this three-dimensional war beneath the waves.

Between the wars research languished. But after the Second World War some researchers, especially in the United States, maintained and developed links with the Navy - the source of funds and ships. This uneasy alliance between many oceanographers, seeking pure knowledge of the ocean, and the Navy, striving for an edge in future submarine warfare, persisted.

Using sound to detect submerged submarines started in the First World War and developed in the Second. Both passive and active sonars were used. Passive systems listen for sounds generated by the vessel. Active sonar emits a pulse and computes its target's range and bearing from the return echo. Sound travels a long way through water and at a speed, on average, four times faster than in air. But differences in the water's salinity, density, and temperature vary the speed. The sound may also be reflected, refracted, or absorbed by the water surface, sea floor, chemicals, gases, or living matter. Other noises from marine life, waves, or other ships, including the searching vessel, may mask the target's signal. So scientists worked to achieve accurate and timely detection in spite of these difficulties.

After World War II the submarine threat escalated dramatically. The Allied shock at discovering the high speeds of the submarines the Germans were developing at war's end spurred research into fast accurate long-range detection. The bar was raised again when the revolutionary USS *Albacore* exceeded 30 knots submerged in 1954. Better steels and design meant submarines of the 1950s could also dive deeper.

Then came the greatest advance. Up to then all underwater craft had not been true submarines. They were submersibles, basically surface ships that could submerge for a short time until they had to surface to charge their batteries quickly depleted, especially by high speed.

On 17 January 1955 the US Navy commissioned its first atomic submarine, USS *Nautilus*. The atomic power plant and systems for crew support meant it could remain submerged and travel at high speed for months. In 1958 the USSR atomic submarine programme also swung into gear. In 1955 the American Project NOBSKA studied the implications of these submarine advances on undersea warfare. Gary E. Weir, in his *An Ocean in Common* quotes a telling sentence from the NOBSKA report, ... *Experience to date indicates that almost any aspect of oceanography, either physical, chemical, geological, or biological has some bearing on undersea warfare.*

The Americans concentrated their research on the Atlantic and north Pacific Oceans. From 1959 the RAN ships carried scientists to study our adjacent oceans - the south Pacific and Indian extending well south of the continent. The work covered the whole spectrum of oceanographic research sometimes in association with American, British, and New Zealand personnel and vessels. One organisation, Australia's Weapons Research Establishment which operated on *Diamantina*, stated in its 1967/8 Report that its research into Australia's ocean environment was ...*aimed at gathering a better understanding of the phenomena affecting undersea sound propagation over great distances.*

In the August 1977 issue of the Australian Defence magazine, *Triad*, Bruce Davis detailed *the importance of oceanography in assisting the RAN [to] improve its anti-submarine warfare capability.* He listed the RAN's objectives in oceanographic research as including:

- assisting the prediction of sonar performance in different areas;
- assisting in the design, selection, and tactical use of the RAN's anti-submarine warfare equipment;
- investigating energy exchange just above the sea surface to improve the detection of sea-skimming missiles;
- facilitating such civilian oceanography aims as production of an oceanographic atlas, and study of oceanic resources and water masses.

The last objective illustrates the difficulty of differentiating between civilian and military research. For example, warm water oceanic eddies appeared to focus sonar beams. There was however, much pure civil research too. Harry Jitts, one of the CSIRO team that took the first oceanographic readings from *Diamantina*, sailed on many cruises. In his chapter 'Frigate Days' in *CSIRO at Sea*, Jitts paid tribute to the Navy's contribution when he wrote, ...*the two frigates, HMAS* Diamantina *and* Gascoyne *sailed on into oceanographic history. Our waters went from Mare Incognitum to some of the most studied in the world.*

Yet, it seems that pure and applied civil science were not the driving force behind the research. *Diamantina*, which had figured prominently at the end of the Pacific War was also at the forefront of the Cold War; 80-90% of all US oceanography at this time, Weir reports, was funded by the Navy. It is reasonable to assume the same applied in Australia. We too seem to have taken to heart President Kennedy's message to Congress on 29 March 1961, less than two years after *Diamantina* recommissioned in her oceanographic role, *Knowledge of the oceans is more than a matter of curiosity. Our very survival may depend on it.*

1960

With the annual refit and long leave extending from the end of each calendar year into the next, the story of *Diamantina*'s second commission falls neatly into year chapters.

The year 1960 opened with *Diamantina* secured alongside 10A Wharf, North Fremantle. In a sombre start to the year, a party, on 6 January attended the funeral of Sub-Lieutenant Mauritz.

Between 11 and 16 January, on the South Slipway, the hull was scraped, anti-fouling and zincs renewed, and the propellers and all underwater fittings examined. The ship's staff also replaced the anti-submarine dome, damaged by the keel blocks while under the Dockmaster's control. While on the slip, a new AS49 depth recorder was fitted.

The Canteen Flat was put to an unusual use on 12 January when three deserters from HMS *Centaur* were detained there until the Navy Police returned them to their ship next morning. A more pleasant connection with *Centaur* was the cricket match against 801 Squadron, which *Diamantina* won.

In six days from 18 January, a new crankshaft section was fitted to the troublesome port engine. Full power trials north-west of Rottnest Island on 26 January put it to the test. It failed. The high-pressure bottom bearing again overheated. Two days later Cockburn Engineering discovered and removed paint chips in the system and subsequent full power trials up to 18 knots produced no recurrence of the problem.

The annual small arms practice at Swanbourne Rifle Range on 20 and 21 January, was another event in this month of 'inactivity' which culminated in an inspection on the 29th, by the Naval Officer in Charge, Western Australia, Captain Wright.

On 2 February, with five CSIRO Department of Fisheries and Oceanography researchers aboard, *Diamantina* sailed south on her second oceanographic cruise - D1/60. In 16 days, including two of cold, dense fog in the Roaring Forties, the ship gathered plankton and took deep-water readings. As well, there were practice shoots of the 4-inch and 40/60 guns. The new AS49 depth recorder operated continuously. At 3.50 pm, 7 February, 620 nautical miles west of Cape Leeuwin it indicated a depth increase from 2,500 to 3,400 fathoms. The next morning the figure plunged to 4,400 fathoms. This, the greatest depth then recorded in the Indian Ocean, the Navy Board named the Diamantina Deep. On modern maps and charts it appears as the Diamantina Trench or Diamantina Fracture Zone.

After a week in port *Diamantina* put to sea again on 26 February. For three days she conducted seismic and hydrophone tests in association with the United States Research Vessel *Vema* in the Geographe Bay area. By 11 pm, 29 February, the ship was back at No. 3 North Wharf. But this cruise's importance far exceeded its short duration. The DCNS noted on the Report, *An interesting report of work with* Vema.

Vema itself was interesting. The iron hulled three masted schooner built in Copenhagen in 1923 had been first owned by E.F. Hutton, founder of the New York stockbroking firm, and uncle of the Woolworth heiress, Barbara Hutton. Renamed *Vema* by its new owner in 1934, it crossed the Atlantic in 10 days 10 hours. She spent

World War II as a requisitioned floating barracks at the Merchant Marine Academy. Professor Maurice Ewing of Columbia University's Lamont Geological Observatory saw the ship's potential in a charter cruise in 1953, and the Observatory later bought and refitted it. Ewing worked the ship hard. Each year she averaged 30,000 miles and 10 months at sea.

On this voyage, studying sea floor structure *Vema* had left New York the previous October and sailed via Brazil and South Africa before reaching Fremantle from Mauritius on 22 February. After its three days with *Diamantina* the research vessel continued its circumnavigation via Cape Horn to return to New York in August. Panama registered and crewed by 19 Nova Scotians, the diesel-engined vessel with its Columbia research team was financed by the United States Navy and the National Science Foundation.

A typical *Vema* research profile of 30 miles with *Diamantina* took up to 12 hours. The receiving ship hove to and lowered a hydrophone while the other followed a prescribed course away dropping explosive charges ranging from a half to 300 pounds at determined times. Echoes from the varying strata were recorded for later analysis. At the extreme range the 'shooting ship' became the 'listener', quiet on battery power and the process was repeated. One Australian researcher later recalled his almost constant seasickness during the three days and the meticulous care of *Vema*'s powder monkey who he had been detailed to assist. The American always stationed his Australian assistant at a safe distance during dangerous procedures. Some years later, the assistant heard of his companion's death in a premature explosion.

Vema had heard of the Diamantina Deep discovery while on passage from Mauritius and had diverted to investigate it. Harry Jitts reported in *CSIRO At Sea*, the search was fruitless. He went on, "*...the American crew dubbed it the Diamantina A...hole and the frustrated cruise leader speculated that a Soviet submarine had run off with the thing. Fortunately he was later proved wrong.* One wonders if the cruise leader's joking reference to a Soviet submarine might point to a military application for the information gathered on his ostensibly scientific cruise financed by the United States Navy.

Only 21 hours after docking, *Diamantina* put to sea again, this time for Adelaide. Deep water readings, plankton sampling, and 4-inch and 40/60 shoots were interspersed with two more periods of seismic profiling with *Vema* before the ship tied up at No.1 Berth, Port Adelaide at 4.50 pm, 13 March. The first rendezvous with *Vema* had been at noon on 2 March at 35 degrees South and 115 degrees East - just south of Cape Leeuwin. Two days of seismic profiling followed with Mr. J. Hennion of Columbia University and Mr. E. Jesson of the Australian Bureau of Mineral Resources and Mr. H. Doyle of the Australian National University making up the team on the Australian ship.

Diamantina next met her American consort south-west of Kangaroo Island at 7 am on 11 March. Professor Nafe of Columbia University joined the team for two more days of profiling. On the morning of 13 March, between Capes Forbes and Torrens the ships anchored while the seismic equipment was returned to the schooner. *Diamantina* then weighed to berth in Adelaide that afternoon. *Vema* arrived next morning to tie up astern.

In Adelaide, the Australian scientists and Mr. Hennion disembarked. On 16 March LCDR Gordon left the ship to take up command of HMAS *Anzac*. LCDR G. Jude was his replacement. In one of his last acts as *Diamantina*'s captain, LCDR Gordon addressed a problem that had come to a head on the latest cruise - the demise of the Wardroom Pantry's refrigerator. In a request for a 7 cubic foot refrigerator, he pointed out the inadequate capacity of the ship's 12 domestic refrigerators and the age of the Wardroom Pantry appliance - *it is pre-1945 construction*. New refrigerators were supplied.

LCDR Jude took his new command to sea for Fremantle at 1 pm, 16 March. Tracking west along 37 degrees South Latitude, *Diamantina* made full oceanographic stations on every second meridian between 132 and 118 degrees East. As well, there was a daily 10 am net tow to sample productivity and plankton. Regular bathythermograph and soundings readings were also made.

Then, at 33 degrees 13 minutes South and 113 degrees 43 minutes East (south-west of Cape Leeuwin), *Diamantina* fired shots literally 'heard around the world'. From 2.55 am, 22 March, at five minute intervals, three depth charges were dropped. The detonators, supplied by *Vema*, exploded them at 800 fathoms to be detected by United States Navy SOFAR monitors on the Atlantic Ocean bed off St. David's Lighthouse, Bermuda. SOFAR (Sound Fixing and Ranging) experiments explored the possibility of using Professor Ewing's discovery of a deep sound channel in the ocean to detect vessels up to thousands of miles away.

LCDR Jude reported each depth charge contained 300 pounds of Amatol explosive and was fitted with three pressure detonators, two primers, one one-and-a-half pound charge of TNT and one pound of plastic explosive. They were fired while the ship was steering a course of 235 degrees at a speed of 4 knots. The centre charge was fired on the designated position, and all were dropped in water 1,350 fathoms deep. Greenwich Mean Time firing times were 19 hours 4 minutes 11 seconds, 19h. 9m. 43s. and 19h. 14m. 7s. The next day, at 11 am, the ship tied up at the now familiar 10A North Wharf, Fremantle. A week of dumping of surplus ammunition outside the 300 fathom line began on 28 March.

10 April was a festive day on board. The Navy Reserve chaplain, Rev. C.W. Chetwynd, christened Deborah Jane Terry. Deborah, daughter of LT Terry, was the first to be christened on board in *Diamantina*'s second commission and afterwards *The baby's head was well wetted.*

With a SAS officer and seven other ranks together with four boats embarked, the ship sailed the next day for the previous year's survey area. After overcoming a recurrence of the engine bearing heating problem a stop was made at Onslow for fuel. Off Derby, seven more SAS troopers came on board, and the survey began on 16 April. In sketchily surveyed waters of the Admiralty Gulf, Vansittart Bay area, the soldier surveyors, carrying five days' supply of food and water in their Zodiac boats, went about their task. *Diamantina* made its contribution with the echo sounder mounted in the motorboat and the ship's anti-submarine team 'pinging' ahead.

Then, torrential rain and winds to 50 knots on the night of 25/26 April reinforced cyclone warnings. With surveying out of the question for the immediate future and a broken refrigerator pipe threatening the perishable food, the captain made for Darwin.

In a day alongside Stokes Hill Jetty, M.(E). I.D. Weir was landed to hospital with appendicitis, the ship refuelled, a new pipe fitted, and the refrigerator topped up. On the return voyage the 4-inch and 40/60 gun crews carried out firings. By 29 April the surveying parties were back at work.

The week's work between Vansittart Bay and Prince Frederick Harbour was followed by a return to Darwin for four days of make and mend. HMAS *Melville* provided opponents in cricket, water polo, soccer, and tennis matches. Other groups ranged further afield to Howard Springs, Rum Jungle, and Humpty Doo.

At 4.10 pm on 11 May, *Diamantina* sailed to resume surveying. At Montague Sound and Prince Frederick the SAS parties returned aboard. They reported the helicopter landing pads had been completed and five drums of AVGAS had been airdropped to each. The Montague Sound party had more to report. While two troopers had been fishing from their Zodiac rubber boat, a crocodile had jumped in. The quick thinking pair left their unwelcome visitor in sole occupancy and began swimming for shore towing the boat. Once the boat grounded the troopers headed inland at speed while the crocodile returned to the water. Next day the SAS returned armed and disposed of the hitchhiking reptile.

The Navy and Army parties, in spite of the cyclone delay, finished their survey two weeks ahead of schedule. On 19 May the Derby SAS party disembarked and, after anchoring in Shark Bay (a noted fishing spot) on 23 May, the ship ended its 5,802.2 mile cruise at 10A North Wharf at 8 am, 27 May. Here Major Lionel Sprenger of the Royal Australian Army Survey Corps and the remaining SAS troopers disembarked at the end of a most successful and harmonious cruise.

Captain Jude put on record some lessons learned from this joint operation in the remote north-west. Like the crocodile, he was impressed with the Army's Zodiac boats. Tips from Western Australian State Shipping Service captains had facilitated his investigation of Sampson Inlet. And a tip from a much older captain had also been useful. Noting that Captain Stokes had reported in 1821 that Port George IV had *a fine beach for the seine*, *Diamantina* had used its net there to catch enough sea mullet to feed the whole ship's company.

June was a 'quiet' month. It began with the ship providing a Guard for the Western Australia Foundation Day ceremony on 6 June. The NOIC's annual inspection followed on 13 and 14 June. After the Ship's Company's Ball at the Pagoda Ballroom came a period of leave and self maintenance that had the ship on the slip on 28 June.

Trials followed unslipping on 5 July. *Diamantina* then sailed into a westerly gale on Oceanographic Cruise 2/60 on 11 July. This was a preliminary to a larger UNESCO multi-ship survey planned for the next year. Sea boat races relieved the monotony when the ship stopped to take readings from 5.30 am on 16 July until 7 pm next day. More such stations followed as the researchers investigated currents, water composition, temperature, and plankton.

Early on 27 June, in pouring rain, *Diamantina* entered Sunda Strait, passing to the south of Krakatoa before dawn with the eight-breadth sea ensign floodlit. Crossing the Line was marked with due ceremony the next day, and, at 9.20 am, 29 July, the ship tied up alongside HMS *Dampier* in Singapore. Here, while the crew enjoyed leave, local technicians repaired the defective radar and refrigeration. The captain later noted the improvement in morale from the run ashore and the ship's presence in a large fleet. No leave breaking or drunkenness was recorded in Singapore.

After slipping at 2 pm, 2 August for Jakarta, *Diamantina* was joined for a time by an uninvited consort, *Vedyansk* of Leningrad (now St. Petersburg) *while cameras on both ships worked overtime*. More hydrology stations, gun shoots, and shark fishing (one on 7 August provided the ship's company with breakfast) occupied the crew. The log also records that on the same day that the shark fed the crew, *a whale made use of the ship's bottom in assisting its toilet*.

Arriving off Jakarta at 8 a.m., 12 August, *Diamantina* joined three Indonesian Navy ships waiting for the pilot. The Australian vessel was taken straight in. Although leave was restricted to organised parties, the crew enjoyed two days of visits to hill stations and Australian Embassy staff homes. The captain and the senior scientist, Mr. H. Jitts, made official calls. The Chief of the Indonesian Navy's Hydrographic Section, and the Director of Maritime Research, at the Australian Government's invitation, joined the ship. At 9 am, 14 August, *Diamantina* sailed to continue the survey towards Port Moresby.

The routine of oceanographic research was interrupted by a call at Thursday Island for gas for the troublesome refrigeration system before the ship began an enjoyable three days in Port Moresby on 27 August. On the cruise's next leg to Darwin a gunnery shoot was carried out and the scientific work continued. Recurrence of the radar and refrigeration problems meant, during the five days in port from 6 September, a new condenser was fitted and the radar was partially repaired; 1,000 seed coconuts, brought from Port Moresby for a trial Aboriginal plantation were landed.

After another scientist joined and the Indonesian observers disembarked, the ship sailed for Fremantle. Before the most concentrated scientific work of the cruise began an exercise with a RAAF Lincoln aircraft and a ship's concert occupied the sailing day and evening.

Radar and refrigerator repairs, trials, the embarkation of new training classes, and a Family Day on 6 October, whose 80 guests included the anti-submarine officer's grandmother, occupied the time from arrival on 26 September, until the ship sailed again on 16 October.

Cruise D3/60 settled into a routine of oceanographic stations and gunnery and small arms shoots. The log on 21 October recorded the ship's second whale close encounter of the year, *1815 Whale swam into the port side of the ship*. No damage to either party was noted.

On the 31 October, the ship made its usual refuelling stop at Onslow. Later that morning the Governor of Western Australia, Sir Charles Gairdner, arrived, inspected a Guard of Honour, and embarked for the Cocos Islands. During the six-day passage, His Excellency, quartered in the captain's cabin, took a keen interest in the scientific work. After a short call at Christmas Island, *Diamantina* came to anchor at Cocos at 9 am, 7 November - the first Australian warship to do so since the islands came under Australian sovereignty. Two days of official calls, visits, a ship's cocktail party, and cricket and soccer matches followed. (*Diamantina* lost the soccer, 10-0)

At 8.30 am, 9 November, *Diamantina* landed a Guard on Direction Island. Two hours later Sir Charles unveiled a memorial to the World War I *Sydney-Emden* action - the Royal Australian Navy's first victory. HMAS *Tingira* Old Boys' Association had provided the bronze plaque set above high water mark at the spot where the German party had landed to destroy the cable and wireless station. *Tingira* was the original RAN training ship and 60 of its old boys had been in *Sydney's* crew.

With the visit's purpose completed, course was set for Fremantle. A 4-inch shoot on 11th punctuated the scientific work, and the ship tied up at 10 am, 15 November. A 102-man Guard of Honour of HMAS *Leeuwin* Junior Recruits met the Governor as he was piped ashore; 50 Junior Recruits who had sailed on the cruise later returned to *Leeuwin*.

The year was ending. The ship's Christmas Ball at the Pagoda took place two days after the return. Long Leave began. The 4-inch gun was landed for modification and a new barrel while the deck below it was renewed. Other work included a larger oceanographic area on X Deck, air conditioning and extra space for the laboratory area, re-bricking the furnaces, tiling the bathrooms and heads, overhaul of the washing machines and water coolers, and installation of a deep freeze, and ice cream and soda machines. Father Christmas visited the children's party on 7 December. After time on the slip from 12 to 21 December, *Diamantina* saw the year out at 10A North Wharf.

It had been a varied, busy year ranging through the ceremony of the *Sydney-Emden* memorial unveiling, recruit training, coastal survey, and scientific work off the south, west, and north coasts. The CSIRO's assessment of the 1960 cruises' value was unequivocal. The head of hydrology, Mr. D. Rochford stated they had ...*put Australia* in the forefront of international research in the Indian Ocean. *Diamantina's* crew had played no small part in the successful research. But the work had also benefited the ship. The captain reported the increased canteen sales resulting from army, sea cadet, and CSIRO spending had given ship's funds a healthy boost. This paid for the ice cream and soda machines and helped pay the extra film rental charges incurred by the long oceanographic cruises.

1961

In a quiet beginning to 1961, seamen trainees joined early in January, while the refurbished 4-inch gun returned to its position on 13 January. The ship loaded ammunition on the morning of the 24th. Later that day the duty watch had their mettle tested when the Ministers for the Navy and Civil Aviation together with their wives, made an unannounced visit on board from 4.40 to 5.20 pm.

Trials that began the next day culminated in a full power run on 27 January, that produced a *remarkably free of vibrations* nineteen and a half knots at 178 rpm. The class of ME2s that had joined the day before saw what the engines could do.

With loading of ammunition completed on 2 February, *Diamantina* sailed two days later, flying the broad pennant of NOICWA, Commodore R. Rhoades, to combine sea trials with the role of safety ship in the Fremantle to Bunbury Yacht Race. On the one-day trip, which also provided sea training for five Reserve officers and 12 ratings, 4-inch and Bofors shoots were fired.

The final civilian worker on the refit stepped ashore as the brow came in on sailing day of the year's first oceanographic cruise on 14 February. The work had taken the entire refit period and it was worth it. The CSIRO leader, Mr. Rochford was impressed with the new laboratory.

Hydrology and plankton tows were not the only work of this cruise. The ship had been ordered back to the Diamantina Deep. Neither Russian nor American searches had been able to confirm the discovery. Indeed, *Diamantina's* captain, on 27 January, reported, *Having searched without success, Argo stated quite categorically that the Diamantina Deep does not exist.* (*Argo* was first commissioned in 1944 as the Salvage Vessel, USS *Snatch*. When it was converted to a Research Vessel in 1959-60 for the Scripps Institution of Oceanography, University of California, its name was changed to that of Jason's ship in which he sailed in search of the Golden Fleece.)

Argo's doubts after a fruitless 16-hour survey on New Year's Eve raised hackles on *Diamantina* and, at a cocktail party during *Argo's* packed 90 hours stay, the Australians challenged the Americans on their precise figures for great depths, asserting an EDO echo sounder was only so accurate to 600 fathoms. The American scientist readily agreed the machine, as built, had this limitation, but went on ...*I changed ours to read to 6000 fathoms with $US 10 of additional parts.*

Next morning *Diamantina's* captain sent Dick Lamb to Professor Robert Fisher on *Argo*. Dick recalls Fisher happily writing instructions for the modification for him and also asking that a copy be sent to *Gascoyne*, the other Australian oceanographic vessel. Professor Fisher's modification later spread from *Diamantina* throughout the Australian fleet.

But Fisher's generosity did not result in the hoped for immediate confirmation of the Diamantina Deep. In bad weather and visibility between 15 and 19 February a definite location fix could not be obtained until the afternoon of the second last day. Then the gyro compass malfunctioned. Disappointed, the captain ended the search at 1.10 pm on the 19th. His report concluded, ...*If it does exist, it must be very small indeed.*

Later exploration confirmed that, rather than a 'Deep' the area was, as it is now named, the 'Diamantina Fracture Zone.'

The cruise had two bright spots. On 21 February, the day before tying up in Fremantle, the captain presented the coxswain with his "well earned" Long Service and Good Conduct Medal. And the CSIRO principal research officer pronounced *Diamantina's* two new laboratories made her *the best equipped ship of her size in the world for this kind of work.*

Diving and oceanographic practices filled the time until the ship sailed again at 9.30 am, 25 February, for Stage II of the cruise to research plankton and the position of the Tropic-Antarctic Convergence. A new crewman was Leading Airman Met II Rule. Rule was to raise the ship's already high standing with the Perth Meteorological Office by taking weather readings in hitherto uncovered areas and radioing them in. The quality of observations would further increase when radio-sonde equipment, planned for later in the year, allowed upper air readings.

High-speed plankton sampling and practice shoots varied the oceanographic routine under CSIRO plankton specialist, Mr. David Tranter. Stations as far as 46 degrees South were occupied in some rough seas before return on 10 March.

On 12 March, *Diamantina* was at sea again - this time as safety vessel for the Cape Naturaliste Yacht Race. At 2.40 am, the watch investigated a flashing white light and red flare astern to assist the badly leaking yacht, *Thea*. The short seas from the Force 5 wind had opened a butt joint in the previous month's Bunbury Race winner. *Diamantina* towed her to Bunbury before returning to Fremantle.

Exercises and another round trip to Bunbury with 56 Junior Recruits, the first to go to sea in the RAN since the *Tingira* scheme ended in 1926, were followed by a round trip to Albany between 24 and 30 March. On both cruises the Junior Recruits took the places of the ship's Ordinary Seamen and ME2s who worked towards their higher rates at *Leeuwin* ashore. The trainees worked in all the ship's departments on deck and in the engine and boiler rooms in four watches. Sea boat, sentry, guard, and side boy duties were also included.

The Albany cruise was a rude introduction to ocean sailing for the class of 31 JRs whose previous time aboard had been in sheltered Gage Roads. Three-quarters of them became so badly seasick the ship put into Frenchman's Bay seeking calmer waters. This was better, but the whaler was still swamped by the seas. The return leg, in 'moderate seas' saw a recurrence of the sickness. Unlike the trainees, the regular crew welcomed these visits to Western Australian ports as a change from oceanography. The people of the towns were also enthusiastic - 2,000 visited the ship on its March visit to Bunbury.

29 Junior Recruits swapped places with the Ordinary Seamen class for the five-day cruise to Geraldton beginning on 6 April. A dentist, Surgeon Lieutenant A.L. Kidd, was also aboard to raise the standard of the crew's dental fitness. When, after casting off, Kidd discovered no dental anaesthetic was in the stores, the ship hove to while an unusually enthusiastic boat crew rowed ashore to remedy this deficiency. The prospect of dental work without anaesthetic would have cast a shadow over the very pleasant weekend of sport, an official dinner and 1,500 visitors at Geraldton.

Another 30 JRs, two instructors and two officers were aboard when *Diamantina* sailed on 13 April, for the annual Monte Bello Islands radioactivity check. The moderate seas on the way laid low all but one recruit. On 16 April, as parties checked the warning notices and LCDR Andrews took his readings, morale and health were restored when sporting parties landed on radiation-free South-East Island.

The recruits disembarked in Fremantle on 19 April, a day after a shipwright's report to their commanding officer at *Leeuwin* had stated *Diamantina's* 27 foot whaler, No. 846, built at Garden Island in 1944, was in moderately fair condition, and essential repairs would cost £200 ($400).

NOICWA inspected the ship on the 28 April; three days later, with five CSIRO scientists aboard, Cruise D2/61 began. After first readings at the Reference Station at 32 degrees South, 111 degrees 50 minutes East, the ship followed the 1960 second cruise's route to arrive at Darwin in the afternoon of 12 May. Several days later, hydrology stations and plankton tows resumed en route to Surabaya via Lombok Strait.

The crew had time ashore on 23 May, before the ship sailed for Singapore the next morning with LT A.L. Lumanauw of the Indonesian Navy aboard. 'King Neptune's' Court came board at 2.30 pm on 26 May, and *Diamantina* tied up in Singapore at 9.05 am, 27 May. Four days later she sailed for more stations on the way to Jakarta. The two days in port included visits to the Indonesian Navy's Hydrographic Office, homes, and the cricket club as well as bus tours. An on-board cocktail party returned hospitality.

Sailing at 10 am, 4 June, the ship transited Sunda Strait before resuming the scientific programme 70 miles west south-west of Krakatoa. A 4-inch and Bofors shoot was conducted on 7 June. A ship's concert supplemented the unusually good range of films embarked in Singapore for carriage to the Fourth Submarine Division before the cruise ended on 12 June and a self-maintenance period began. On the slipway from 29 June, the ship was fumigated on 7 July. Three days later the ship's company enthusiastically obeyed the order 'Splice the Mainbrace' to celebrate the RAN's 50th Anniversary. The slip was cleared on 14 July and trials continued until sailing for Darwin a week later.

This cruise involved two traverses of surface water and plankton. The first was west to the Reference Station. The second tracked from the 50 m depth line just off Port Hedland to about 60 miles south of Java before turning east to Roti Island. Two days out came a reminder of the hazards involved in oceanography. On the Reference Station a 24 hour plankton sampling had begun at 10.30 am in a Force 7 northerly wind and steep seas. As Mr. Tranter continued his work, the weather deteriorated with the wind increasing to Force 9 by 3 pm. Then, as a net was being recovered, a guy wire on the after davit parted, and the snatch block hit Tranter on the head. Surgeon Lieutenant Harrington inserted 14 stitches in the wound but after four days the scientist returned to work. In addition to the injury the net, kite and two sinkers were lost. But it could have been worse. Procedural changes included stronger wire and the suspension of future operations in such conditions.

Apart from this incident, the long drift stations were boring times. To counter this inter-mess competitions in a number of events were organised. A trophy was bought, and the Diamantina Shield competition was keenly contested from then until the end of the ship's commission.

With the final station completed off Roti Island on 2 August, course was set for Darwin. After *Diamantina* tied up beside her sister ship, *Gascoyne*, in Darwin at 10.55 am on 5 August, there was an exchange of scientists including the replacement of the now completely recovered Mr. Tranter by Dr. John McIntyre. The technicians, who made up the majority of most scientific parties, remained.

When the ship sailed on 8 August, three Australian, one New Zealander, and two German scientists were aboard as well as Mr. J. Utting and G. Halverson of the Department of Works. The last two were engineers who were to survey Ashmore Reef and Cartier Island for an automatic cyclone warning station site.

By 13 August, Ashmore and Cartier were astern and hydrographic work continued until Broome was reached several days later. The engineers disembarked and, after two days of enthusiastic hospitality, the ship weighed anchor to complete the successful cruise in the early afternoon of 27 August. The captain's report noted the scientists from Kiel University, Dr. Eric Hagmier and Mr. Uwe Rabasch had fitted in well on the ship. Training of men to advance from Ordinary to Able Seaman had progressed. And 9 Seamen's Mess had won the Diamantina Shield.

Then, at 8.30 pm on 5 September, LCDR J.G. Yule from HMAS *Torrens* joined the ship. Two days later LCDR Jude left and Yule assumed command. Junior Recruit training and ammunition dumping north-west of Rottnest Island in 310 fathoms extended past month's end. In the four weeks to mid-October, 500 tons including depth charges went over the side.

The fifth and final class of Junior Ratings was on board when *Diamantina* slipped for Shark Bay at 9.10 am, 16 October. At anchor in Turtle Bay on Dirk Hartog Island's northern tip on the next day, the ship exercised the recruits in an evening of drills. At 6.15 next morning, anchor was aweigh and the recruits disembarked in Fremantle late on 20 October.

One recruit revisited *Diamantina* in Brisbane in July 2000. He returned a messdeck brush and a book borrowed from the ship's library 39 years before. The 14 Mess member had spent the last six weeks of his draft in hospital with a fractured skull. No overdue fine was imposed.

With 34 Reservists, including six officers, aboard, the vessel put to sea again on 30 October for another training cruise - this time to Adelaide. In an uneventful two weeks the ship spent three days in Adelaide and one in Albany, before the trainees disembarked on 12 November.

The Ship's Ball the next evening was followed two days later by the start of the long leave and refit period. The work included conversion of the Squid magazine to a kit locker flat and refitting of the galley and its range. Unlike most of the ships in the fleet, *Diamantina* did not have a cafeteria. The ship had a broadside messing system with only the wardroom, Chief Petty Officers, and Petty Officers' meals coming in bulk from the galley. The rest of the crew had their plates filled at the galley and carried them to their messes to eat. NOICWA had reported on 31 May that *Senior hands expressed the opinion that smaller mess decks were much more to their liking than the impersonal atmosphere of a cafeteria*. So the ship never got a cafeteria, and until she went out of service her sailors, in all weathers, negotiated the companionways balancing their filled plates.

X Deck became a hive of activity. To improve Met. II Rule's valued three-hourly weather reports, Cockburn Engineering was erecting a new meteorological office and a shelter for filling radio-sonde balloons. When completed the 'elephant hut' had cost a total of £5,602.11.2 ($11,205.12).

Some unplanned work became necessary on 20 November when a coal barge under the control of the tug *Avon* struck the berthed *Diamantina* on the port quarter. Repairs to the tank dented to a maximum depth of six inches totalled £421.14.9 ($843.48).

The ship's armament was inventoried on 9 November. In addition to the Q.F. 4 inch Mk. 16, its associated rocket launcher, and the Q.F. 40/60 Bofors guns, there were two line throwing rifles, four .22 rifles, 25 .303 rifles, shotguns, and Thompson sub-machine guns - a formidable collection, if, for 1961, somewhat outdated.

But the future of *Diamantina*'s research role had opened up. In August, the Minister for the Navy, Senator J.G. Gorton, had announced the RAN would "play a prominent part in an international survey of the Indian Ocean to begin next year." That month *Gascoyne* had taken scientists to a meeting in Honolulu. Her sister had made the glamour preliminary trip, but *Diamantina* was to have the major role in the main event - The International Indian Ocean Expedition.

1962

Diamantina's 10 days on the slipway ended on 18 January when she tied up at H Shed, Victoria Quay. The 74-day refit ended six days later when ammunition was embarked. Next day trials in Gage Roads began. Working up exercises continued at Shark Bay. The highest haul of snapper there was 400 in three hours. On the last day of the month, course was set for Fremantle. Full power trials on 2 February produced over 17 knots at 160 rpm. Then came two days accompanying the Bunbury Yacht race before returning to port.

On 11 February, Mr. Brian Newell joined to lead CSIRO Cruise D1/62 to study water circulation and upwelling together with their effects on productivity during the north-west monsoon. The next day the voyage began.

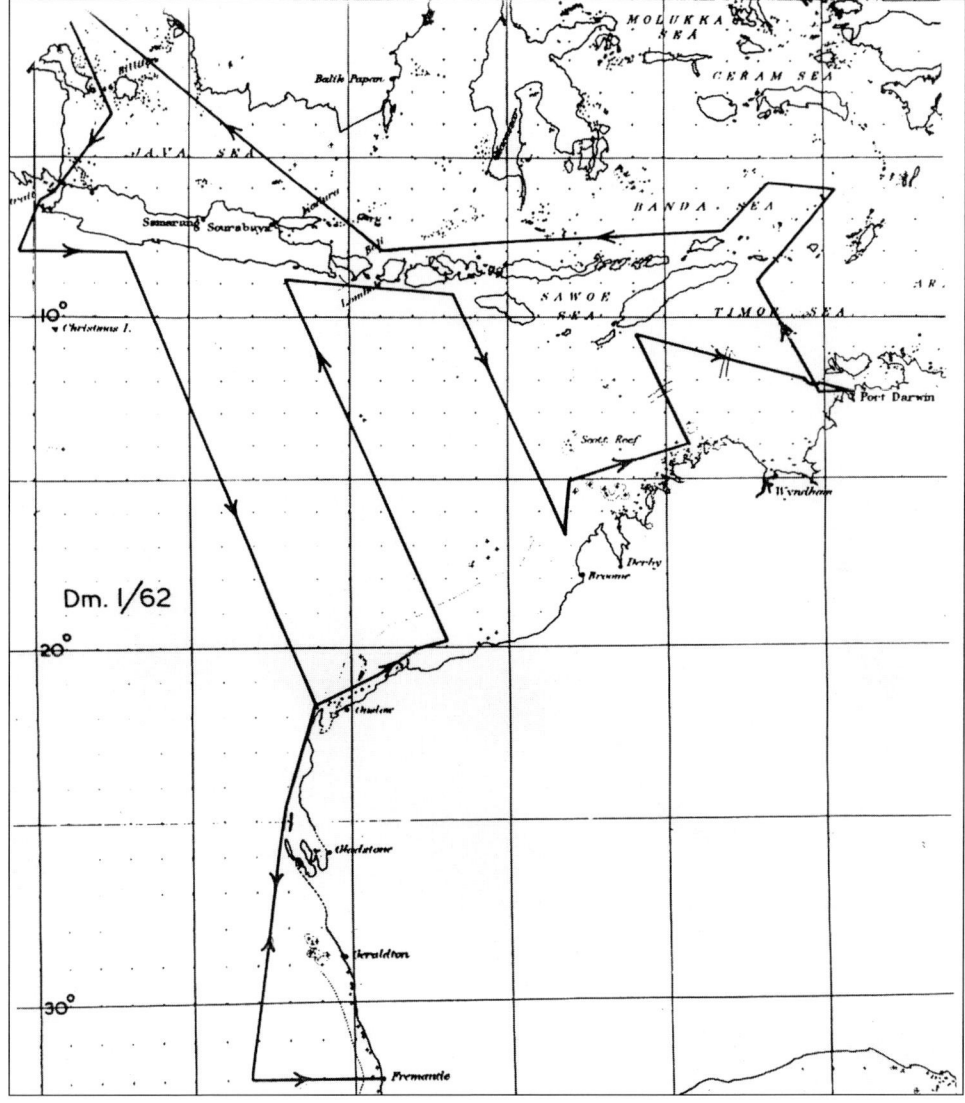

Cruise Dm1/62 track chart (CSIRO)

At 2.40 am, 13 February, the seven hour first station began 200 miles west of Fremantle. Succeeding stations were carried out along three parallel lines north-west from North-west Cape to 60 miles from the coast of Java. Then the ship headed for Darwin where it tied up at Stokes Hill Wharf at 9.35 am, 25 February. Between stations the 4-inch and 40mm gun crews had carried out practice shoots. Another log entry, on 20 February, was rather cryptic, *0645 small shark destroyed by enthusiastic Navigation Officer.*

During the five days in hot, humid Darwin, Mr. D. Rochford replaced Mr. Newell as cruise leader. Wins at volleyball and softball balanced losses at Australian Rules and water polo. On the social scene, three parties visited Howard Springs for barbecues and swimming, the ship hosted a cocktail party, and Darwin High School science students toured the vessel. The cruise resumed at 6.45 am, 2 March, and that leg ended when *Diamantina* tied up at No.6 Berth, HM Dockyard, Singapore, at noon nine days later.

The research's last phase began on 15 March. Steaming via Sunda Strait, North-West Cape, and all the first Reference Station objectives had been achieved when the vessel tied up at Fremantle at 8.30 am on 24 March. The Report of Proceedings noted another achievement - out of a ship's company of 102, there were only four cases of venereal disease contracted in Singapore.

Five weeks of training of five classes of Junior Recruits began on 2 April. The first phase consisted of embarking the trainees each morning, sailing to Cockburn Sound for exercises, and returning them ashore in the evening. An early morning fire in the calorifer room on 30 April caused little damage and barely interrupted the routine.

Commodore Marks made his Annual Inspection on 10 May. The day after NOICWA's assessment a relaxed Families Day cruise in Cockburn Sound included launching of a meteorological balloon and the 'rescue' of a man overboard. An unscheduled part of the day was the grounding of the ship aft at noon. There was little damage. Junior Recruits were aboard when the ship sailed for Albany at 12.20 pm, 14 May. Before the training cruise ended eight days later, visitors had inspected the ship in both Bunbury and Albany. In the latter town, volunteers under LT R.S. Blue painted Mrs. Dorothy Trowbridge's house, and cleared the grounds of Mr. Claude Bathalier and Mrs. Walker's residences.

There was a more solemn duty. In *Diamantina's* first burial at sea, the ashes of RNVR (Ret,) LCDR William Wilson were committed to the deep.

After five days in port, *Diamantina* put to sea to visit again the 1952 and 1956 British atomic test sites in the Monte Bello Islands. The crew worked for six days from the early morning of 31 May, with LCDR Bird RN and his party to monitor radiation and renew warning notices. A sergeant and 10 other ranks of the SAS practised landings and instructed the crew in the use of the Self Loading Rifle, Owen Gun, and Browning automatic pistol. As usual, swimming and fishing in radiation free areas were popular. On the run home full power trials produced a speed of over 16 knots.

Arrival in Fremantle at 11.30 am, 8 June, began a period of self-maintenance. Loading of oceanographic wire on 7 and 8 July began the return to service routine of loading ammunition and trials that included an overnight cruise to Bunbury. There was also training with the SAS and sporting contact. The captain reported on a 4 July Rugby match, *The Special Air Service were not superior players, but were certainly very much fitter.* In a not surprising result, the SAS won, 26-6.

On 15 July at 3 pm, Joanna Hardy Yule was christened on board by Canon J. Halley. This joyful event marked the end of the time in port. The next day Cruise Dm2/62 began. The CSIRO's Mr. Bruce Hamon and his team of five had settled in with their equipment over the previous four days. Beginning at the now familiar co-ordinates of the Reference Station at 30 degrees South, 111 degrees 7 minutes East, they studied currents, their boundaries, and associated biological systems. Readings were taken at 20 stations northward along the meridian of 100 degrees East from 25 degrees South to 4 degrees South-west of Sunda Strait. The last station was completed on 26 July, and *Diamantina* secured alongside HMS *Cassandra* in Singapore at 9.20 am, 29 July.

Phase 2 of Dm2/62 ran from 5 August. The 20 stations northward along 95 degrees East from near the Cocos Islands to off the northern tip of Sumatra were completed in five days, and the ship tied up in Singapore at 9 am on 12 August.

The cruise's last leg began when the ship sailed at 8.05 am, 15 August. After lifeguard duty along the route as the King and Queen of Thailand flew from Singapore to Darwin on 17 August, the research resumed at stations south along 105 degrees East from 7 degrees 45 minutes South to the 57th, and final, set of readings at the Reference Station , completed at 5.30 am on 24 August. The quarterly full power trials producing a speed of over 17 knots helped the cruise to end at 8.30 am, on the following day.

Junior Recruit training and dumping of ammunition, including 680 depth charges and 161 x 500 lb bombs were the duties until mid September. The ordnance went over the side into 390 fathoms of water 20 miles west of Rottnest Island. At the end of manoeuvres with sister oceanographic research ship, *Gascoyne*, three CSIRO researchers transferred to *Diamantina*. Four days later the cruise leader and three more CSIRO personnel embarked. The following day, 24 September, after a visit from the Hydrographer of the RAN, Dm3/62 began.

In investigating zooplankton species distribution and their relationships with subtropical and subantarctic faunas the first readings were taken at the Reference Station, 32 degrees South, 110 degrees 50'E. The ship then occupied stations about 84 miles apart on the 110 E meridian southward to the most southerly one at 8 pm on 30 September. This was at 45 degrees South, well into the Roaring Forties. More stations were occupied on the return north until Station 125 was completed on 5 October.

The cruise plan had included four stations in a diamond pattern from 44 to 46 degrees south. In the appalling weather the ship could not maintain position and the southernmost stations were not occupied. Throughout these extreme conditions the Petty Officer Meteorologist continued recording observations. On return to Fremantle on 6 October he reported to the Perth Weather Bureau with his tabulated readings, however, the staff was reluctant to accept the accuracy of his figures. The ship's coxswain tells what happened when LCDR Yule accompanied his meteorologist on a return visit to the Bureau. *'Jock' was not averse to calling a spade a shovel when required*, the cox'n recalls. *I'm not aware what was said at the meeting but let it be said we had no further problems in that area. I think if we said we had a snow storm going through Sunda Strait they would have accepted it.*

After nine days in port Mr. Harry Jitts led aboard a team including Mr. K. Chan of Hong Kong and Mr. B. Wauthy of France for Cruise Dm4/62. Sailing at 3 pm, 15 October *Diamantina* headed first for the Reference Station before taking readings at 90 mile intervals northward along the 110 E meridian until 1.15 pm, 26 October. Two days later the ship was in Singapore.

At 9 am, 1 November, the ship put to sea to resume Dm4/62. The next day a 'distressed' fishing boat stopped the ship and food and rice were passed down. The crew's good feeling evaporated when, on getting underway, they saw a boat in the distance change before their eyes from a purposeful working vessel into a piteous hulk with a starving crew. *Diamantina* was not fooled twice.

Drift and hydrology stations and plankton net tows resumed at 11.30 am, 3 November. They continued down the 110 meridian to the Reference Station and the cruise ended at 10A North Wharf at 8.30 am, 13 November. The six scientists left that day. On the succeeding days the ammunition was landed and the first draft began their long leave. The refit began on 19 November. In a busy successful year, the weather balloon 'elephant hut' had proven its worth to the Weather Bureau with 80 successful ascents furnishing upper air information from remote previously unrecorded sites.

In December, Adams Electric Company played a major part in the refit, replacing batteries, and installing a new 974 radio and other equipment in the radio room, as well as setting up a new diesel generator outside. In other work the 20" searchlight platform and the port forward heavy derrick were removed. The ship's Land Rover would, in future, be handled by the small starboard side boom.

Diamantina also contributed to the success of the Perth Commonwealth Games. The officers of the visiting submarine, HMS *Taciturn* were accommodated aboard the frigate. As well, many of the ship's company worked as ushers at Games events. This wholehearted participation in Perth's big event was not surprising. Two-thirds of the ship's six officers and 100 sailors, including the captain, were West Australians.

Yet another, greater success was building. Much of the year's work had been part of Australia's contribution to the International Indian Ocean Expedition. The IIOE (1960-65), sponsored by UNESCO and the Scientific Committee for Oceanographic Research, was organised by the Intergovernmental Oceanographic Commission. Of the 23 participating countries, 13 furnished 40 vessels ranging from the USSR's 6,400 tons, 109.4m *Vityaz* to the 15m *Conch*, one of India's ships.

The intensive phase had begun in 1962. *Gascoyne* played a part in turning the world's least known ocean into its best understood. But *Diamantina* was by far the major Australian participant. Harry Jitts, who made many cruises on *Diamantina*, wrote later: *Let it be noted with pride that Australia made the major contribution to the work of the IIOE. Our main contribution was to occupy a line of stations along the 110 degrees East meridian from Java to well south of Australia on a regular monthly basis for well over a year. At these stations we measured the physical, chemical, and biological properties of the ocean, which enabled us to construct a time series of the seasonal variation of all these properties over a significant expanse of the Indian Ocean. This in turn was of material assistance in integrating the huge amount of data collected by all the participating nations in the IIOE who, of necessity, had each collected their data at different times of the year. There is an apocryphal story that a further result of our work was a noticeable ridge on the seabed along the 110 degree East meridian, consisting largely of tangled wire, expensive equipment and discarded tin cans and beer bottles. Of course it is not true, especially the bit about beer bottles.*

1963

January 1963 saw *Diamantina* make history again. But this time it was not at the cutting edge of technology or science.

It happened on 7 January as the ship moved to the slipway. With the boilers being cleaned, the silent vessel, under the control of a harbour pilot, was being towed by two tugs. When he believed *Diamantina* might swing into a moored ship the pilot hastily ordered both anchors dropped to halt the ship. With the crisis over, a new problem became apparent. Before the tow could be resumed the anchors had to be raised. And the ship had no power. The Engineering Officer later recalled: *A series of blocks and tackles were run along the deck. Then it was all hands - everyone aboard, regardless of rank or rating - working in relays on the blocks and tackles. We'd gain a couple of feet, lock the anchor chain, reposition the blocks and tackles and then start pulling again. The procedure of shifting ship from wharf to slipway, which normally took one to two hours, took 10 hours. I do believe* Diamantina *would have been the last naval vessel to weigh anchor by hand, and probably the only steam driven naval ship ever to do so.*

On 14 January, with the ship still on the slipway, ME1 Porter broke his kneecap in a fall on board. A more serious event was the fire in the calorifer room on No.2 deck, port side amidships, at 12.35 am on 27 January. After fighting the fire for 15 minutes the crew was joined by the Fremantle Fire Brigade who had the blaze under control by 1.15 am. Internal damage was confined to the room and the bathrooms' passage. In addition the ship's side was slightly buckled, and stokers' overalls and boots, drying in the room, were destroyed. The repair bill topped £1,400 ($2,800). The stokers found a new drying room in the gland space. The inquiry next day found the rating responsible failed to turn the hot water boiler off on leaving. Subsequently, overflowing fuel ignited.

With post refit trials completed, the ship sailed on 31 January, with its refurbished funnel and newly painted pennant numbers on a cruise to southern Western Australia ports. The 'show the flag' visits passed in a round of ship inspections, dances, and receptions in Esperance, Albany, and Bunbury on 2, 4, and 6 February. Esperance's 600 visitors included a group of children who had made the long trek from Kalgoorlie. At Bunbury the captain and navigation officer were invited on a kangaroo shoot. The ship's company was less than impressed with the hunters' bag - two rabbits.

A266 with 'elephant hut' balloon filling shelter, gas bottles and Land Rover on deck. (RAN)

Between 8 and 10 February, *Diamantina* carried out its familiar role as 'watchdog' and communications link for competitors in the Bunbury Yacht Race. Two days of exercises around Turtle Bay on Dirk Hartog Island preceded putting into Onslow on 20 February. There NOICWA, Commodore W.B.M. Marks, Brigadier G.P. Hunt, and Dr. G. Georgeff, 'a noted big game fisherman' came aboard. The ship then sailed to the Monte Bello Islands, anchoring in eight fathoms at Parting Pool at 7 am, 21 February.

Here, as the crew prepared for the Annual Inspection, working parties replaced the multi-lingual warning signs on Burgundy Beach, Alpha Island, while off duty personnel tried their luck in fishing. The ship sailed for Shark Bay at 6.45 pm the day after arrival. There more drills, and fishing filled the time until departure for Carnarvon early on 25 February.

In port until 9 am on the 27 February, the ship welcomed visitors while crew members enjoyed a Rotary lunch and a Civic Reception. The Brigadier and Dr. Georgeff disembarked. The social round was repeated in Geraldton from 28 February to 2 March; with 15,000 visitors coming aboard in one day.

The captain's monthly Report of Proceedings, addressed to NOICWA, noted other happenings in Geraldton: *...the yacht, Sarnia,...secured alongside the ship, and, under your direction, sir, was prepared for the passage to Fremantle*. It went on to record *Sarnia's* sailing for Fremantle at 8.20 am, 2 March, with NOICWA, a keen yachtsman, and a RANR rating among the crew and *Diamantina* following, maintaining radio contact until berthing at 9 am, next day. When the report reached Melbourne some senior officers' endorsements questioned the carriage of passengers and work on the yacht. Another wrote, *... see no error in what has been done*. He was in the minority.

Seaboat exercises, Royal Visit practices, and duty in the Cape Naturaliste Yacht Race occupied most of March. The practices included the ship standing in for the Royal Yacht at a rehearsal for the Queen's arrival when a RAANC officer 'Queen' landed from the ship to inspect the Guard and meet dignitaries. Practice became reality from 8.45 am, 25 March, when *Diamantina*, dressed overall, and with the sides manned, joined HMAS *Anzac* to escort *Britannia* into Fremantle. *Anzac* berthed astern of the Royal Yacht, and *Diamantina* ahead. At noon Queen Elizabeth landed and the escort ended.

Cruise Dm1/63 began at 3.30 pm, 28 March. Congratulations from the Queen on the ship's escort were received as work at the Reference Station ended. The crew was happy to comply with her final order, 'Splice the Mainbrace.'

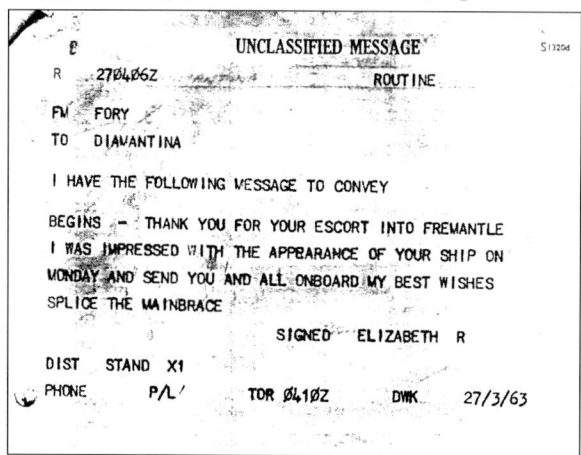

Well done (QMM collection)

Bathymetric dips and trawls were made at stations northward along 110 degrees East until the northern Reference Station at 9 degrees South, 105 degrees East was completed at 3.30 a.m., 8 April. Passage through Sunda Strait had *Diamantina* begin five days in Singapore at 2.15 pm, 10 April.

Only 10 hours after sailing on 15 April, course was retraced at 17 knots to land POM(E) D.J. Norling for treatment ashore for acute appendicitis. At 10.50 am, 18 April, stations down 110 degrees East were resumed and the cruise ended at 6.30 pm, 27 April. Unlike an earlier visit to Singapore, there were no VD cases.

Following a small arms shoot and fumigation of the ship the cruise was repeated from 6 May. After four days in Singapore, the return leg down 110 degrees East began on 23 May. There was some variation from the previous trip. Submarine photometry was added to the measurements. And high winds and swells to 15 feet forced stations to be abandoned before the ship reached Fremantle at 2 pm, 3 June.

There were major changes during the self-maintenance period. LCDR R.B. Nunn took command from LCDR Yule on 7 June. At 33 years of age, Nunn, who had served with Yule during the Korean War, became *Diamantina*'s youngest captain.

A more obvious change was the removal of the 4-inch gun to store at the Byford Armament Depot. As well, 600 rivets in 7 and 9 oil fuel tanks were renewed, and the galley range rebuilt. An Army mobile field kitchen fed the crew until the range was restored. Tests followed unslipping on 24 June. During sea trials on 8 July, Chaplain Chetwynd officiated at the scattering of the ashes of CPO (Ret.) J.A. Laughton, RN. In a more happy ceremony, on the previous Sunday, Rev. Chetwynd had christened Frayne Summers and Erica Bartlett in the ship's bell.

CSIRO Cruise Dm3/63 sailed at 3 pm, 9 July, to follow along 110 degrees East in the wake of the previous cruises. A firing practice at a meteorological balloon with the ship's last remaining gun, the Bofors, on 16 June, came four days before the second Reference Station's readings were completed at 1.45 am, 20 July.

Then came another change. Course was set, not for Singapore, but for Bali. At 7.30 pm, 23 July, *Diamantina* anchored in 43 fathoms only 2.8 cables from the shore at Buleng. Captain N. McDonald, the Australian Navy Attache, and Indonesian officials boarded to begin a packed day; 80 boxes of Red Cross and medical supplies went ashore for the victims of the recent volcanic eruption. Parties visited refugee camps and took short bus tours. Australian Embassy staff and eight local officials lunched on board. But the day's highlight was a display of Balinese dancing. In 1999 the cox'n recalled it as ...*a great and enlightening experience...I still see in my mind's eye, even after all these years, the building, the concert, and the wonderful people who entertained us*. After presenting a *Diamantina* crest, the ship sailed for Singapore at 11.15 pm.

Five days after arrival the return leg of the cruise began on 30 July. Rough seas forced the cancellation of Station 16 and the Reference Station and the ship came alongside 10A at Fremantle at 10.30 am, 11 August. In the short port time, sea cadets and Junior Recruits came aboard for training. There was also an addition to the ship. When she sailed on 20 August for Dm4/63, *Diamantina* had a depth charge chute welded to the quarterdeck and carried six depth charges and a supply of hand grenades.

There were four research tasks: to find and measure West Australian crayfish larvae; to determine whether deep water prawns lived near the continental shelf's edge; to sample the shelf's sediment; and to explode the depth charges. The Bureau of Mineral Resources would use stations at Mundaring, Grass Valley, Narrogin, and a mobile one to study the earth crust's structure by analysing recorded echoes. However, bad weather forced the ship back to Fremantle on 23rd with the work incomplete. The three days port time was filled with cadet and recruit training and a visit by 40 country schoolchildren. Then, at sea between 27 and 29 August, Dr. Chittleborough and his party completed their tasks and the charges were fired. *Diamantina*'s old consort, *Vema*, was in company for some of the firings.

On 1 November the Director of the Bureau of Mineral Resources wrote to the Secretary of the Department of the Navy conveying his thanks for the Crustal

Preparing to drop the first depth charge - Cruise 4/63. (L. Spanton)

Structure Project's 'very successful outcome.' He stated the three depth charges dropped south of Geraldton and the other three detonated south of Fremantle yielded such good results *mainly through the full co-operation of the ship's staff.*

After more day training cruises, Dm5/63 began on 4 September with departure for the Reference Station followed by more stations to the north - north-west. En route, the ship disproved the existence of the Maria Augustina Bank. On 10 September, LT A Summers, the Diving Officer, cleared a net from the port propeller, and a mortar was test fired from the quarterdeck. After Station 157 was completed on 11 September, at 9 degrees South, course was set for Singapore. *Diamantina* tied up at No. 6 Dockyard Basin at 7.30 am, 14 September.

Three days later, with refrigeration defects made good, the ship set off for Bali. In this period following the sacking of Britain's Jakarta embassy, *a state of defence preparedness [was] assumed, [and] the ship's firepower doubled by the mounting of Bren guns.* This heightened security continued during Indonesia's 'Confrontation' with Malaysia. In these years, crewmen later recalled, armed guards were posted in Singapore, lookouts were on alert, and Sunda Strait transits were made with gun crews closed up.

In the event the precautions were unnecessary, and *Diamantina* was welcomed to Bali by the Indonesian Navy Riga Class escort, *Ngurah Raj*. At Buleng, 33 cases of Red Cross stores and six cases of kitchenware, clothing and toys collected and donated by the Nedlands Rotary Club, were landed. The ship then sailed that evening to continue the cruise.

During three days in Darwin, 14 high school students inspected the laboratories and Dr. Chittleborough and his party of five researchers embarked. The ship sailed on 1 October. Crayfish, prawns, and sediment were again the research subjects as the cruise progressed south-west to anchor off Onslow on 5 October. Here mail and the scientists were transferred. A week later, at 8.45 am, 12 October, the cruise ended alongside H Shed.

The year then wound down. Junior Recruit training and NOICWA's Annual Inspection were completed. A Cockburn Sound Family Day on 18 October included weapons firing and a chicken lunch. On 7 November the ship dumped a ton of miscellaneous explosives and 186 Squid projectiles. Seven days later a letter from NOICWA to the captain underlined the ship's status when he stated, ...*As the ship is no longer regarded as having a capability in war...*

But *Diamantina* was still valued. NOICWA had written to the Hydrographer on 6 September asserting *Leeuwin*'s Junior Recruits' ...*periods of training in* Diamantina *are absolutely essential.* He went on to point out the ship's achievement in balancing this role with the others of hydrographic research and 'showing the flag.' NOICWA could not defend his ship all the time. Another letter to the Navy Department had him lamenting, *It is unfortunate that HMAS* Diamantina *has somewhat of a history of canteen losses.*

The year which had begun with a mixture of farcical and more serious incidents ended the same way. On 11 November, 24 Salvation Army children were entertained at a successful Christmas Party. On 31 December on the slip the Log records; *0855 unauthorised female discovered on board.*

The day before a firing party and escort had attended Karrakatta Cemetery for the funeral of Ordinary Seaman G.A. Hughes, who had been killed in an accident on Christmas Day.

1964

Amid the bustle of unslipping and preparing the ship for another year, LCDR P.E. Holloway took command on 18 January. Five days later *Diamantina* was en route for Bunbury's Annual Marine Festival. Nine drums of cyanide were on board under the supervision of Instructor Lieutenant V. Uksi. In another example of service to the civil authorities, Uksi supervised, on behalf of the Swan River Conservation Board, the dumping of the drums in 1,400 fathoms. After two pleasant days of a Civic Reception, cocktail party, and visits, the ship sailed for Fremantle at 6 pm, 26 January. Both the crew and the townsfolk always enjoyed these small port visits.

Two days later, at 8 am, CSIRO Cruise Dm1/64 began. Dr. G. Chittleborough and three other researchers, in a series of traverses, studied West Australian rock lobsters (Panulirus cygnus), and water and sediment composition on and adjacent to the continental shelf between North-West Cape and Cape Naturaliste. Chittleborough's work in this and subsequent cruises in unravelling the life cycle of the lobster's larval phases was, in Harry Jitts's words, *beautiful*, and research...*that will stand the test of time.* A whale was pursued on 5 February so the scientists could use a special marking gun to tag it. The whale easily eluded its chasers. Next morning, at 6.30, the cruise ended at Berth 10A.

Two days later Bunbury Yacht Race duty had *Diamantina* at sea for a day. On 11 February, a four-day round trip with two days in port at Albany began. The scientists returned aboard on 15th for the completion of Dm1/64 around Cape Naturaliste by 18 February.

A memorial service for the victims of the *Voyager* tragedy was held during the port visit to Esperance on 21-24 February. Once back in Fremantle on 26 February, four weeks of Junior Recruit and Ordinary Seaman training began. Sea time was built up during the Cape Naturaliste Yacht Race, and a quick run to sea on 1 March to take in tow the dismasted yacht, *Kirribilli*. The Annual Dance was a pleasant diversion at this time.

CSIRO Cruise Dm2/64 got under way at 9 am, 24 March. Mr. D. Rochford and his team of four sampled water characteristics and zooplankton at stations 60 miles apart along the meridian 95 degrees East to and from, and in the region of, the Equator. As usual some analysis of samples was carried out on board, while laboratories at Cronulla (NSW), and Cochin (India) performed later studies.

The first of two interruptions to a smooth flow of work came on 2 April, when a break caused the loss in 2,750 fathoms of 1,500m of wire and 11 Nansen bottles. The next day 'King Neptune' boarded the ship to induct the Medical Officer and 22 Ordinary Seamen into his court.

Three enjoyable days at Penang which included games against RAAF Butterworth, ended when *Diamantina* sailed on 9 April to begin the cruise's second phase. A smooth run had the ship tie up at Fremantle 12 days later. Fumigation and Junior Recruit training followed.

So far, in its second commission, *Diamantina* had been the venue for christenings, and funeral services. On 27 April the ship hosted celebrations of the third major stage of life when the wedding reception of Sub-Lieutenant and Mrs. Stuart Wilson was held on board.

Harry Jitts led a team of six on Cruise Dm3/64. Sailing on 4 May, they investigated an upwelling of water south of Indonesia. Readings were taken en route; and then 13 stations carried out in the 5,910 square mile area confirmed the presence of the upwelling. On 15 May, the day before the last readings were made at the Reference Station at 9 degrees South, 105 degrees East, SS *Durango* contacted the ship with a request for charts. They were freely given.

After three days in Singapore, a new course was laid at 12.30 pm, 21 May - for Bangkok. Three stations later the ship tied up at No. 9 Berth, Bangkok Naval Harbour at 9.30 am, 24 May. While the seven officers and 117 sailors enjoyed a new port over the next three days, official calls were made and returned and over 2,000 visitors inspected the ship.

Lieutenant Nirun Patamsing of the Royal Thai Navy's Hydrographic Service was aboard when the vessel sailed at 12.45 pm, 26 May. He disembarked two days later after observing the stations on the way to Singapore. On the last day of May, *Diamantina* steamed out for a second investigation of the upwelling. A wry entry appeared in the log next day, *1920 approx. Log damaged by floating log.*

Thirteen stations in the area found a decrease in the upwelling. Then course was set to reach Fremantle at 8.15 am, 12 June. The scientists pronounced the cruise a success. The officers were pleased, too. The Wardroom had won the Diamantina Shield yet again.

After the mid-year refit, CSIRO Cruise Dm4/64 investigated crayfish, the continental shelf and water to North-West Cape between 20 and 29 July. A short spell of Junior Recruit harbour training preceded departure on CSIRO Dm5/64 on 10 August. The ship had a brush with fame when a TVW-7 cameraman embarked for the first two hours to take wake and bow shots for a film on the *Sydney-Emden* clash.

On the 10 day run to the Cocos Islands the five-man scientific team studied the sea's particulate matter's variations with latitude and depth. Five and a half to seven hour stations were made from Reference Station 1 at 32 degrees South, 110 degrees 50 minutes East to Reference Station 2 at 9 degrees South, 105 degrees East. Then course was set for Port Refuge, where the ship came to anchor in six fathoms at 7 am, 20 August for a day of visitors and sport.

Sailing via Sunda Strait, *Diamantina* reached Singapore on 25 August. When the ship put to sea again, CDR H.W. Dillon, the RAN's Deputy Hydrographer, was on board. There was one station from 2 to 6 p.m. on the last day of the month before the ship made for Christmas Island. CDR Dillon began a special survey around Christmas Island at 1.05 am, 1 September. At 7 am, the vessel secured to C Buoy, Flying Fish Cove. Over the next two days survey cruises circumnavigated the island while sports, dances, calls and school visits took place. Then the last leg of the cruise to Fremantle began. But, over the years to come, the frigate's visits to the island would be more frequent and lengthy.

From 10 September to 8 October, Junior Recruits trained while the crew carried out maintenance and completed a small arms practice. The next week was one of sea training of Junior Recruits and Reservists in some heavy weather around Shark Bay. This was the year's last cruise.

Until *Diamantina* was secured on the slip on 1 December, there were short trips for explosives dumping and Junior Recruit training, the NOIC's Annual Inspection, a Family Day, and a Christmas Party for 60 orphans.

Two important unofficial events occurred in November. On Saturday the 8th, the Dean of Perth, Rev J. Payne, christened in the ship's bell, Timothy, the third child of LCDR and Mrs. Holloway. Later in the month the Wardroom presented to the Royal Fremantle Golf Club the Diamantina Trophy. The large cup surmounted by the figure of a golfer rests on a stand. It was given in appreciation of the continued honorary membership granted by the club to the captain and officers. Over the years the names of the winners of the annual 18-hole Stableford competition have filled all the space available. Now a mounted engine plate from 'The Grey Ghost of the West Coast' performs that role. Until *Diamantina* sailed from the West for the last time, a ship's representative, wherever possible, competed for and presented the trophy. The continuing competition for the trophy every year keeps the memory of *Diamantina* alive.

1965

In 1965 *Diamantina* ranged further west than ever before. The RAN Hydrographer's 43/135 letter to the Secretary of the Navy explains the CSIRO requested a triangular cruise to Mauritius to further investigate information gathered on the British RRS *Discovery's* recent voyage. Specifically the cruise would investigate:

a. the source of a 300m deep counter current of oxygen rich water - especially around the Maldive Islands;
b. the path of Red Sea water east of 70 degrees East;
c. the path of Banda intermediate water westward of 90 degrees East;
d. the northward movement of Antarctic Intermediate water in the central southern Indian Ocean.

The Hydrographer pointed out Australia's *unique opportunity and responsibility* for this work and noted *the Australian frigates are, by world standards, amongst the best fitted* for such work. The cruise was approved. But it was three months into the year before it began.

Another funeral began the year. On 7 January the ensign was half masted and an escort and firing party attended the last rites for A.B. Keith Wood who had been killed in a car accident three days earlier.

With the ship off the slip on 15 January, the routine of fumigation, trials, and the loading of ammunition and supplies filled the rest of the month. The familiar successful visits to the southern ports followed. A Bunbury cruise from 5-8 February was followed by one to Albany between 23-25 of that month. Junior Recruit training and overseeing of the Bunbury and Cape Naturaliste Yacht Races were other regular tasks. A more sombre event was the scattering of Keith Wood's ashes at sea north of Rottnest Island on 19 February.

The annual trip to the Monte Bello Islands was different this year. In the early 1950s, Sir William Penney had led a British team there to test three low yield atomic weapons.

The first, detonated in *Diamantina's* sister River class frigate, *Plym*, had vaporised the ship off Trimouille Island at 8 am, 3 October 1952. In 1956 the two devices were on a metal tower on Trimouille, and below a balloon tethered above Alpha Island. After the tests the islands were abandoned and warning notices erected to deny access.

But, after the petroleum exploration group, WAPET, discovered oil on Barrow Island, just 15 miles south, the Monte Bellos became a prime site for exploration. So, in February 1965, a RAN party of three flew to Barrow Island to embark on a WAPET barge for the Islands. Their radioactivity survey found only a small area to be dangerous.

From 14 March, when *Diamantina* anchored in Parting Pool and began unloading with the help of the WAPET barge *Jarrah*, Operation Cool Off followed up their work. Over six days a combined army and navy party under Captain Rex Rowe of the Royal Australian Engineers camped ashore. With each man wearing a personal radiation detection unit they erected apron mesh and barbed wire fences around the 'hot' spots - 200 x 200 yards on Alpha Island, and 100 x 100 yards on Trimouille. The men further contained the danger areas with fences across the islands' narrowest parts - 300 yards long on Alpha, and 500 on Trimouille. As the parties drilled and blasted holes for pickets and radiation warning notices geiger counters monitored the dust. The work, estimated to take 10 days, was completed at noon on 19 March, in half the planned time. It was just in time for *Diamantina* to withdraw in the face of danger from nature - Cyclone Mavis.

Next day off Onslow two familiar faces appeared on board, Commodore Marks and Brigadier Hunt. As the ship headed to continue the training cruise in Exmouth Gulf, Mavis asserted herself and the decision was made to curtail the cruise. Looking a little the worse for wear from her work in the Islands and brush with the cyclone, the ship tied up in Fremantle at 9.30 am, 24 March. After the senior officers, recruits, and army party disembarked, the crew set about refurbishing their ship.

The first half of April saw more Junior Recruit training. Preparations for the long cruise also went on. On 8 April, after the full power trial, all the hydrology winches passed tests. Two days later divers scraped the screws.

CSIRO Cruise Dm1/65 sailed on 17 April. In early stages of his work on water masses around Australia that Harry Jitts later labelled 'monumental', Dr. Rochford's team occupied stations en route to Cocos Islands where the ship came to anchor at Port Refuge on the 24 April. The usual port visit activities of calls, games, and parties were enjoyed. An unarmed platoon took part in the Anzac Day march. Early next morning anchor was aweigh for a new port - Colombo. With four stations daily taking a total of seven hours, it was a leisurely transit. The 17 knots reached in the full power trial on sailing day showed speed was available if needed.

Berthing at Queen Elizabeth Quay, Colombo at 8.55 am, 3 May, came close on the heels of riots in the city. But these did not affect the three days of this 'good visit.' Both cricket and rugby matches supplemented the usual calls, visits and cocktail party.

The three-legged course to Port Louis, Mauritius, occupied 12 days from 8 am, 6 May. There were between two and four stations each day with those on 9 May, arranged around the Crossing of the Line Ceremony.

The quay at Port Louis took *Diamantina's* lines at 8.15 am, 18 May. As the captain's Report of Proceedings later put it, the island was *in a state of unrest* and some calls were considered paid and returned. However, the trouble was mainly outside the city, and the Coldstream Guardsmen, flown in to help control it, were relaxed enough to compete against the ship in a rifle shoot, which *Diamantina* won.

In the event, the visit, enthusiastically endorsed by the island's government, was a resounding success; 60 attended the cocktail party, visitors included school groups, and the crew hosted a party for orphans. Bus tours and sport helped the sailors enjoy their run ashore.

The cruise's final leg to Reference Station 1 and home began at 10 am, 23 May. Occupying two stations each day the ship tracked eastwards. On 28 May, the CSIRO gun successfully tagged a hapless whale '19095.' With bad weather forcing the abandonment of Station 96, the ship, with its seven officers, 136 sailors, and four scientists, completed its triangular traverse of the Indian Ocean at 8.40 am, 3 June. The scientists pronounced the cruise, *most successful*. Diplomatically, too, it had exceeded expectations. The captain added his compliments, reporting all the crewmembers except one had been *most pleasing*.

During the midyear leave and self-maintenance period, LCDR P.G. Duncan relieved LCDR Holloway as commander at 9 am, Tuesday, 8 June. Two days later, 10 members of the South African Rugby team were entertained on board ship. The Springboks had just defeated Western Australia 104-0.

A day later the tug *Wilga* collided with *Diamantina*. The buckled Frame 57 and sprung plates were repaired in four days on the slipway. With trials completed and a new Type 771 echo sounder replacing the Type 765, the ship sailed on Dm2/65 on 17 July. The cruise was to further knowledge of West Australian crayfish, hydrology, and the circulation of ocean water masses. The 10 days of scientific work ended successfully on 29 July. There was another success. The dentist embarked for the voyage had produced a dentally fit crew.

Day trips providing sea training for Junior Recruits were followed by a *most enjoyable and successful* visit to Geraldton from 24-29 August for the Sunshine Festival. To the usual events of a port visit were added boxing, a rifle shoot, and visits by outback children.

Three days before the Annual Inspection a deserter voluntarily returned. This unusual event was followed by a change in the Inspecting Officer. Instead of NOICWA, the Flag Officer Commanding the Australian Fleet, Rear Admiral O.H. Belcher came aboard on 9 September. Admiral Belcher concluded his report:...*Diamantina, considering her age and her wartime design, is in excellent shape and appears to be capable of continuing her oceanographic and training role for some years to come. In spite of her lack of bunks and modern messing arrangements, her company like serving in her, and she is a happy, well-disciplined ship. Hard work has been done preparing for my inspection, and, generally, she was well up to Fleet standard. It gave me much pleasure that the last ship I will inspect in the Royal Australian Navy was clean and keen, and obviously of high morale. I made the following signal on completing my inspection.'Your company has worked very hard and successfully to produce a very clean ship for my inspection. She is wearing well and should have many more years good service left in her. Well done.'*

Two days later, at 10.30 am, 11 September, 'The Grey Ghost of the West Coast', which for six years had operated alone as an oceanographic vessel, sailed on a new task - to carry out soundings, and in consort. The task was *to establish a safe approach for heavy shipping to the Port Hedland channel*. In five weeks 'interesting surveying' *Diamantina* teamed with her sister oceanographic ship, *Gascoyne*, the survey vessel, *Moresby*, and the smaller HMAS *Bass*, which concentrated on the inshore soundings.

The novel work, the company of other RAN ships, and inter-ship visits all had a decidedly positive effect on morale. Runs ashore at the previously unvisited Port Hedland for basketball and barbecues were further bonuses. However, the ship's weather observer got little pleasure out of one trip ashore. On 24 September, Leading Airman B.S. Blackwell was landed to hospital with appendicitis.

Soundings sometimes continued into the night. By 16 October the three larger ships had completed surveying the area from north of Rowley Shoals to Bedout Island, while *Bass* had finished the inshore work.

On the 17th NOICWA came aboard off Dampier to carry out the annual sea inspection. The scenario for the exercises at the time of the Malaysia-Indonesia Confrontation was an interesting one. *Diamantina*, at Action Stations while transiting Sunda Strait, suffered damage and casualties aft and on the bridge from an aircraft attack. Later a submarine made a torpedo attack on the ship. The frigate's reply was to ram and board the enemy. Commodore Marks was generally well satisfied with the crew's response to the situation. He made especial note of an incident during the hoisting of the submarine boarding party's whaler, *The for'ard fall parted whilst the whaler was being hoisted. Serious accident was averted by the quick thinking and action of the Leading Hand of the boarding party in the bows of the whaler who successfully choked the lower block.*

The next day Commodore Marks directed Acting Leading Seaman A.V. Hann be confirmed in the rate immediately and recommended him for a Naval Board commendation. Hann's prevention of the accident had been at the risk of serious injury to himself as he caught the tail of the broken fall.

The Commodore was also 'impressed' with the Meteorological Department. The two qualified Leading Airmen under the Navigating Officer operated the only station making upper air observations off the Western Australian coast. NOIC praised the *valuable material to the body of scientific data being collected in sparsely settled regions.* In commenting on the 10 failures out of 44 radio-sonde ascents he made the point, *...This would be regarded as a small failure rate on a shore station where conditions and facilities are vastly superior.*

Four days after reaching Fremantle on 19 October, CSIRO Cruise Dm3/65 sailed with four CSIRO researchers, nine Reserve sailors, and 26 Junior Recruits aboard. All the planned 47 stations had been completed - the first full programme for some time - on return to port on 5 November.

A Full Power Trial during the Family Day on 10 November produced a creditable 18.8 knots. The Ship's Ball next evening heralded the work year's end. On the slipway after 18 November, the ship's side was cut open to fit the new 114Q Sonar. As well, many rivets were replaced before the vessel re-entered the water on 1 December. The refit then continued.

At year's end the Ordinary Seamen's Mess held the Diamantina Shield. They had won a keenly fought competition involving a quiz, darts, quoits, uckers, Indian wrestling, rifle shooting, boat races, and a tug-of-war contest using ropes rigged through loading blocks on the quarterdeck. Ashore, at the Fremantle Golf Club, Mr. Tony Kelly was the first winner of the Diamantina Trophy.

1966

The new class of Ordinary Seamen joined in January. The young O.D.s, some not yet 17 years old, settled into their first ship. Bernie Rogers ('Rogo') recalled, more than 30 years later, boarding around midnight after a long flight from Melbourne to find an unexpected welcome - his hammock was already rigged. Grateful, he quickly stowed his gear and swung himself into it - to find himself dumped on the deck. It had been rigged with slipknots.

January days were filled with chipping, painting, and other preparations for the year's cruises. O.Ds, the Navy's second lowest rank, were lowest in *Diamantina*'s hierarchy, and they were never allowed to forget it - until the lowest ranks arrived. Then, on the day and overnight cruises the O.D.s played 'old salts' to the Junior Recruits. The O.D.s, many of whom had been J.R.s only a year before, happily initiated their juniors in such unpopular tasks as laundry and chipping. With the wisdom of their extra year they freely offered advice to the young sailors struggling to master a whaler in Gage Roads - a much more difficult task than in the tranquil Swan River. Yet O.D.s were also there to learn. So they attended classes to prepare them to advance in rate. Their junior status was apparent, too, off duty. All sailors not on duty had leave every night. But the Ordinary Seamen's was 'Cinderella Leave'. It expired at one minute to midnight.

With the refit and trials completed, February began with Junior Recruit training and ammunition dumping. All hands spent 12-13 February at HMAS *Leeuwin* while the ship was fumigated. On 25 February, with Commodore Marks embarked, the ship sailed to investigate and then disprove a report of a shoal 50 miles north-west of Fremantle. Even in the heavy seas the Commodore took the opportunity to investigate the fishing possibilities.

CSIRO Cruise Dm1/66 sailed at 9 am, 3 March. The party of five studied crayfish and water masses over the next 18 days to as far north as 22 degrees South. The *most successful and valuable cruise* ended at 10A North Wharf at 3 pm, 21 March. A night at Geraldton, a Bofors shoot at a meteorological balloon, and the quarterly full power trial which produced over 16 knots at 160 rpm were fitted among the 72 stations.

Among further trials and Junior Recruit training, the crew manned the ship on 1 April to cheer the Queen Mother. Then, at 9 am, 12 April, with three Reserve officers and eight sailors embarked, Dm2/66 began. Only one CSIRO technical assistant was aboard. That was not the only variation. After revisiting the Diamantina Deep, the ship steered not for its usual areas, but headed south, then east through mountainous seas for Port Lincoln in South Australia. Here a pod of killer whales escorted the vessel into harbour. After the other four scientific team members joined, *Diamantina* sailed *to examine the chemical and physical environment during the South Australian tuna season.*

From 17-21 April, observations were recorded at 48 sites in Spencer Gulf before tying up at the fuel wharf in Port Adelaide. South Australian crewmembers enjoyed four days 'natives' leave' while off duty watches were granted day leave. Sport included an Australian Rules game, narrowly lost, against *a team of VFA standard.*

Diamantina sailed for home at 8 am, 25 April. In a smooth passage across the Bight the echo sounder operated continuously. One dawn the watch on the small lone ship detected another vessel approaching on the opposite course. When it resolved into a huge Soviet container vessel the captain was called. The signal was made, 'This is warship, *Diamantina*. State destination and ETA.' No response came as the colossus passed close down *Diamantina*'s side. Whether the signal was not seen, understood, or just ignored, there was no point in further action. Canberra was notified and the captain went to his delayed breakfast.

From arrival at Fremantle on 29 April to departure on 9 May for the year's first cruise 'up top', the most notable events were the Ship's Ball on 5 May, and the loading of 8,000m of new hydrology wire. Seven Reservists including one officer were embarked along with the CSIRO team of six. They studied plankton, crayfish, and aspects of the Western Australian coastal gyre, as the ship steered various courses before securing to C Buoy, Flying Fish Cove, Christmas Island at 4 pm, 18 May. The Police Superintendent then boarded to brief the crew on local laws and customs before a packed two days of calls, sport, a dance, and a cocktail party began. In addition, 150 school-children toured the ship.

Phil Collins, one of the Ordinary Seamen class on his first visit 'up top', did not take long to exhaust the small island's sights of the phosphate loader, salt-water swimming pool, and open-air movie theatre. So he and his three mates readily accepted a well-dressed man's offer of drinks at his home. It was a pleasant change from the crowded mess deck to be on the balcony of a two-story home high above Flying Fish Cove. At 11.30, after exhausting their host's food and drink, the four took the last liberty boat back aboard. Much later Phil learned the identity of their host. Locally known as 'The Gov.', he was the Island's Administrator.

At 8 am, 20 May, course was set for Singapore. Stations continued towards Indonesia. In this time of the Malaysia-Indonesia Confrontation, the captain wrote later in his Report of Proceedings of, ...*the northerly passage of Sunda Strait, steaming on modified and not obvious defence watche*s. An Indonesian patrol boat made a brief appearance during the transit but there was no incident.

During the three days in Singapore the captain attended meetings on a future task - Operation Monsea to take place from August to November. Reflecting the heightened security during Confrontation, the ship's sentries were armed and the seaward side floodlit. Ashore, the Ordinary Seamen enjoyed their first taste of Asia on 'Cinderella leave', with sightseeing and duty free shopping.

After sailing on 26 May, Diamantina stopped 30 miles south of Java Head two days later for the first scientific station. Then stations were carried out every six hours on a dogleg course until the ship came to anchor at Port Refuge, Cocos Islands, at 9.30 am, 31 May. During this short stay leave was restricted to the cricket team and four tennis players. Phil Collins nominated for tennis, and, to his surprise, was selected. The Cocos Islands team of four ladies from Perth quickly noticed Diamantina's four did not possess a single racquet between them. This brought up the reasonable question of whether they should attempt to play or watch the cricket. Immediate agreement was reached and all adjourned to the oval. Phil does not recall who won. But he vividly remembers the drinks and export quality steaks consumed between the match's end at 4 pm and return to the ship at dark. Choppy seas made the anchorage uncomfortable, so the cruise resumed as soon as the sportsmen boarded.

Stations to the northern tip of Sumatra were interrupted when 'King Neptune' admitted 52 new members to his Court on 4 June. A canvas swimming pool on the quarterdeck was filled with seawater, flour, sugar, sauces, food colouring, and other additives. Then 'Clear lower decks of all Ordinary Seamen,' was piped. Appropriately clad in shorts and sandals only, they obeyed. 'Neptune' and his court then initiated his new subjects. The call then went up for "Mr. Jitts." The CSIRO chief scientist, as usual, impeccably dressed in suit, white shirt, and tie, was brought before the Court. When he could not produce a certificate to substantiate his claim of previous initiation, 'Neptune' ordered him thrown into the pool. Mr. Jitts took the ducking a lot better than his suit.

After two days at Penang that included sport against teams from RAAF Butterworth, the cruise's last leg began on 8 June. Crayfish larvae trawled 700 miles off the Western Australian coast - at double the previous known range - was just one highlight of a *most successful cruise*. The Seamen's Mess celebrated too. They were the winners of the Diamantina Shield. Leave and self -maintenance followed arrival on 19 June.

This involved more than usual activity. While the ship was on the slipway from 21 June to 7 July, 1,646 rivets were replaced and a further 3,000 were marked for renewal at the annual refit. As well, a strong point for refuelling at sea was fitted to the wheelhouse, and a new Type 975 radar installed with displays on the bridge and aft of the wheelhouse. Then, Mr. W. Harper of the Royal Australian Navy Experimental Laboratory arrived on 28 June to *supervise the installation of special equipment for the forthcoming participation in Operation Monsea.* The biggest task was running cable from the sonar station to the laboratory. Clearly Monsea was an operation out of the ordinary.

After satisfactory trials *Diamantina* sailed at 11 am, 19 July for Darwin. Eight days alongside Fort Hill Wharf from 25 July during the Darwin Festival were filled with calls, visitors, a cocktail party, a civic reception, and sport. The crew appreciated their captain's attendance at their many different matches where they acquitted themselves well against quality opponents.

Twelve hours after sailing at 6.30 am, 2 August, the ship rendezvoused with HMAS *Vampire.* Mail was transferred to the destroyer and the Fleet Dental Team was welcomed aboard. They added to the other extra personnel embarked - three Bureau of Mineral resources geologists, and LCDR M.W. Varley of the Hydrographer's Office, *joined to assist RANEL personnel.*

Christmas Island was reached at 6.30 am, 2 August. Two years earlier, with the RAN's Deputy Hydrographer aboard, the ship had made a detailed offshore survey. Now, until they disembarked on 9 August, the geologists took and analysed bottom samples while the ship made thousands of soundings ostensibly *to establish the genesis and distribution of phosphate deposits on the island.*

Soundings continued en route to Sunda Strait. After the transit between 11 am and 4 pm, 10 August, course was set for Singapore. *Diamantina* tied up alongside HMS *Dampier* at Berth 12 in the Singapore Naval Base at 11 am, 12 August. *Dampier* bore the name of the 17th century navigator and hydrographer, William Dampier, the author of the first English description of Western Australia. The white painted ship, completed in 1948, and previously named *Herne Bay* and *Loch Eil*, was of the modified Bay class, a development of *Diamantina's* River class.

On the day of arrival, Mr. J. Milton, Principal Scientific Officer of the Admiralty Underwater Weapons Establishment (AUWE), and Scientist in Charge of Operation Monsea, visited the ship. The next day three RANEL scientists came aboard and Replenishment At Sea (RAS) trials were carried out alongside and outside the harbour. Scientific and recording equipment was fitted, connected and tested.

On Monday, 22 August, at A Buoy, 4,000 one-pound explosive charges were loaded. Trials at sea with *Dampier* and the Royal Fleet Auxiliary *Brown Ranger* took place between 24 and 28 August. On the first morning *Diamantina* successfully completed its first practice Replenishment At Sea.

At 8 am, 29 August, *Diamantina* put to sea with *Dampier, Brown Ranger, Verulam,* and the submarine, *Andrew,* that had played USS *Scorpion* in Stanley Kramer's 1959 film of Neville Shute's end of the world novel, 'On the Beach'. Operation Monsea's aims were simple and also looking to the future. The ships were to *gather environmental data in possible operation areas of the next generation of sonars.* That afternoon the first charges were detonated.

The flotilla worked in two groups. The veteran submarine, *Andrew,* was teamed with HMS *Verulam,* commissioned in 1943 as a destroyer and described in 'Jane's Fighting Ships' as converted to a trials ship for testing new antisubmarine equipment. *Dampier* and *Diamantina* made up the other group. Working in adjacent areas, but 50 miles apart, the ships detonated the one-pound charges as acoustic sources. As in her work years before with *Vema, Diamantina,* acting as transmitting ship, would make a run of 20 to 30 miles from a stationary *Dampier* dropping charges at preset times and ranges. Then *Diamantina* would stop and the roles reverse with *Dampier* closing. The whole sequence took 8-10 hours. Then the ships would move overnight to the adjacent area to begin again at about 8 am, next day.

In addition to the Monsea observations (MOSOBS), *Diamantina* had RAN tasks (RANOBS). These involved bathymetric dips, hydrology casts, underwater camera observations, and, using a special buoy, readings of remote ambient sea noise. After zigzagging through one degree squares across the shallow sea, *Diamantina*, *Dampier*, and *Brown Ranger* refuelled simultaneously on the morning of Saturday, 10 September from the Royal Fleet Auxiliary, *Tide Pool*. Then, with typhoons to the east and north, they made for port.

At 2.15, that afternoon, *Diamantina* secured alongside *Dampier* at the United States Naval Base at Subic Bay in the Philippines. *Verulam* was inboard of *Dampier* at No.13 and 14 Berth, Rivera Point. LCDR Duncan along with CDR P. Cardno of *Dampier*, LCDR D. Watts of *Verulam*, and LCDR M. Sizeland of *Andrew* called on the Base's Chief of Staff on Monday morning. Host ships, assigned to the visitors made the crew's stay pleasant, but with the typhoon generating very heavy and rising seas and winds some berths became untenable. As the weather deteriorated, HMAS *Parramatta* and HMS *Delight* joined the three already at Rivera Point. On 13 September, the ships were glad to sail for Monsea's next phase towards Hong Kong from 14-21 September.

In two days of runs over a known acoustic range interested new researchers were Mr. F.E. Hale of San Diego on *Dampier*, and Mr. R. Wyber, the RANEL's Principal Research Scientist, on *Diamantina*.

The routine of operating hydrophones, buoys, underwater cameras, and other instruments, was interrupted at 2.30 am, 16 September when Monsea's commander received a distress signal. The 10,000 tons ore carrier *August Moon* was aground on Pratas Reef, 250 miles away. CDR Cardno ordered his ships to proceed at best speed into the rising swell from Typhoon Elsie. The venerable *Dampier*, in the act of changing boilers, connected both by 4.12 am, and increased to 15 knots. *Diamantina* maintained 14 knots while its second boiler was brought on line. Then it cracked on the pace. At 8 am, about to pass its Royal Navy consort close on the port side, the older Australian ship made the cheeky signal, 'How do you get these things out of second gear?' CDR Cardno later reported, *By now the swell from Typhoon Elsie had become quite steep, and both ships were clambering up the crests and plunging down into the troughs, proving once again their excellent hull design. So we continued for an hour, in bright sunshine, with a feeling of excitement in the air, and, it must be admitted, a feeling of escape from the daily oceanography.*

But, at 10 am, *Diamantina* received a signal that helicopters from USS *Oriskany* were flying to the rescue. The Monsea duo then reduced speed and, in the 15-foot swells, returned to oceanography.

Two weeks in Hong Kong began on 22 September. With a peak presence of 12 RN and RAN warships there were a number of changes of moorings before sailing on the next Monsea phase at 8.10 am, 6 October. This involved the duo ranging to within 150 miles of the southern Philippines and off the coast of Vietnam as they recorded the results of tests, ambient sea noise and other marine characteristics. Bernie Rogers remembers one clear night seeing sustained flashes on the horizon. On another occasion a giant American B52 bomber made a low daylight pass over the ship. Another sailor recalls the navigator covering a chart of the Vietnam coast as he approached. The leg ended at Singapore on 18 October.

Hong Kong 1966. The ship's painters pose in front of LCDR P. Duncan and the crew. (RAN)

Five days later the four vessels transited the Straits of Malacca. Phase Three had the two groups, about 100 miles apart, probing the sea from just north of the Straits of Malacca south across the Equator, and then north to the southern edge of the Bay of Bengal. *Verulam, Andrew*, and *Brown Ranger* again made up Unit One, and *Dampier* and *Diamantina* Unit Two. The research was carried out at areas about 180 nautical miles apart.

On 3 November a RAF Shackleton dropped containers of mail to the ships. After recovering hers, *Diamantina* began drawing away to the next position. An urgent signal from *Dampier* brought her hurrying back. The mailbags' labels had been reversed. The bags were exchanged.

Monsea's final readings were made on 4 November close to the Thai coast, north of Penang. *Dampier* then farewelled *Diamantina* with a salvo of firecrackers. *Andrew, Verulam*, and *Diamantina* proceeded to Singapore. Just before they tied up a helicopter photographed them steaming in company. The 'Scrap Iron Flotilla' (*Andrew* and *Dampier* had been completed in 1948, *Diamantina* in 1945, *Verulam* in 1943, and *Brown Ranger* launched in 1940) had done well. In Monsea's two and a half months the only equipment on *Diamantina* that had given disappointing results had been the underwater camera. *Dampier*'s had covered this deficiency. *Diamantina* steamed 15,000 miles, took 423 bathythermographic dips, and detonated over 5,000 acoustic charges to achieve outstanding results.

Dampier's captain put his assessment of *Diamantina* in his Report of Proceedings: *...It would be impossible to imagine a better ship to work with. She has played a faultless part in the combined work although often wrestling with defective equipment, and her irrepressible humour has helped along rainy and sunny days alike...*

The O.Ds, told little of the cruise's purpose, made deductions from what they saw and heard. Phil Collins believes it tested a new British sonar fitted in *Verulam*. Collins recalls *Dampier* and *Diamantina* spending mornings drifting tied together; the ships sailed close together with fenders out and heaving lines helping to maintain a single silhouette. *Diamantina* would be dead in the water while a rifle was fired vertically into the water in timed sequence. He also recalls an American Chief Petty Officer radioman at Subic Bay thanking him for "being out there with us," and then replying to Phil's puzzled "Out where?" with "Vietnam, of course. I heard you on the radio."

Ordinary Seaman Collins' most exciting time on the cruise came during the passage of the Straits of Malacca. He was on duty in the wheelhouse when the steering failed in one of the world's most crowded shipping lanes. The quartermaster quickly moved to the aft steering position leaving Phil in the wheelhouse. But the emergency steering gear also malfunctioned. Phil had a hectic 10 minutes relaying orders as Captain Duncan on the bridge above used the main engines to avoid a rusty merchantman by 20 metres before the rudder answered again.

The five scientists and their equipment were offloaded in a day at Singapore. Then, at 5 pm, 8 November, course was set for home. A search for the Maria Augustina Bank well and truly disproved its existence when the minimum depth in the area was recorded as 1,480 fathoms. 19 knots on the full power trial helped have the ship alongside 10A at 1.45 pm, 16 November. After her four months absence on the most successful 6,000-mile cruise there was a large welcoming crowd.

Two days after arrival, LCDR Varley was discharged to the Hydrographer's Office in Sydney. He would return four years later as captain. Refit and leave began. On the slip work began on replacing 3,500 rivets. A second diesel generator was installed on the starboard side. Refrigeration and laundry deficiencies were made good.

The oceanographic equipment, including the 771 echo sounder and an EDO and Precision Depth Recorder were checked. The PDR had been supplied in August, and, along with the EDO was housed in the bridge's cramped sonar compartment. A letter of 10 November approved the replacement of the Type 974 Radar with a Type 975.

On 4 December, stores of a different kind were offloaded. The 325 toys bought in Hong Kong with money raised by a levy on canteen sales were delivered to the Child Welfare Department. These Christmas gifts then went to Fremantle's underprivileged children.

On 20 December, LCDR M. Ward replaced LCDR Duncan in command.

The Ordinary Seamen also departed to leave and courses in the eastern states. Phil Collins and Bernie Rogers looked back on a hard full year of long hours and spartan living conditions. To escape stifling conditions in the mess decks they had often slung their hammocks or set up 'click-click beds' (banana lounges) on the upper decks. As the ship's Landrover, C81868, took him to the airport for his next posting Bernie caught a last glimpse of *Diamantina*'s stern on the slipway. He wrote in 1999 that the year aboard that had begun with his stern crashing to the deck as his hammock collapsed had been *the best twelve months of my life.*

1967

Before *Diamantina*'s 1967 programme meeting in July 1966, the RAN's Hydrographer wrote to NOICWA. There was a notable suggestion in his letter - moving the ship to the east coast for six months. His reasons included, *...the priorities for RAN oceanographic work lie mainly off the east coast,* and *The allocation of ship time to CSIRO and the eastern universities is expected to result in useful work for the RAN in addition to the work of the cruise leaders.* Quite rightly, the Navy wanted to gain as much as possible from *Diamantina*'s work.

The ship was dressed overall on 30 January for Australia Day at the end of a month of preparations. All activities went as usual, except the record of fumigation has the wry postscript, *with only moderate success.*

On 13 February, after two weeks of Junior Recruit training and ammunition dumping, with two wooden rails added to the quarterdeck, the ship took on 12 depth charges. The next day, with five more depth charges and Junior Recruits aboard, *Diamantina* sailed to play its part in the Bureau of Mineral Resources' Fremantle Region Upper Mantle Project (FRUMP). Building on knowledge gained in the ship's 1960 work, FRUMP was to investigate the earth's crust offshore for oil potential in the arc from Fremantle to Albany.

From 13-19 February, Petty Officer Corkhill of HMAS *Leeuwin* armed and dropped all 17 depth charges in designated positions south-west of Rottnest Island, and off Albany and Cape Leeuwin. Flying the international signal for survey operations and the red code flag, 'Bravo,' *Diamantina* detonated the 300 pounds Mk.7 depth charges singly on the sea- bed at the locations:

32 degrees 10'S, 115 degrees 15'E (west of Rottnest Is) on 13th and 14th; 5 shots.
31 degrees 35'S, 115 degrees 10'E (off Yanchep) on 15th; 5 shots.
35 degrees 10'S, 118 degrees 30'E (S of Albany) on 17th and 18th; 5 shots.
35 degrees 15'S, 116 degrees 15'E (SE of C. Leeuwin) on 19th; 1 shot.
34 degrees 20'S, 114 degrees 40'E (NW of C. Leeuwin) on 19th; 1 shot.

The vessel returned to port on 20 February. Mr. I.B. Everingham, Senior Scientist at the Mundaring Geophysical Observatory, reported the results had exceeded expectations.

While Junior Recruit training proceeded, an upgrade of the laboratory was completed. This was to allow *study of the growth of organic matter in a duplicated sea environment on board*. The Royal Australian Navy new Ensign was hoisted for the first time on 1 March. The event coincided with the completion of Commodore Stevenson's Annual Inspection. Both events were celebrated at 2.55 pm, when the crew wholeheartedly obeyed the order, 'Splice the Mainbrace.'

After CSIRO personnel and Dr. Christopher Von De Boch of Flinders University's Horace Lamb Institute had finished equipment installation, and the ship's Land Rover had been hoisted inboard, *Diamantina* sailed at 10.30 am, 6 March for Adelaide. The cruise's main aim was to test CSIRO's new light bath. Dr. Von De Boch was searching for undersea canyons stretching at right angles from the coast. Regular hydrology stations were also made to collect the usual data. The Flinders researcher was more than satisfied with the cruise. About 25 miles off Esperance, he discovered a 20 mile long, 6,000 foot deep canyon. This feature, named after the town, plunged 1,000 feet deeper than California's Monterey Canyon, until then the world's deepest known Continental Shelf canyon - another 'first' for *Diamantina*.

Two days in Adelaide began at 8 am, 11 March. Here more personnel from Flinders University and the RAN Experimental Laboratory replaced the CSIRO group before the ship slipped from North Parade Wharf for the Southern Ocean. Until the echo sounder became unserviceable three days out it recorded continuously. The cruise followed the meridian 135 degrees East south to 44 degrees South. Then the ship sailed east to run up 138 degrees East. Hydrology stations every two degrees of latitude as the vessel tracked south and north along the meridians yielded good results, even with the ship rolling through 25 degrees in the seas. In three hours at Port Adelaide Outer Harbour on the afternoon of 19 March, the satisfied scientists disembarked.

Eight years after she had left to begin her second commission, *Diamantina* returned to Sydney Harbour on 22 March, berthing alongside her sister ship, HMAS *Culgoa* at Garden Island's Fitting Out Wharf.

Six days later Dm2/67 began. In this interrupted cruise, water samples were taken to a depth of 2,500 fathoms to detect and measure the East Australian Current. There were also experiments with neutral buoyancy floats, and Geomagnetic Electro Kinetographs (GEKs) and hydrophones were streamed and recovered before Cyclone Glenda forced a return to Sydney a day early on 6 April. From 10 to 18 April the ship probed the main stream of the current on and below the surface. 'Pingers' measured to depths of 3,000m and drogues to 1,000m. The Reference Station was east of Sydney at 34 degrees South, 153 degrees 20' East. Over the study area from the coast to 160 degrees East and from 27 to 37 degrees South the East Australian Current was measured as about six miles wide, set on a course of 170 degrees, and running at up to four knots.

Print and television reporters interviewed both the captain and cruise leader on their return. The 14 confirmed and nine suspected cases of rubella that manifested themselves during the cruise featured prominently in the reports. The 'pingers', GEK, and hydrophones did not. Less than a week later, at 9.30 am, 24 April, Dm3/67 began for Fiji, Manus Island, and Darwin. Daily stations at 8.30 am and 9 pm sampled the water and made subsurface photometry readings. As well, in the laboratory, marine organisms were grown under simulated conditions.

The first leg's weather was poor as *Diamantina* tracked to Fiji making continuous soundings. In two days at Suva the crew enjoyed the usual port events. The Fiji Police Band played the ship out at 10 am, 3 May. The nine-day leg to Manus Island saw stations continue with a Bren gun, Thompson sub-machine gun, rifle and pistol shoot interlude on 7 May. The stay at Manus was brief. The ship tied up at Lombrim Point Jetty in Seeadler Harbour at 9.30 am, 12 May and sailed at 9 am next day for Darwin. The cruise continued its uneventful course through two days in Darwin from 22 May, and transit of Torres Strait via Prince of Wales Channel, to the final station's completion on the morning of 3 June. Next morning *Diamantina* tied up alongside *Vendetta* at Garden Island's Cruiser Wharf at 9 o'clock.

The winners of the Diamantina Shield for the first half of 1967 were the members of the Engineering and Electrical Mess. The Press, however was more interested in the cruise reports of the captain and Mr. Jitts, the Cruise Leader. They made the point that this cruise, one of the longest in Australian oceanographic history, had made notable progress in the nine-year-old project of mapping Tasman and Coral Sea resources. As well they pointed to the discovery of a 4,000-fathom deep 250 miles east of Noumea.

After the long self-maintenance ended in mid-July, trials included testing of sonar buoys and RANEL equipment loaded for the next cruise. Then 30 tons of TNT-RDX explosives made up into charges ranging from a half pound to 68 pounds were loaded. At 1.30 pm, 12 July *Diamantina* cleared the Heads for a six weeks seismic survey off the Barrier Reef. Mr. L.V. Hawkins led the University of New South Wales team on board. The ship was to work again with *Vema*, carrying a party of scientists from the Lamont Geological Observatory.

At Townsville, on 16 July, equipment was transferred to *Vema*. As well, a University of New South Wales scientist joined the Research Vessel, and Dr. M. Ewing, the Director of the Lamont Observatory, and another scientist embarked on *Diamantina*. The next day, in Challenger Bay, Palm Island, the frigate transferred half of the explosives to the 583 tons, 200 foot, three-masted schooner. The 23 Nova Scotians and six scientists stowed the 15 tons of explosives aboard the vessel.

The first shots to plot seismic refraction profiles were fired at 8 am, 19 July. It was a very similar process to the previous work with *Vema* and the sonar development Monsea exercise with *Dampier* the year before. One ship stopped and listened through sonobuoys and hydrophones while the other used satellite navigation to follow a determined course to up to 50 miles away while firing charges. Then the roles were reversed. The University of New South Wales sonobuoys' performance fell short of expectations. Still, Dr. Ewing, a founder of modern oceanography, *commented highly* on *Diamantina's* work. In turn, the Australians were very impressed with the Lamont hydrophones.

27 July was spent in Cairns. Then, two days later, work with *Vema* resumed at 3 am, until the survey ended on 8 August. The ships expended 950 charges in making 19 profiles, most around Willis Island. Co-operation between the ships was excellent and included the exchange of officers for periods of up to 48 hours. LCDR Ward made particular mention of the usefulness of *Vema's* satellite navigation system.

Debriefing was in Townsville on 9 August. *Diamantina* then sailed for Sydney. There, from 13 August, the scientists and their equipment went ashore. As well, the class of 40 Ordinary Seamen, who had successfully completed their final tests on the previous day, were posted out to be replaced by another class. There were more replacements. The ship's old .303 rifles and Bren guns went ashore, and Self Loading Rifles and LIA2s came aboard.

A short CSIRO cruise in two parts from 21 August-1 September, and from 4-15 September, measured hydrology and currents using remote 'pingers' and a temperature recorder. The full power trial produced a creditable 18 knots. The east coast interlude ended when, with equipment for the Horace Lamb Institute aboard, course was set for Adelaide at 9.30 am, 18 September. From 21 to 25 September the HLI scientists embarked as the crew enjoyed Adelaide hospitality.

The cruise from 25 September to 2 October took place in weather ranging from 'rough' to 'appalling.' At 45 degrees South a break lost 1,400m of wire and seven Nansen bottles. Nevertheless the team leader, Dr. J.A. Bye was greatly satisfied with the results of their study of the dynamics of the Southern Ocean in spring.

In three hours in Adelaide Outer Harbour on 4 October, the HLI team was replaced by four other scientists from Flinders University, before the ship sailed for home. Hydrological readings along the 2,000 fathom line were made across the Bight. A fault in the Precision Depth Recorder hampered the search for more underwater canyons. A seven months absence ended when *Diamantina* returned to No. 9 Berth, Fremantle at 10 am, 9 October. The ship quickly resumed the routine of day training of Junior Recruits. Family Day and the Ship's Ball were other familiar events.

Five CSIRO researchers under Dr. J. Rochford further studied the Western Australian crayfish and Indian Ocean dynamics between Bunbury and North-West Cape in the cruise from 30 October to 17 November. In 24 hours in Geraldton from 9 am, 7 November, two sailors were transferred to hospital while the rest enjoyed time ashore.

The full power trial on the run south produced 19.5 knots. More pleasing to the CSIRO team was the first development in captivity of a larva to a young crayfish. The momentous metamorphosis took place unobserved during the night and the historic specimen's life was short-lived. But it was an event of such magnitude the five scientists 'celebrated with drinks.'

The record steaming year ended with the arrival at G Berth. 36,456 miles had been covered with 6,738 of those in May alone. *Diamantina* began the annual leave and refit period. The ship was on the slip from 24 November to 19 December. The varied cruises had produced good results. The community of the ship's company had changed as Junior Recruits and Ordinary Seamen's classes had been posted in and out. As with all communities there had been ups and downs. A fire in the victualling store had, fortunately and suspiciously, been confined to the records. Correspondence had flowed back and forth over the loss early in the previous year of £100 from the Commonwealth Bank agency. Eventually the Bank had made up the loss.

Death had come again to the community. On 14 December, colours were half masted for the funeral of Junior Recruit Bridgland. The ship, too, passed a milestone. Byford Depot still held the 4-inch gun. On 12 December the Navy Board approved the captain's request of 8 March ...*to remove and land A Gun Deck complete with barbette*. LCDR Ward's reasons, considering NOICWA's 14 November 1963 assessment, ...*the ship is no longer regarded as having a capability in war*, were sound. He wanted to use the man-hours expended on maintaining the gundeck on ...*the many more essential items in the ship*.

One O.D.'s Cruise

As well as research cruises, *Diamantina*'s other tasks included training of Junior Recruits and Ordinary Seamen. Peter Dales recalls his O.D. Cruise from 6 June to 14 August, 1967. Ordinary Seaman Dales was late for his cruise. After spending six weeks in hospital at HMAS *Cerberus* with hepatitis followed by two weeks leave to recuperate, he was eager to join his first ship. *Diamantina*, with its World War II origins, small size, and hammocks seemed an interesting posting. At Sydney Central Station, just off the 'Spirit of Progress', he met another new man for the ship at the RTO - a RANR lieutenant. The officer shouted the new rating a ride in his cab to Garden Island where the ship was in self-maintenance. Peter soon found himself chipping and painting on the forecastle under the watchful eye of POQMG Jack Edwards. Bert Krollig was the 'killick' of his Mess - No. 8, Port. The raw Ords, many of whom formed lasting friendships during this cruise, learnt more than Navy lore alongside. When *Diamantina* entered the Captain Cook Dock, one of the cooks, Jim McVeigh, took a container to collect some of the fish stranded as the water drained. The painters and dockers soon made the ownership of the fish clear to Jim. Fish wasn't on the ship's menu that night.

Peter found leaving harbour for the first time a 'real buzz' in spite of the Ords...*stumbling about with heaps of enthusiasm, but not too much achievement...Out past Pinchgut, the ships in mothballs, Bradleys Head, The Sow and Piglets, then through the Heads into the gentle swell of the Tasman Sea.*

In his first time at sea Peter was initially also metaphorically 'at sea.' *We assumed sea routine with watches to stand, part of the ship to be worked, and the usual 'for exercise, for exercise, for exercise, man overboard, fire,' but I don't recall an 'action stations.' It took a while to get used to watchkeeping, often forgetting to muster, or being adrift. I'm sure my ear was bent severely many times before I got into the swing of things, and relieved the previous watchkeeper the customary 10 minutes early. Getting used to life aboard took a while. Slinging hammocks, having your locker in another area from your mess, collecting your meals from the galley and taking them back to your mess were problems, but with L/S Bert Krollig's guidance as sea-daddy to us raw Ords and that of the other AB killicks and POs it wasn't too traumatic.*

There were simple unexpected pleasures - 'scoring' a freshly baked roll with a mug of ky [Navy cocoa - other spellings are ki, kai, and kie] on a cold night in the 'guts' watch at sea was one. Other times, like standing first watch on deck as his 19th birthday dawned, were less pleasant.

It was not all practical work. Afternoons were spent in the 'elephant hut' learning general and specialist Navy lore. On 9 August, after mastering the skills of *"...keeping the ship on a steady course, responding to the officer of the watch's orders, using the telegraphs, and resisting the urge to chase the lubber's line,* Peter received his Helmsman's Certificate.

The work with *Vema* provided experiences not available on other ships, including the regular thumps when four of the 68 pound explosive charges were lashed together and detonated.

Port calls introduced more variety. At Cairns Peter had a busy time as wharf sentry complete with heavy rifle. He found the only way to avoid a pestering bunch of children was *...to keep marching back and forth from stem to stern.* Although the Quartermaster, ABQMG 'Shorty' Gibson later praised his handling of the situation, Peter's main lesson learned was *...there were better duties to cop than wharf sentry.*

The Townsville calls produced two memorable incidents. A dance at Brothers football club erupted into an alcohol fuelled brawl between the uniformed sailors and some disgruntled locals. Peter, restricted to soft drinks by his recent bout with hepatitis, found himself cold sober beside his mates in a situation where they were *...heavily outnumbered and the immediate future didn't look too promising.* The RAAF came to the rescue of Peter and some of the crew, bundling them into cars and back to the ship. The rest, after the police had calmed the situation, rode back in a paddy wagon. Lost caps and dirtied, torn uniforms were the night's main cost!

Then teetotal Peter, recalls the next incident more clearly than most other participants. Returning with his 'almost legless' messmates early from a night on the town he turned in shortly after 9 pm. In port, to escape the heat, their hammocks were slung on the upper deck. There was a wardroom cocktail party that night. A foursome passed by on a tour of the ship. The ladies were struck with the quaint sight of the hammocks and discussed them loud and long. One occupant, already suffering from alcoholic remorse, snapped at this added torment and loudly and clearly requested them to "p— off." Their sub-lieutenants quickly escorted them back to the party. Over the next few days no mention was made of the incident. But the ratings received some hard stares.

Peter ended his account 33 years after his first cruise: *I think most of the Ords were posting off when we returned to Sydney, so we were in high spirits on the trip back with the knowledge that we were off to the various training establishments for our branch training. Entering the Heads, and lining up for Procedure Alpha was a more polished performance by the Ords under training, than when we left Sydney Harbour. I made many new friends and acquaintances in* Diamantina *and learnt a lot about seamanship and being at sea. My sea time as an Ord under training was very short compared to many, but I was extremely glad that I spent it in* Diamantina.

1968

1968 was the second year in succession *Diamantina* operated mainly off Australia's east and north coasts. NOICWA, Commodore J. Ramsay, was aboard on 30 January when the ship put to sea for the first post refit trial. As part of the refit, six bunks had been installed for the scientists. On 2 February the captain ordered innerspring mattresses for them.

At 8.45 am, 5 February, *Diamantina* cast off to monitor the Monte Bello test sites. That evening, at 6.42 pm, in three-foot seas and an eight to ten foot south-westerly swell, the ship rolled heavily in a big swell tipping 17-year-old ORDWM Richard Wojcik off the port side of the quarterdeck into the sea. Immediately the lifebuoy sentry, ORDSA Alfred May, a classmate of Wojcik, let go a lifebuoy and sounded the alarm - installed in the recent refit. When Wojcik surfaced to starboard after feeling the beat of the ship's screws as he passed completely under the hull, the lifebuoy was in the next trough and out of his sight. He spent an anxious time treading water watching his receding ship and wondering if he had been seen. He was soon reassured. Within half a mile *Diamantina* turned and hove to 60 feet to starboard. With the prevailing sea conditions and a 20-knot wind no boat was launched. A/LSCD E.C. Sporer went over the side on a line. After only 10 minutes in the water the relieved Wojcik was back on board.

The heavy weather had effects below deck as well. Warren Treadgold who served on *Diamantina* as a stoker from July 1967 to April 1968, as a Leading Hand from February 1969 to September 1971, and Petty Officer from May 1973 to 1975 remembered in 1998: *Brian (Nobby) Norman was the 'messdeck dodger' (cleaner) at one stage around this time, in fact it was from Brian that I got my nickname of Twiggy. Twiggy was the high profile English model with the waif-like figure. I was 6 feet tall and built like a racing greyhound, hence the nickname. During Nobby's stint of messdeck dodger, he decided to paint the mess and he proceeded to get stuck into it by removing any thing that was a temporary fixture. Some of the lockers that held our kit and belongings were not always fixed too securely and there was one set, on the starboard side at the bottom of the ladder, that had been wired to a pipe or something. Of course Nobby removed the wire during the painting and had forgotten to put it back.*

Some of the blokes in the mess decided instead of sleeping in a hammock, they would put down stretchers on vacant areas of the deck and sleep there. After a few months in the mess, I managed to secure an area on the floor where I also could put a stretcher and it just happened to be right next to this set of lockers, between them and the ladder which led down from the mess above. Everything was OK until one night while at sea and everybody was sound asleep, including me. It got a bit choppy and the ship started to move around; to this day I do not know what woke me but something did and I woke in time to catch this set of lockers as they fell on top of me. They were pretty heavy but I had woken up in time to put my hands up and break the fall and with my elbows by my side, wedged into the stretcher, I managed to hold the lockers just off my chest until my yells for help alerted the blokes asleep in the mess to my plight. Nobby very quickly secured the lockers back in place after that, apologising profusely.

One of the characters onboard at this time was A/ERA George Forbes. Unfortunately George suffered chronic seasickness; the ropes only had to be slipped from the wharf and George would be sick and he would remain that way until we were back alongside or we had anchored somewhere, on this occasion, at Monte Bellos Islands. The most amazing thing with George, however, was that he had a great sense of humour and could make light of any situation. As I recall, we encountered some pretty rough weather on this trip. We didn't see too much of George because he spent most of his time, while the ship was underway, in his hammock or in the sick bay. A short time later, he was transferred to the Sydney *and some time after that was medically discharged.*

The ship came to anchor in the Monte Bellos two days after Wojcik's ducking. From 8 February, CPO Richard Bartlett, in baking heat, led his 12-man team in monitoring radiation and taking 69 soil and rock samples. The crew honed their skills in demolition, boat, and small arms exercises. Off duty, in the beautifully hued water of the bays, the many anglers found a variety of fish *almost jumping onto the rods.*

The shore parties, many of whom paid the penalty for inadequate sun protection, found radioactivity continuing its decline, but the Ground Zero site on Trimouille and Alpha Islands still dangerously 'hot.' As well, the fence separating the closed northern part of Trimouille from the oil exploration area on the south had been breached. In the closed area were remains of beach campfires and an unregistered, servicable four- wheel drive vehicle with fuel in the tank. This, along with a 'hot' 1926 Australian two-shilling piece, was left undisturbed. With the fence repaired and notices renewed, the anchor was weighed at 1.15 pm, 11 February, and the voyage ended at No.5, North Wharf, at 8.30 am, on 14 February.

Five days later CSIRO Cruise 1/68 began. Mr. R. Cowper's team studied hydrology and the Western Australian rock lobster. An uneventful first leg ended at No. 2 Berth, Geraldton at 9 am, 27 February. Early next afternoon, the work resumed. By 7.30 that evening off the Abroholos Islands the ship was rolling in heavy seas as she made east-west trawls. During the night the weather deteriorated. Ordinary Seaman Michael Boyd, who had slung his hammock outside under the 'elephant hut', was later grateful to the Coxswain who disturbed his sleep with a forceful, "Get your **** inside." Seas, which had begun washing over the side, soon were regularly breaking on deck. Many of the crew became seasick in the 'extremely uncomfortable' conditions that persisted for the rest of the cruise, as the ship rolled through 65 mile trawls in beam seas. Still, the scientists were happy with their results from the curtailed cruise when the battered ship tied up at 9.05 am, 10 March. The crew then repaired the storm damaged buckled breakwater and shattered quarterdeck locker.

Until the next sailing, on 18 March, Horace Lamb Institute researchers loaded equipment, and the Annual Inspection took place. Commodore Ramsay carried out his sea inspection en route to Bunbury. There he disembarked while the crew relaxed with cricket and a bus tour. The guests at the ship's cocktail party arrived at the gangway by special train along the jetty. The Mayor entertained the ship's company at a Reception next day. At 8.30 am, *Diamantina* sailed for Sydney.

Stations in the often stormy Southern Ocean were a change from those on the year's first cruise. Although the weather was cold and grey, seas were calm. Acting Sub-Lieutenant Andrew Morling, on his first ship, recalled the beauty of albatrosses trailing in the wake before flexing wings to ride air currents past the bridge. While appreciating the view from the bridge he also remembered his responsibilities, especially in the light of the previous month's 'man overboard' incident. In his early solo bridge watches he repeatedly mentally rehearsed the drill.

In the ideal sea conditions the cruise plan, at first deemed too ambitious, was not only completed by the now experienced HLI team, but time was found for an additional station. Soundings were made continuously. Before tying up at Garden Island's Fitting Out Wharf on the morning of 29 March, the log was calibrated on the measured distance off South Head.

As the scientists disembarked the Ordinary Seamen gleefully headed for their first leave in Kings Cross. Older, more prudent, hands ranged further afield. Over the next four days the captain attended meetings with University of NSW, RAN Experimental Laboratory (RANEL), and CSIRO researchers. The upcoming cruise had multiple aims. CSIRO was to study Tasman Sea dynamics; the Bureau of Mineral Resources planned to test a towed array that would allow seismic soundings by a single ship; and the RANEL wanted to test Towflex, an experimental towed array sonar, similar to the BMR array.

In Cruise 4/68 from 2 -10 April Mr. Bruce Hamon's CSIRO team took magnetometer readings and investigated Tasman Sea and Eastern Australian Current dynamics, work that, when completed, Harry Jitts stated …*changed the face of dynamic oceanography*. As well, they sampled crayfish and prawn larvae up to 220 miles out to sea. Their research area was off the Queensland and New South Wales coasts between 26 and 33 degrees South. As on most cruises, 40/60 shoots were carried out.

During the self-maintenance 12 days from 11 April, BMR and Department of National Development equipment was installed. The RANEL was also busy with Towflex and a Towed Acoustic Array.

The BMR towed array was repeatedly streamed and recovered off Sydney Heads during the afternoon and night of 24 April. The crew wrestled with the 6,000 ft long apparatus that was up to four inches (10 cms) in diameter. At 3.38 am a recovery ended with only 1,500 feet aboard. A search ended at 5.20 am when a skilful radar operator picked up the missing 4,500 feet among the wave top 'clutter.' It was hauled aboard, and the weary crew and relieved scientists returned to Garden Island.

Cairns was the destination when the ship sailed, the morning after Anzac Day. Until it was recovered for the last time at 12.30 pm, 1 May, Towflex was streamed and recovered on *most satisfactory* operational and research trials. There was other work, too. The Ordinary Seamen attended daily classes; the echo sounder operated continuously; and radiosonde and other meteorological readings were regularly reported.

While the crew enjoyed leave and games in Cairns from 1 to 4 May, RANRL teams changed for the cruise's next leg which began with 31 T.S. *Endeavour* sea cadets sailing aboard at 9 am, 4 May, to return to Cairns with the pilot. Then course was set for RANEL hydrographic and acoustic stations every 90 miles to the 2,000m line. Traversing the waters where she had worked with *Vema* the year before, *Diamantina* tracked to Noumea. On 12 May a *very successful…acoustic propagation experiment* was completed with a RAAF maritime reconnaissance Neptune aircraft north-west of Noumea.

A security talk preceded arrival in Noumea on 16 May. Visits, a cocktail party, and a rugby match were some of the planned activities before the *most successful* visit ended after four days. Andrew Morling recalled the contribution of two persons to the success. The first was *Diamantina*'s Royal Navy navigator - the only fluent French speaker on board. The other was the cheerful, extrovert Australian consul who was tireless in his efforts on the unofficial as well as official levels. Memories of an evening at the Biarritz nightclub, which included dancing a spirited Tamure with the grass-skirted performers, remained long with some officers.

Sailing for Sydney on 20 May, the ship made sovereignty visits between 26 and 29 May to islands in the Diamond, Magdelaine, and Tregrosse Groups preparatory to the assertion of Australian sovereignty over the Coral Sea Islands Territory the next year. Gardiner Bank was also on the itinerary before the cruise concluded at Garden Island on 31 May when the leave and self- maintenance period began.

From 1 April to 27 May, when the last hydrogen bottle had been emptied, 48 radiosonde ascents had been made with 41 successfully transmitting readings from areas ranging from off Sydney to Noumea. These, and the six hourly reports of surface weather conditions, had been of great value to the Sydney Weather Bureau. During the refit, Mr. T. Donald of the Sydney Office overhauled all the meteorological instruments. As well, 402 megacycles radiosonde equipment replaced the 72 megacycles apparatus. Tests, including flights over Sydney, were successful. At year's end the captain wrote to the Flag Officer Commanding the Australian Fleet requesting another upgrade in this valuable department of the ship - replacement of the potentially explosive hydrogen gas with inert helium.

In late June, the Ordinary Seamen who had joined the ship in January, left for leave and their new postings. The new class of 32 former Junior Recruits replaced them for Common Sea Training. Then, at 12.05 pm, 9 July, the ship sailed on a RANEL/CSIRO cruise.

Before the four days in Cairns from 22 July the ship occupied stations between 153 and 158 degrees East, and 29 and 18 degrees South. Here samples, readings, and bathydips measured salinity, oxygen levels, and other water qualities. Some researchers disembarked at Cairns before the leg to Port Moresby began. After two days there course was set on 30 July for Rabaul. Arrival on 1 August was followed by departure next day for Manus Island. *Diamantina* tied up at Lombrum Wharf, HMAS *Tarangau*, on 3 August.

Here, the next day, the RANEL team embarked. From the 7 -14 August, *most satisfactory* Towflex trials were carried out. In work with HMAS *Samarai* and a RAAF aircraft operating from Lae over 500 charges were expended. Course was set for Singapore on 15 August as the regular radiosonde ascents continued. 'King Neptune' came aboard three days later, and the ship came alongside HMNZS *Otago* at the Singapore Naval Base on 23 August.

After a period of self maintenance, *Diamantina* sailed at 10 am, 2 September, on Operation Puccini V - a Royal Navy study of the dynamics of the north-eastern Indian Ocean between 5 degrees North and 10 degrees South, and 90 and 105 degrees East. Mr. A. Folkhard of the British Ministry of Fisheries and Agriculture led the embarked scientific team of CDR. E.R. Whitemore, RAN, and two RN ratings trained in oceanography - a Leading Seaman and a Leading Airman. The first phase of hydrology readings in which the researchers studied internal waves, sub-surface currents, and made bottom soundings, ended in Penang on 16 September.

Passage north-west through the Straits of Malacca was interrupted when a length of scrap engine room pipe thrown over the side damaged the starboard propeller tips. Sub Lieutenant Andrew Morling later remembered the details: *Rick Waring, the engineer, was a jovial sort of bloke who seemed quite happy with his role of looking after the oldest ship in the Navy. He referred to the engines as his elbow joint turbines. When something needed to be repaired he believed in doing it thoroughly. He once shut down the ship's only evaporator while we were at sea and completely overhauled it. In fact* Diamantina *was one of the few ships which actually gained water while it was at sea, because the evaporating capacity was designed for a much bigger complement than she had in 1968. There was another occasion when he wanted to repair the wheel. I don't know what was wrong with it, but he took the wheel off and the helmsman steered the ship with a big adjustable spanner for most of the day.*

There was a lot of obsolete stuff on the ship and Rick took great delight in tracking down unused bits of machinery. He would find a pipe that wasn't connected to anything so he'd track it down and find the other end wasn't connected to anything either, so he'd chop it off and chuck it over the side. On one occasion he got a great big length of pipe up from the engine room. He heaved it over the side and it hit one of the screws. There was a tremendous vibration that you could feel through the quarterdeck. We had to stop and put a diver over the side. The tip of one blade of the screw was bent over, throwing it out of balance. Anyway we went on for a bit and the tip broke off, which reduced the vibration considerably.

The work continued. The next day, the world's biggest ship, the 210,000 tons tanker *Idemitsu Maru* dwarfed *Diamantina* as it made its laden eastbound passage half a mile on the starboard beam. Puccini V recommenced when *Diamantina* sailed from Penang on 18 September. The first station was occupied two days later at 1 degree 30' North, 93 degrees, 20' East - off the west coast of Sumatra. Five days later the last readings were recorded at 6 degrees 31' S, 103 degrees, 34' E - north-west of Christmas Island. Then course was set for Fremantle.

A large crowd greeted *Diamantina*'s eight officers, 117 sailors, and six scientists at H Berth, Victoria Quay, at 9.30 am, 1 October. In six and a half months away the vessel had covered a wide circle from the Southern Ocean to the South China Sea. And all that time the sounder had charted the sea bottom and the normal routine of shoots and promotion classes continued.

115 guests were aboard for a very successful Family Day on 9 October. Next day Dm6/68 began. In four phases, 10-19 October, 22 October-1 November, 4-12 November, and 15-20 November, the researchers completed a variety of tasks in studying hydrology and the West Australian crayfish. In phase three, for example, evening and morning hydrology stations were separated by night-long mid-water trawls. Phase four involved four hydrology and 36 trawling stations in a 50 mile square area south of Geraldton from Jurien Bay to Port Denison.

The 1968 cruise programme ended when the ship tied up at H Berth, Victoria Quay, at 8.30 am, 21 November. Long leave and annual refit began. On the slipway from 27 November the starboard shaft was faired, and its damaged propeller replaced. Also, three new plates went on the port and starboard sides of F strake, and another in the starboard cable locker area. The Ordinary Seamen began posting off, and another class joining from HMAS *Leeuwin*.

1968 had broken the previous year's record. 39,714.5 miles had been covered in 3,894.5 hours under way. In September's 672 hours, 632 had been spent on the move to steam 7,486 miles.

1969

December 1968's Report of Proceedings, whose last paragraph had ended, *...conditions onboard are good and well maintained although overall accommodation and amenities are well below present day standards*, was signed, not by LCDR Ward, but by LT K.H. McGowan. Murray Ward's two years in command were over. On 5 January 1969 LCDR James Buchanan, who had been First Lieutenant when *Diamantina* recommissioned in 1959, joined from *Queenborough*. Next day, at 2 pm, he assumed command. It wasn't the ship's only change. When it returned to the water, two days before the new captain arrived, the bow carried the last of its four hull numbers - GOR 266.

All the new class had joined by 7 January and the last of the previous group was posted out four days later. The training routine settled down. On the first post refit sea trial on 10 February, armament stores were dumped in 300 fathoms west of Rottnest Island. Further trials followed. On one of these the ship was at anchor in Geographe Bay off Busselton at 7.50 pm, 15 February when the watch sighted a red flare to the north-west. Steam was raised, and, at 10.30 pm, the drifting cabin-cruiser, *Bowerbird*, was found and taken in tow. Later, the launch with its disabled engine and three holidaying fishermen, was passed to a rescue craft from Busselton.

More short training cruises followed until Cruise Dm1/69 sailed at 9.30 am, 15 March. Dr. J. Bye led a team from Adelaide's Horace Lamb Institute to successfully revisit the sites of their cruises of the preceding two years en route to Sydney.

After *Diamantina* tied up at Garden Island's Cruiser Wharf at 1.30 pm, 24 March the HLI scientists disembarked. Six RANRL researchers under Dr. W.F. Hunter then began loading Towflex equipment together with sonar listening, monitoring, and recording apparatus for Operation Fasor (Forward Area Service Research) III. In the morning of 28 March, *Diamantina* moved to No. 2 Buoy. Here Underwater Sound Signal charges were embarked before the ship sailed for Station E1 - 33 miles east-south-east of Macquarie Light. The preliminary stage of Fasor III was about to begin. From 3 pm, at E1, the RANRL's pipe noisemaker was hoisted inboard, and the scientists made measurements of sea noise, bottom reflection, and sound scattering until 8 pm.

After moving to Station E2, 105 miles east of Macquarie Light, overnight the team successfully tested Towflex from 5 am to 12.30 pm. At 11 am, the array picked up, at an initial range of 140 miles, low frequency sound transmissions from the approaching USNS *Charles H. Davis*, an eight-year-old Conrad class research ship, the first type specifically designed and built by the United States Navy for oceanographic research. Like *Diamantina*, her pennant number, 5, was prefixed with the letters, GOR. Manned by a civilian crew of 26 under Captain R. Fosse, she could carry up to 15 scientists. Her gas turbine auxiliary engine allowed quiet operations when main engine power would interfere with research. A bow thruster allowed precise manoeuvring.

From 12.30 pm, 31 March, *Diamantina* ran south-west to Station E20, 92 miles south-east of Macquarie Light. Towflex was streamed throughout the passage monitoring *Davis*'s low frequency transmissions. At 2.30 am, 1 April, the array was recovered and course was set for Sydney. Fasor III's preliminary phase had been successful.

Operation Fasor III began in earnest on 13 April, at Station E4. East of Newcastle at 33 degrees South, 153 degrees, 20′ East, *Diamantina* had investigated the sound scattering layer, bottom reflection, and sea noise for 15 hours before streaming Towflex at 8 am. *Davis*, at Station C, 100 miles away, transmitted low frequency sound while steering various courses and speeds. Towflex was recovered at 4 pm. Operations moved north. After a day in Brisbane from 9.30 am, 16 April, *Diamantina* closed Mooloolaba next afternoon to land an ERA with a heart condition. Then stations were renewed.

Station F from 10 am, 20 April, was well out in the Coral Sea at 16 degrees 40′ S, 160 degrees E. Here *Diamantina* and *Davis* worked in company with the submarines, HMAS *Otway*, and USS *Baya* (CDR W. White). (Fasor tested long-range active sonar detection and *Baya* was on her third FASOR cruise. The first in 1964, following evaluation the previous year of the BQS-5 active sonar system, had ranged from Indonesia to Japan. The second, from February to August 1966, had tracked down East Asia from the Aleutian Islands to the South China Sea. During Fasor III Baya sailed from Pearl Harbor via American Samoa, Sydney, Singapore and Colombo to Hong Kong. *Baya*'s decommissioning programme stated, *Fasor cruises were the first effort to test long range active sonar detection in the Pacific and Indian Oceans in order to better understand the environmental effects on acoustic propagation.*)

Baya, AGSS 318, was a Balao class submarine, a year older than *Diamantina*. After sinking four enemy vessels in five World War II patrols, she had, like *Diamantina*, been placed in reserve in 1946. The submarine's inactive period was much shorter than our frigate's with the second commission beginning on 10 February 1948. *Baya*'s 1969 Cruise Book, which refers to *Otway*, but makes no mention of *Diamantina*, takes up the story...*Since recommissioning, Baya has provided service to the US Navy Undersea Research and Development Center, San Diego, California, acting as an undersea laboratory for testing and evaluation of many types of underwater research equipment...This book is the story of the* Baya, *her crew, and Fasor III, third in a series of oceanographic expeditions in support of the programs of the US Navy Undersea Research and Development Center.*

Before her career ended in 1972, seven years earlier than *Diamantina*, *Baya*, like the Australian frigate, had undergone many changes in profile. The 1958 change was the most radical. In a complete reworking to test LORAD, *an experimental long range sonar*, a 23 foot section and the trademark bulbous bow were added to house the *massive sonar equipment*. Quarters and laboratories were provided for 12 scientists. In 1964 a second set of LORAD hydrophone 'wings' was added to the BRASS-II sonar equipment. In 1967, two years before this cruise the ship was completely demilitarised by the removal of all weapons equipment and became a pure research vessel.

Diamantina was the only one of the four vessels with a medical officer aboard. At 10.30 am, the ship rendezvoused with *Otway* to transfer a sailor by boat for treatment. Then, after a Towflex calibration run, course was set to the north-west for the Solomon Sea. VLF sound transmissions were recorded every six hours. From 23 to 25 April the frigate operated south-east of New Britain at Station G, 8 degrees 21' S, 152 degrees 55' E. As well as making Nansen, sound and Towflex measurements, *Diamantina* dropped charges. *Baya* used these to assess bottom bounce sound characteristics. Then, in response to a call from *Baya*, *Diamantina* set off southwards at 8 pm, 24 April, at 18 knots. An officer on the submarine had a head injury. Five hours later the submarine cancelled the emergency, and *Diamantina* returned to Station G.

The vessels met at 10 am, Anzac Day. *Baya* transferred EDO echo sounder parts to the frigate before assessing, that afternoon, sound bottom bounce from charges *Diamantina* dropped at agreed times while steaming at 12 knots. At 7.30 that evening a boat returned the recovered *Otway* sailor to his submarine. Three days later *Otway* needed help again. A 9.30 am, signal had *Diamantina* abandoning readings at Station H, south of New Guinea's eastern tip, to aid a seriously ill sailor. Five hours later, heavy seas at the rendezvous prevented the transfer of either the doctor or patient. The decision was made for the vessels to proceed in company to Port Moresby. Next morning, in slightly improved conditions, the doctor made a hazardous crossing to the submarine in a 20-man life-raft streamed behind his ship. He recommended hospital treatment. As *Otway* did not have Port Moresby charts, *Diamantina* led her in. They were tied up by 7 pm. The submarine sailed four hours later. *Diamantina*, in port 36 hours earlier than planned, decided to remain and repair Towflex and the oceanographic winch.

So the planned port visit stretched from 29 April to 5 May. In spite of the heat in the messes, the crew enjoyed their stay with visits, tours, and sports. *Baya* and *Davis* arrived on 2 May and stayed for four days. The locals, too, took advantage of the visit.

Acoustic research submarine USS *Baya* alongside *Diamantina*. (QMM collection)

On the open day, 4,500 people flooded the ships. *Baya's* cruise book's photos show her and *Diamantina's* decks completely covered with visitors.

On 4 May, to commemorate the Battle of the Coral Sea the Australian and American commanding officers laid wreaths at the Port Moresby War Memorial. From 7 to 13 May the three vessels worked westwards through Torres Strait and the Arafura Sea before tying up together in Darwin on 14 May. Although the crews found this port every bit as enjoyable as Port Moresby, they were relieved, even if slightly disappointed, at one difference. Territorians were more blasé on open day - only 350 visitors crossed the gangways.

Departure was again staggered with *Baya* and *Davis* sailing on 22 May, a day after *Diamantina*. Fasor III resumed on 22 May at Station K1, 10 degrees 30' S, 125 degrees 30' E. From this point south of Timor, the ships moved westwards to occupy 26 more stations. The work did not exclude other activities. On 26 May the regular 40/60 firing exercise was followed by a clay pigeon shoot and night small arms firing using tracer ammunition.

At 10.30 am, 31 May, *Baya* requested assistance with a sick sailor. At the rendezvous south of Java seven hours later at 10 degrees, 49'S, 109 degrees 29' E, the man was transferred to *Diamantina* for observation, and the vessels returned to their tasks. Next day, at 1 pm, the medical officer decided surgery was necessary. Towflex was recovered, and the ship sped west at 18 knots to tie up at No.2 Buoy, Flying Fish Cove, Christmas Island, at 7 pm. That night, at the invitation of the hospital's doctor, Surgeon Lieutenant S. Leitl successfully operated. The recovering American remained in hospital when the ship sailed at 2 pm, next day.

Diamantina's role in Fasor III ended on 3 June when Towflex was recovered after the last VLF experiments at 7 degrees 18' S, 105 degrees E - off the western entrance of Sunda Strait. The ship's excellent relations with the RANRL team and the two American vessels had contributed greatly to the operation's excellent results. The ship headed to Jakarta where 4-8 June were spent alongside at No. 3 Basin, Tanjung Priok. Hospitality was generous and returned with a 6 June party on B Deck for children of Indonesian Navy personnel.

The run back to Fremantle began with a station south of Christmas Island on 9 June. Until RANRL Cruise 5/69 ended at 7 pm, 17 June, seawater temperature, salinity, oxygen and silicates content were measured by taking water samples to depths to 5,000m. As well, each day from an hour before sunset to an hour after, acoustic readings were taken of bottom reverberation, reflectivity, and volume reverberation.

The long cruise ended at 10.10 am, 20 June. At F Berth, Victoria Quay, the 31 Ordinary Seamen class was replaced by a new one of 35. The leave and self-maintenance period began. On 2 July a *Daily News* report stated *Diamantina, Baya*, and *Davis* had ...*co-operated in gathering a wide range of scientific data for naval and civil use*, not exactly detailed reporting.

Cruise Dm3/69, whose budget of $250,000 was partly funded by oil companies, began on 29 July. Dr. W. Ludwig of the Lamont Doherty Geological Observatory and five other scientists from the University of NSW under Professor L. Hawkins were aboard. The international team aimed at determining sediment thickness and the crustal structure of north-west Australia's continental shelf and adjoining seabed. Continuous soundings, magnetometer profiles, and echoes were to provide the information; 22.5 tons of explosives were embarked as sound sources. As well, an air compressor was secured near the engine room skylight to power a 'gun' to provide safer underwater sound. Other additions were a 50-foot radio antenna on the balloon shelter and two 10-foot booms for towing hydrophones.

Malfunctions in most of the equipment, especially the compressor, forced a return to Fremantle within two days of sailing; 24 hours later, a new start was made on 2 August. At 10.25 am, next day the first soundings were made. When the first leg ended at Port Hedland at 9 am, 8 August, the compressor-powered air gun had produced some of the sounds. The 'Spinifex Festival' enlivened the four days in port. On 12 August Leg 2 began. Compressor problems affected the generally successful 10 days of work to Broome. The three days port stay ended when the last leg began at 6.30 pm, 25 August.

The routine 40/60 shoot was held on this run. It produced a high level of accuracy - two meteorological balloons were destroyed. The high standard of gunnery did not transfer to the compressor where faults recurred. Overall, the scientists pronounced the cruise highly successful when the six weeks ended at 8 am, 4 September with *a large balance of unused seismic charges*. The captain's report focussed on other matters. While noting the scientists were *friendly and co-operative,* he pointed out the crew had expended considerable effort trying to remedy faults in the complex equipment. Singling out the overused compressor's problems, he suggested two improvements - preliminary trials, and a second compressor.

CSIRO Cruise Dm4/69 between 9 and 21 September studied crayfish larvae and water masses. The NNW-SSE traverses between 111 and 113 degrees East and 29 and 31 degrees South, included a return visit to the 55 miles square area at Jurien Bay and Port Denison.

After the Annual Inspection, the next CSIRO Cruise followed the same path with the addition of measurement of surface currents by towing a Geomagnetic Electro Kinetograph. Dm6/69, from 22 October to 3 November, curtailed by bad weather, went over the same area again. The scientists were happy with the results - discovery of a clockwise ocean swirl between 29 and 31 degrees South and 110 degrees 30' East and 112 degrees 30' East.

These repetitive cruises saw increased interest in 40/60 and small arms shoots, and the Diamantina Shield competition. About 30 crewmembers actively participated in the scientific work. As well, the usual duties were interspersed between the cruises. Junior Recruits trained aboard and the Family Day took place on 20 October. A more sombre occasion was the scattering of the ashes at sea of two retired naval men on 16 October.

Death came home to the ship on 11 November. Early that morning the 31-year-old First Lieutenant complained of chest pains. At 11.20 am, LCDR Robert Crawford was found lying on the floor of his cabin. Rushed to Fremantle Hospital, he was pronounced dead on arrival. Chaplain F. Lyons officiated at the Requiem Mass next day for the "fair and well respected nice bloke."

Two days later the ship sailed for Adelaide. A diversion to Kwinana loaded 30 tons of explosives. These were dumped that afternoon at 32 degrees 10'S, 115 degrees E. Across the Bight the five scientists made hydrology and photometry readings on the continental shelf and trenches to 3,000 fathoms.

At Adelaide the team was replaced by six Horace Lamb Institute researchers. They took bottom cores and made observations of deep ocean circulation on the way back across the Bight before the cruise ended on 4 December.

In the year's last cruise from 8 to 13 December, CSIRO Dm9/69, four scientists revisited the 55 miles square on a crayfish and water circulation investigation. On the way back, a distressed cabin cruiser was taken in tow. The hard year had ended late. The 32 ordinary seamen were posted off. Annual leave began. But there was no refit.

CHAPTER 8

1970-1979

1970

There was a simple reason for no annual refit at the end of 1969. With the decision taken to prolong *Diamantina*'s life until, at least, 1975, a major refit was scheduled. In spite of Fremantle maritime workers earnest representations that this could be carried out locally, Williamstown Dockyard was chosen. So, at 9 am, 7 January, the ship sailed for Port Phillip Bay. En route, there was one stop. Three days out, well to the south of the Great Australian Bight, at 37 degrees 5' S, 130 degrees E, five hundredweight of marine dye from the RAN Depot, Byford went over the side. Two days later, at 4.30 pm, the ship tied up at Outer Nelson Pier, Williamstown Naval Dockyard.

Between 14 and 19 January the crew moved to the accommodation ship, *Gascoyne*. On 15 January at 7 am, *Diamantina* went out of port routine. The refit began two days later. It was to stretch through five months at different berths and in the Alfred Graving Dock. The captain's May Report of Proceedings touches on the ship's company during that time when he wrote they, *...bore up well under substandard living conditions...and morale is most satisfactory.* Warren Treadgold, then a leading hand stoker, recalls the time as *a lot of hard work, and a lot of fun,* with *...a pub on every corner and one in between.* One particular publican, Yvonne, of the 'Britannia', endeared herself to the crew as a 'lovely lady' always ready to help the sailors out with a loan.

The work involved extensive changes to improve the ship's capability and accommodation. These included:

Capability

Replacement of the condemned 25-foot motor cutter with an upgraded motor whaler from HMAS *Leeuwin*;

Replacement of 1,000 rivets, renewal of wasted deck, blasting and preservative treatment of underwater areas;

Rewiring of much of the ship;

Installing a new 'bathy' winch on X Deck, an oceanographic winch from HMAS *Anzac*, replacing the minesweeping winch, overhauling the capstan;

Overhauling the generators;

Overhauling the main engines;

Re-bricking and re-tubing No. 2 boiler, and partially re-bricking No. 1;

Rebuilding the laboratory area to provide separate compartments for electronic equipment, chemical analysis, and Nansen bottle storage as well as a stable AC power supply, and an intercom linking all spaces to the bridge;

Securing the off-line communications office, removing two B40 receivers and a Type 86M transceiver, and fitting a R1051 receiver with Koden selective calling device, and an AWA Carphone on the bridge for contacting civilian harbour control and merchant ships;

Installing a prefabricated enclosed bridge (described in the captain's later report as *worth its weight in aluminium, if not gold*).

Accommodation

Replacing the ship's company bathroom's three shower open area with five shower
cubicles, and installing modern basins and exhaust ventilation;

Improving ventilation in the heads;

Air-conditioning and insulating all accommodation (except the scientists' six-berth
cabin), sickbay, wardroom, off-line, and wireless office;

Fitting a new range, deep fat fryer, steaming oven, and a bain marie from *Quickmatch*
to the galley;

Converting the port after passageway messdeck to a recreation space with tables,
chairs, library, movie, and TV facility;

Installation of 108 bunks to complete the change from hammocks, removal of
redundant messdeck fittings including gun supports, and installation of smaller
messdeck tables to seat half the occupants at a time, and provision of built in seats
with backrests in most messes.

Not surprisingly, not all work went smoothly. Warren Treadgold remembered flashing
up No. 2 boiler one day in Williamstown: *No.1 boiler was on load and I was bringing on
No. 2 to take over. Every thing appeared OK from where I was. On either side of the boiler, at
the front was a mirror which was angled so that we could look through a tube and hopefully
see a light which was situated at the rear of the boiler. The idea was that between the mirror
and light was the area where the smoke and gases from the furnace went on its way to the stack
(funnel). If, by looking at the mirror, you could see a white haze, this indicated you were making
white smoke which usually would indicate too much air was getting in; if you couldn't see the
light at all or only intermittently, it would probably mean black smoke and not enough air.
Either way it meant incomplete combustion one way or another.*

*Rob Scott came down to relieve me shortly after I took over the load and Brian Jones, who
was in No. 1 boiler room, had shut down and left the space. Rob said that he had noticed I
was making a bit of smoke and so I looked into the mirror and noticed a white haze. I said
I couldn't understand why that was because the fuel/air ratio was appropriate. I had a look
into the boiler and got the shock of my life. The brick floor inside the furnace had buckled
with the heat and lifted about a foot so, instead of the flame burning cleanly, it was bouncing
off the floor and going straight up though the uptakes. The next 30 minutes or so was quite
humorous. I immediately got in touch with the engine room and told John Mills that I was
shutting down the boiler because the floor had lifted. John didn't completely understand what
I meant and I didn't have the time to draw pictures. Of course what he was worried about
was that the steam generators were taking the ship's full electrical load and he wanted time
to get someone to start up the diesel generators or someone else to transfer the load to shore
power, unfortunately I couldn't give him that time.*

*Someone was trying to get hold of Brian Jones to flash up No. 1 again and of course the
lights were getting dimmer and dimmer; in the end we were working in the dark which would
not have been easy in the engine room because some of the floor plates had been lifted to do
some work in the bilges. After about 30 minutes Brian had the other boiler on line and took
the load so we could again see properly. About an hour and a half after shutting down No.2
and after the fans had been running flat out all of this time, Trevor, George and myself (the
ship's brickies) figured that things should be cool enough to get inside and have a look at the
problem. On inspection, we determined that when the contractors had renewed the floor, they
hadn't put in an expansion gap which meant there was no room for it to move when it got
hot. We cut an expansion gap there and then and solved the problem once and for all. It had
been an interesting time though.*

With the work almost completed, *Diamantina* sailed for sea trials at 1 pm, 8 June. They continued over four days, interrupted on 9th by a dockyard worker's mild heart attack on board. The trials verdict was *most satisfactory*, so the ship sailed at 8 pm, 12 June for Fremantle. The few unfinished tasks were to be completed en route. The weather changed that. Steering into Force 8 headwinds, at 7.40 next evening, the quartermaster was dealt a compound fracture of his right thumb by the wheel. Course was reversed, and best speed was made for Adelaide. The patient was landed, fuel taken on, defects in the bridge sonar compartment made good, and hull leaks stopped; 21 hours later, at 8 am, 16 June, *Diamantina* sailed again into the Force 8 headwinds.

For most of the passage the weather decks were out of bounds as crashing seas buckled upper deck lockers and split the breakwater base allowing water to flood the mess below with every breaking wave. The 10 days after reaching port on 20 June were first spent on voyage repairs, then on completing the dockyard tasks. The crew was not happy when the ship was put on alert to aid the liner *Oriana* south of Fremantle. Nobody wanted another battering. There was a sigh of relief when the job was given to another ship.

Maintenance and leave filled the time in home- port. Commodore and Mrs. Ramsay attended an onboard cocktail party on 24 July. It was a farewell. On the 27 July course was set for Sydney. On 7 August, five days after arrival at Garden Island, came calibration trials off South Head. Three days later, five RANRL researchers joined as loading of equipment was completed. Next day *Diamantina* loaded explosives at No.3 Buoy before putting to sea at 1.10 pm.

RANRL Trial 9/70 studied and assessed the performance of the TOWFLEX towed hydrophone array in detecting medium and long- range sound propagation off Sydney, Brisbane, and Cairns. The work 26 miles east of Sydney included successful exercises with a RAAF Orion aircraft at ranges up to 150 miles. Still more successful Orion trials took place 20 miles east of Cape Moreton from 16-17 August.

On passage to the next site, spare time was put to good use. From 10.30 am to 5.30 pm on 19 August, the ship anchored north of St. Bees Island off Mackay while the crew enjoyed a beach barbecue and skindiving. The successful test series continued on 20 and 21 August. Five miles north-east of Grafton Passage the ship worked with a Neptune aircraft before arriving in Cairns at 9.15 am, 22 August. Here, while 300 visitors toured the ship and the crew enjoyed three days in port, the Towflex team was replaced by a four-man group to study hydrology.

This RANRL Trial 10/70 investigated water masses entering the Coral Sea from the north and east. Between 28 August and 4 September 12 hydrology stations were made on each of two axes - a north-south one between New Caledonia and San Cristobal/Guadalcanal, and the other running west from San Cristobal to the Louisiades. Station 1 began north-west of New Caledonia at 11 am, 28 August. Station 24 was completed at 10.45 pm, 4 September. Throughout the cruise the sounder operated continuously. On this cruise the Diamantina Shield competition events were; tug o'war, uckers, 500, bridge, euchre, and chess.

The researchers changed again in Port Moresby from 6 to 14 September. Five men from the Weapons Research Establishment at Salisbury South Australia replaced the RANRL hydrologists. Among the usual port visit activities there was an important visitor. Accompanied by his wife, Mr. Walter Rice, the United States Ambassador, was entertained on board.

Diamantina sailed at 11.30 am, 14 September, to begin Operation Barrabool. RAAF Long Range Maritime Patrol aircraft, RAN patrol boats, and hydrophone arrays were deployed, and explosive charges detonated in this assessment of the acoustic characteristics of the waters in the shipping lanes north of New Guinea. Venue A was 50 miles south-west of Port Moresby. Here, the day after sailing, the acoustic array was streamed and a RAAF Neptune aircraft dropped calibration charges to a range of 100 miles. Sea noise, temperature, and other water characteristics readings were also made at different depths. The process was repeated at Venues B, F, E, D, on 18, 20, 22, and 24 September off New Guinea's north coast. A Neptune, an Orion aircraft, and HMAS *Samarai*, worked at separate time with the ship. The venues ranged from 40 miles south-east of Lae to 20 miles north of Wewak.

At F, *Samarai* deployed a sea noise buoy. On 24 September, a civilian transferred from the patrol boat before the ship began three days at HMAS *Tarangau*, Manus Island, next day. Project Barrabool ended at Station H, 40 miles north of Finschhafen, at 5.30 pm, 1 October. Station C, 15 miles east of Madang, had been completed two days before. At Darwin from 7 to 12 October, while the crew enjoyed a port visit, six RANRL researchers replaced the WRE team. The new task was to acquire oceanographic and acoustic data from the Java Trench, Sunda Strait, and Cocos and Christmas Islands areas. Another aim was ...*to provide information required for the proposed laying of deep hydrophone arrays on the ocean bed north of Christmas Island.* (Gary Weir in his 2001 book, *An Ocean in Common*, refers on p. 217 to the development in the early 1950s of the...*acoustic ocean sound surveillance system (SOSUS)* for ...*direct detection of a submerged adversary at previously unimaginable ranges. Diamantina's* operations from 1970 at Christmas Island, so close to the bottleneck of Sunda Strait suggests she was involved in this Cold War activity.)

Having surveyed 12 stations, the ship tied up at C Buoy, Flying Fish Cove, Christmas Island, at 11.45 am, 18 October. Then, in round the clock work over three days, the ship ranged off and on the island laying current buoys, taking bottom cores, dredge samples, underwater photographs and readings of other water characteristics with bathythermographs and Nansen bottles. As well, surveys ashore found a site for an acoustic receiving laboratory, and manoeuvring trials were carried out with the island's tug barges.

On 23 October, course was set for Singapore. Here, midway through the stay from 26-30 October and five days after his wedding, Leading Sick Berth Attendant Frank Stephens joined. A Royal Navy driver met Frank off the direct Melbourne flight at 10 pm, and took him the 20 km through the steamy Singapore night to the ship at Sembawang. Assigned a bunk in the Sick Bay for that night, Frank had little sleep. It was caused by a combination of new surroundings, some jet lag, and calls to treat the 'walking wounded', returning through the night from the bright lights of Singapore. The next morning Frank moved to the Forward Seamen's Mess. Since the previous Sick Berth Attendant had left three weeks before, Frank spent the rest of the time in port restocking and refurbishing the sickbay. On the second day out from Singapore, Frank found time to visit the ship's barbershop - a stool inside the engine room starboard hatch. There the Chief Air Handler listened patiently to his instructions before ignoring them completely in favour of the style laid down by the Chief Coxswain.

En route to Christmas Island, the ship took readings at more stations. The work at the island was completed on 4 November. Next day *Diamantina* sailed for Fremantle occupying more stations until she joined Task Force 334 on 9 November. Exercise Swan Lake involved the usually solitary ship in two days of fleet work and, with nine other vessels, manoeuvres including towing the much larger destroyer tender, *Stalwart*, 40/60 firing, and underway replenishment exercises, including one, off

Rottnest Island, when two RANRL researchers transferred to the Royal Fleet Auxiliary, Resource.

Throughout the exercise *Diamantina* proudly flew her Western Australian Navy (WAN) pennant - a black WAN and swan on a yellow background. The one ship WAN's pride was dented, however, during the Fleet target shoot competition. In front of the assembled Eastern Australian Navy and British ships, *Diamantina's* single gun crew at last had the opportunity to show the results of their hours of practice. As the ship steamed down the range to open fire, the gun jammed. *Diamantina's* score was zero.

The RANRL men and their equipment disembarked soon after arrival in Fremantle on 11 November. On 13 and 19 November, followed the Annual Inspection, and a very well attended Ship's Ball at Subiaco Town Hall. Three days before the Ball, LCDR Buchanan was relieved by LCDR, M. Varley. LCDR Varley had served on the ship four years before when he had been detached from the Hydrographer's Office for Operation Monsea. With the Christmas Island work imminent, the appointment of a hydrographer to command *Diamantina* seems more than a coincidence.

From 23 November to 9 December, with time in port between 28 November and 2 December, *Diamantina* carried three CSIRO and one West Australian Museum researcher on Dm1/70. The cruise disproved the existence of commercial quantities of the West Australian shovel nosed lobster off the coast. As well, a good haul of specimens was made for the Museum. As the 35 Ordinary Seamen were posted out on 9 December, long self-maintenance and leave began. The main task was fitting new equipment in the starboard laboratory. A small fire in a refrigeration unit on 15 December brought the Fremantle Fire Brigade to the ship but there was little damage.

Diamantina's unofficial Ship's Company Galley Public Records Section noted that in 117 days at sea the vessel had steamed 23,761 nautical miles - equal to an Equatorial circumnavigation. Discounting the time at Williamstown, *Tina had spent 50% of the active year at sea - 76 days of that stopped on station.* Less official statistics included the coxswain winning the bridge tea-drinking prize, and three charts ruined by tea. A cryptic entry recorded *The most expensive fish in the Indian Ocean - $6,500 each.*

1971

Variety spiced *Diamantina's* 1971 programme. Activities ranged through the usual civil and defence research, training, and community aid activities along the Western Australian coast. Fremantle slipway time was brief - from 4 to 12 January. By mid-February No.1 Boiler's re-tubing was complete. A new class of 28 Ordinary Seamen joined from HMAS *Cerberus* and *Leeuwin*. On 19 February five crewmen, including Frank Stephens, successfully completed a three-week long intensive Ship's Diver course at *Leeuwin*. It had been a taxing time of day and night instruction that had included a three-km swim against the current, and a jump from *Diamantina's* bridge in full gear. The new divers were well used during the year.

There was another funeral. On 9 February the ensign was half masted and a party accorded Naval Honours at the burial at Fremantle Cemetery of ABUC K.R. Gibsone. He had been killed three days before while hitchhiking home on weekend leave.

Trials ended on 4 March, and day Junior Recruit cruises began the next day. Four days later came a security alert. At 6.15 p.m., 9 March, a steward sighted a wetsuit-clad man swimming astern of the ship. Berthed ahead of *Diamantina* was the US landing ship, *Monticello*. Less than 20 metres away was the Russian freighter, *Novoaltaisk*. In those Cold War days, the alarm was raised, and the area was searched. Divers examined the hulls of the American and Australian ships and found nothing.

Routine resumed. Then, six and a half hours later, at 12.40 am, 10 March, *Diamantina*'s watch again spotted a swimmer. Two *Monticello* crewmen confirmed the sighting. A further search also found nothing. Authorities played down the incidents. They pointed out *Diamantina* and *Monticello* were not 'state of the art' warships. No mention was made of their functions. The generally accepted opinion that the swimmer was a potential prankster whose attempt at slogan daubing was foiled by his sighting was not disputed by officialdom.

After the Family Day on 11 March, Mr. J. McCreddie and J. Gibbins of RANRL began winding onto the quarterdeck's newly fitted mine-sweeping loop winch three miles of four-core armoured cable. Four days later the ship sailed on RANRL Trials 3/71. Work began at 3.30 pm on 17 March in a canyon off Esperance. After the cable had been successfully streamed and laid on the seabed the ship returned to port to repair cable drum defects.

With three more miles of cable embarked, and three CSIRO researchers and their equipment, CSIRO Dm1/71 sailed on 25 March to study rock lobsters and water characteristics. LT SSDH D. Dunlop was also aboard to assess and treat the crew's dental needs. (The frequent short term rotation of civilian and defence scientists aboard during long slow cruises where the ship often spent time stopped on station in heavy seas with most of the crew with time on their hands raises the question of crew researcher interaction). George Humphrey, from his administrator's perspective, wrote, *Our naval-scientific cooperation has been outstanding.*

Frank Stephens gave a sailor's perspective: *Although the CSIRO scientists were not personally disliked by the crew, there was some animosity created by the fact they were entitled to a number of allowances not given to the crew, they only carried out two to three week stretches at sea before being replaced by another group, and, while they were generally busy with interesting oceanographic research, the ship's crew were bobbing up and down in the middle of the ocean, going nowhere, and carrying out routine duties.*

Harry Jitts had another view: *Perhaps a group of now aging scientists learned a little from the RAN of the value of their traditions and dedication, their system of discipline, and of informed chains of command; perhaps a group of RAN officers learned something of the value of untrammelled imaginations coupled with inquiring intellects and a spirit of innovation.*

Until dusk on 1 April the cruise was without incident. Then, 120 miles west of North-West Cape, at 22 degrees South, 112 degrees 4' East, a flare was sighted. The ship closed to find the missing Mr. Neville Sweeny in the prawning research trawler, *Pacific Pride*. The trawler had been reported missing 12 days before when it had not reached Snag Island, north of Jurien Bay on a voyage from Thursday Island. Mr. Sweeny told his rescuers he had drifted for 17 days after his engine had broken down. Dead batteries had prevented him from radioing for help. So the experienced seaman had made the best of his situation. He had supplemented his rations with fish and rigged an awning as a sail to edge towards shore after taking 'a terrible hiding' from Cyclone Mavis.

With the engine beyond immediate repair, the ship took *Pacific Pride* in tow while Mr. Sweeny enjoyed his first hot meal and shower in three weeks. Early next afternoon, the trawler and her captain were transferred to the Markwell Ross trawler, *Biarri*, and *Diamantina* resumed her cruise. At 9.40 pm, 3 April, the ship came to anchor in the Wallabi Group of the Abrolhos Islands after feeling ...*her way in with echo sounder, sonar, Mark One eyeballs fitted with polaroid glasses, and a boat sounding ahead of the ship.* Over the next three days in a landmark archaeological achievement the ship's divers and three from the West Australian Museum recovered cannons and other artefacts from the 1629 wreck of the Dutch ship, *Batavia*.

Netted water-filled 44-gallon drums were attached to a 2.5 ton bronze cannon, two 1-ton iron cannons, and an eight-foot long iron anchor. When air displaced the drums' water the relics were raised and towed to *Diamantina*'s side. There, a wire from the windlass run through the replenishment high point hoisted the heavy weapon aboard. A chain block from the quarterdeck davit raised the others. Bags, continuously sprayed by a fire hose, covered all iron relics on the quarterdeck. Bags and boxes of bricks, pottery, glass, china, cannon balls and other artefacts came on deck from the ship's boat. In the final afternoon the ship's divers recovered more bricks and pottery pieces from the seabed. Surf prevented diving on the wreck itself. The stay ended with the ship hosting the five fishing families of Beacon Island and the Museum divers to dinner and a movie on board.

Ship's Cook and Baker Neville 'Nobby' Clarke recalls a dividend of the dentist's trip: *The dentist proved to be a winner because while we were at anchor at the Abrolhos Islands all the cray fishermen, their wives and children who were resident there also saw him. One of the wives had a tooth pulled and all the children had checkups. Repairs were done to two boat engines by the mechanical personnel, and the Shipwright did minor repairs to their huts. Ice cream was given to the children and cartoons were shown followed by a movie for the parents. In return for this a bag of crayfish was delivered everyday whilst at anchor. I consider myself an expert at cooking crayfish. We would cook a meatboat of crays and leave them on the servery. You could take as many as you wanted.*

In a letter over 20 years later 'Nobby' recalled his vital role in the early '70s: *...Supplies were taken on board - The ship would be fuelled and stored. Swan Beer arrived on a seven-ton truck. Clear lower decks would be piped and the grog stored in the 4-inch magazine. Victuals next. Fuel and water were worked in amidst the chaos. First the meat, frozen vegetables, etc. All were put in the cool room and cold room respectively. The fresh vegetables consisted of 50 kg. bags of potatoes and bags of carrots, wooden crates of cabbages, fruit , and salad vegetables. These were stowed aft of the galley on the port side by the stack in a caged vegetable locker.*

The boffins would finally arrive and settle in forward of the wheelhouse. The first leg was straightforward - leave Fremantle, hard a'port and head south into the Roaring Forties. Ahead east, then west course would be applied with a southerly leg at each change and the Fifties and Sixties would be achieved. All this activity took place below Australia, water temperature at different levels would be recorded - something to do with submarine detection (I think). A northerly course was always welcome as it meant fresh food and shore leave in Port Adelaide.

I have spent many a hot hour in the galley in the northern waters of Christmas Island, New Guinea, and South-East Asia, just to mention a few with a boiler room under your feet and a very hot oil-fired galley range facing you. All of this discomfort becomes somewhat of a pleasant dream when your next trip (of about four months) is going to be in the Southern Ocean.

Cooking in the Southern Ocean was difficult as it was 'rock and roll' without the music. Grooved bars formed a grid around the pots on top of the range to stop sliding meatboats. Gashbins, pots and cooks were buffeted and slid from port to starboard. It was at its worst when the ship was on station taking water temperatures about four hours per station side on to enormous seas. You would actually slide into a trough. The position was kept to keep as little pressure as possible on the cables carrying Nansen bottles to great depths. A seaman operated the winch and the boffins did the rest. The position of the ship was vital and this was achieved by two ever-reliable slow revving steam engines.

I would like to take some time now to explain about the galley - my part of the ship. First, the lighting of the oil fired range. (You had to have a stoker's ticket - well almost). Half a

In the Southern Ocean 'Nobby' Clarke prepares Kye for the middle and morning watches. (N. Clarke)

dozen sheets of greaseproof paper were rammed into the firebox with the aid of a butcher's steel, a little fuel via the sprayer, a sheet of paper rolled into a taper, then lit and rammed into the firebox, turn on the air fan, add a little more fuel, and hope for the best. The Charley Noble [Galley chimney] went from the range then out aft of the galley and to the main stack.

There were two baker's ovens, one above the other. They were brick lined on the bottom and electrically operated. There were 15 bread tins per oven, a batch of 30 loaves at a time. Two batches were proved and kneaded then made to produce 60 loaves - the daily requirement. All this was done by hand. Sweets, pastries and cakes were also the baker's job. This work was carried out from 2200 to 0400 hours and you were required to help serve the midday meal, the duff mainly - you made it, you take the flak, if any. Two steam chests stood on the port side next to the range and one steam copper (cauldron) was brought to the boil by 100 psi. steam pressure. The pressure gauge was on the port side above the sinks.

Diamantina was in my opinion a very good sea ship. In my time aboard her I spent many days in the Southern Ocean, been in cyclones off North-west Cape, and the Coral Sea - from almost unbearable heat in the north to freezing temperatures in the south. Given the chance I would do it all again. But only in HMAS Diamantina.

After embarking the team who had made a 48-hour record of Beacon Island's tides, the ship made its cautious way to sea. Fremantle was reached at 10.20 am, 7 April. Extensive Press and TV coverage of the relics' unloading was well deserved. The ship had recovered and transported a significant part of our national heritage.

Then followed 12 days of Junior Recruit training, ammunition dumping, an underwater survey of Woodman Point jetty, and, on 14 April, a brush with *Koojarra* that left the starboard focs'l guardrails bent. No publicity attended RANRL 5/71's sailing at 1.30 pm, 19 April. Five days later at 8 am, the ship tied up at Christmas Island's Flying Fish Cove. A security briefing was the first item of business. The cocktail party that evening and the attendance of six officers and 30 sailors at the dawn Anzac Day service at the Administrator's house preceded a period of concentrated work. Later on Anzac Day a shore party installed RANRL equipment in a structure near the abandoned 6-inch gun. From this 'Fort Kaye', named after Mr. E. Kaye, the team leader, a half-mile path was cut two days later to link it with Garrison Fissure on the coast.

The ship had taken on fuel and water on 26 April, and carried out acoustic trials the next day. On 28 April, at 5.40 am, *Diamantina* was in position at the datum point, two miles west of South Point. Now the March cable laying practice off Esperance paid off as two hydrophones were laid in 575 fathoms and, with local barges assisting, cable carefully paid out. The operation began at 8 am, and, at a speed of less than one and a half knots, moved to 150 feet off Garrison Fissure. There a ship's boat brought out the shore cable for joining. A test at 1.50 pm was successful and *Diamantina* was back at C Buoy at 2.15 pm.

With the shore installation operating, *Diamantina* took bathymetric readings to 20 miles north of the island on 29 April. On the last day of the month and 1 May the ship made boxing runs on the hydrophone array. Then, on 3 May came a propagation run. Starting at the datum point, the ship sailed towards Sunda Strait dropping explosives at set intervals until Java's continental shelf was reached. The captain later reported the array had successfully recorded them, and the trials were *assumed undetected*.

Off duty, the visit had not begun well. As one crew member put it, the previous RAN crew had "overstayed their welcome," so shore leave was initially restricted to 25 men per night with a 10 pm curfew. *Diamantina* crew's good behaviour quickly allayed the locals' concerns to the extent the captain could later write of ...*many officers and sailors being entertained at dinner in private homes.* So, when the RANRL shore party and equipment came aboard, and the ship sailed at 5.30 pm, 4 May, it was the end of a very successful visit. The shore leave on the island near the Equator was especially welcome as the air conditioning system broke down and could not be fixed. On the way home another search for the reported Maria Augustina Bank again proved fruitless. Shortly after arrival at 9 a.m., 9 May the RANRL team disembarked.

After only three days, CSIRO Cruise Dm2/71 sailed for Adelaide. The five-man team successfully tested a new plankton net, and analysed the waters south of the Great Australian Bight. On the night of 20/21 May the last station was completed south of Kangaroo Island, and the vessel tied up in Adelaide at 1 pm. Among the usual port activities, four WRE and two Flinders University researchers loaded their equipment as the CSIRO team landed. As well, the RANRL Towflex winch and cable went ashore for modification.

On 27 May WRE Trial UDS 3/71 sailed for south-west of Kangaroo Island to make general measurements and test the acoustic propagation of water masses. On 29 May and 2 June, a RAAF Orion aircraft dropped charges to a maximum depth of 1,200 feet and distance of 100 miles. The hydrophones dipped from the ship clearly registered the detonations. The aircraft provided a bonus after the last run. In a low pass it dropped newspapers to the ship.

Back in Adelaide from 3-7 June, a CSIRO Department of Fisheries team replaced the WRE one. Across the Bight they studied water masses on traverses 100 miles apart from the shore to deep water. As well, *Diamantina* continued her soundings and weather observations. The work was interrupted at 2 am, on the 17 June and course was set for Albany. There, at 10.am, ABWMG R. Day was landed to hospital for a successful appendectomy. The ship refuelled and sailed at 4 pm to complete the last traverse off Cape Leeuwin on 18 June, the day before arrival at Fremantle. Long self-maintenance and leave began on 21 June. Before leaving the ship, the crew was given a security talk.

Frank Stephens recalls the Adelaide trip: *During May and early June 1971, Diamantina spent five weeks in the Southern Ocean carrying out further oceanographic research. It was during this time the freezing temperatures and rough seas, the boredom of daily routine, and the isolation of the ship at sea, took its effect on most of the crew. The feeling was of legalized incarceration created by working and living in the same structure, with the same people, day in and day out. Evening movies shown in the port side machinery space flat did however help to alleviate this problem.*

After spending time in the Southern Ocean, Diamantina *pulled into Port Adelaide on 3 June 1971 to refuel and restock with food. After many weeks at sea, some crew suffered a temporary movement phenomenon when they went ashore. Although the ground was stable, the body felt it was still moving like on board the ship at sea. The return trip to Fremantle was again slow as the ship zig-zagged in and out of the Southern coastline. Each morning, the ship's Navigator's assistant would plot on a chart placed on the main noticeboard situated in the main passageway, the ship's position. This information was viewed each morning with great interest by the crew, who then converted the remaining distance into days away from Fremantle. After nearly seven weeks at sea, the crew badly wanted to return to Fremantle to their families and friends. In mid June* Diamantina *returned to Fremantle harbour.*

Living conditions on Diamantina *were cramped, like most warships. However, unlike other EAN (Eastern Australian Navy) ships, there was no central mess deck for the crew to eat their meals, and therefore meals had to be taken from the galley on plates to the respective mess decks to be eaten. This exercise was somewhat exciting in rough weather when crew were trying to hold on to a plate and bowl in one hand and climb down ladders and negotiate passageways with the other. Meals were generally of a good standard and nutritious. However, the most eagerly sought item was the daily fresh cooked bread buns made in the galley bakery.*

After normal working hours at sea, or when not on watch, the crew would spend time in their respective mess decks. Main activities after the evening meal would be cards, mah jong, and other board games. A beer ration of one bottle per person, per night would be issued both at sea and in harbour. On odd occasions there would be visits to other messes for drinks and card games. Some of the better night activities were held in the starboard Stewards mess, where a few extra bottles of beer would appear from nowhere.

One tradition on board Diamantina *was the wearing of 'pirate rig' (civilian clothes), once outside the harbour. Although this was allowed, most times crew wore part navy uniform due to limited locker space to hold extra clothing. Another tradition, as with all other EAN ships, was the annual family day trip. In early 1971,* Diamantina's *family day trip was down to, and around Garden Island. It was a beautiful sunny day, the ocean was calm, and the ship's cooks put on an excellent midday meal. The day was enjoyed by crew and their families and friends alike.*

The usual mid-year duties extended to the first week of August. Ammunition dumping on Junior Recruit days included dropping World War II depth charges at slow speed at 31 degrees 53' S. 113 degrees 30' E. In mid-July the annual small arms course was fired at Swanbourne Range. A more solemn task was the scattering of the ashes at sea on 27 July of Chief Yeoman of Signals (Ret.) A.A. Wilkinson.

CSIRO Cruise Dm4/71 sailed at 10 am, 9 August to investigate zooplankton and the Western Australian rock lobster. Along 110 degrees E from 32 to 20 degrees S, stations were made until 10 am, 19 August. Then the University of Western Australia's new gravity corer was used to recover four-inch cores of the sea floor.

During the four days in Port Hedland from 20 August the crew enjoyed the Spinifex Festival while the research teams changed. Dm5/71 studied water movement in the rock lobster grounds on tracks from the coast to 120 miles off shore from 20 degrees S, with the final station ending off Cape Leeuwin early on 2 September. Late that afternoon the ship tied up.

The Annual Inspection, successfully completed on 7 September, was followed, six days later, by the arrival of an RANRL team. They reinstalled the large quarterdeck loop winch and loaded onto it and into drums on deck miles of cable. On 17 September, at 10 am, the ship sailed on RANRL Survey Proposal 10/71. En route the familiar SCOR/UNESCO Reference Station at 32 degrees South, 111 degrees 50' East was occupied for oceanographic readings. Another familiar location was that of the elusive reported Maria Augustina Bank. Again, only deep water was found. Ammunition dumping three days out at 20 degrees 20' S, 108 degrees 56' E was another routine task.

At Christmas Island, late in the afternoon of 22 September, Mr. Paul Scully-Power joined the ship. Mr. Scully-Power, a 1965 Sydney University Science graduate, had been one of the first to join RANRL on its establishment. He had arrived at Christmas Island on the United States Conrad class, oceanographic research ship *Bartlett* (operated by Military Sea Transport Service for the US Naval Oceanographic Office) and had already tested the shore equipment installed in April. Scully-Power's oceanographic work later took him to the United States where, in October 1984, he became the first Australian-born astronaut.

The nine days before sailing for Singapore on 2 October were busy as the ship laid, tracked, and recovered current buoys. These used a variable depth suspended parachute to measure subsurface currents to a depth of 500 metres. The day before sailing the crew enjoyed the Christmas Island Territory Day celebrations.

From 5 to 14 October at Singapore RANRL equipment came aboard as the crew carried out maintenance. More current drogues were deployed on the three-day voyage back to the island. The RANRL instruments were installed in Fort Kaye on 18 October. For the next three days the ship circumnavigated the island on acoustic trials. On the 22nd, pressure tests on the new cable were successful. The next day the ship laid a second set of hydrophones and ran the cable to shore. Propagation runs were made by a RAAF aircraft dropping charges on the 26 and 27 October. On the latter day *Diamantina* made boxing runs and took soundings to 30 miles north.

On 1 November, after topping up fuel and water, *Diamantina* laid deep hydrophones. Assisted by two local barges, the ship laid the first hydrophone in 2,000 metres of water three mile west north-west of Garrison Point. The apparatus was positioned within 100 metres of its chosen position - equivalent to dropping a ship's anchor into a one-metre circle in 20 metres of water. The second hydrophone was soon on the bottom at its correct distance and bearing from the first. Then, at about one knot, *Diamantina* laid the cable to join the land end at Garrison Point. At 4.10 pm, the ship was at C Buoy.

Less than four hours later course was set for Tanjung Priok. En route the ship dropped charges at set intervals on propagation tests. After four days at Jakarta's port where the visitors included the British Ambassador who showed a keen interest in *Diamantina's antique pieces of machinery* the ship sailed for the island with new RANRL staff. Another propagation run was made as the vessel approached the island in the afternoon of 9 November.

Other runs the next day and a boxing on 12 November produced excellent results. The shore party re-embarked equipment from Fort Kaye - now transformed from a disused bunker to *...an air-conditioned scientific laboratory, complete with lights, running water, gardens, and concrete walks*. Divers made a final check of the position of the

Garrison Fissure cables before the upcoming rough weather of the North-West Season. Frank Stephens remembers diving in perfect conditions and crystal clear water. A wardroom party that evening celebrated the completion of a successful cruise. The next day 100 islanders embarked for a two-and-a-half hour cruise before the ship left for Fremantle at 5 pm.

The cruise year ended at H Berth South Wharf at 2 pm, 18 November. Next day the RANRL team left and the leave and refit period began. On 25 November, 264 persons attended the Ship's Ball at Subiaco Community Centre. The Ordinary Seamen classes changed. There was little for the captain's Reports of Proceedings. At year's end one notable item was the venereal disease cases from the Jakarta and Singapore visits totalled only five minor infections.

1972

Age and hard usage were taking their toll on the ship. In February NOICWA, Commodore P.H. Doyle, wrote to the Secretary of the Navy Department, "...Diamantina *shows all the signs one would expect of a ship of her age. The hull maintenance task, particularly in respect of leaking oil fuel tanks, watertight doors, and lockers, appears to be beyond the capacity of ship's staff...* He then went on, ...*Nevertheless her ship's company appear cheerful and well led, and I am confident* Diamantina *will give good service in her limited role for as long as is required of her.*"

The captain, on relinquishing command five months later, was more cautious, *I hope...she can continue with her valuable oceanographic work until she is replaced by HMAS* Cook *in 1976.* In the event LCDR Varley's hopes were fulfilled and then some. *Cook,* laid down in September 1974, did not join the fleet until October 1980, just eight months after *Diamantina*'s long career finally ended. The purpose-built oceanographic vessel was no match for the frigate in longevity and paid off after only 10 years in October 1990.

1972's programme made no concessions to the ship's infirmities and she rose to the challenge. The ship came off the Fremantle State slipway on 20 January with a new port propeller shaft, and the air-conditioning finally completed with the scientists' six-berth cabin connected. Trials progressed smoothly until 8 February, when steam failed with the ship between the harbour moles. The dead ship was towed back to the wharf where, over the next two days, the contaminated fuel system was flushed. On 11 February the sea trials were completed.

WRE Trial USD 1/72 surveyed seasonal variations in the surface mixed layer of water off south-west Australia. The first station began at 11 am, 14 February at 30 degrees S, 114 degrees E. Nansen bottles, GEK streamings, and expendable bathythermographs were used to collect the data. The first phase ended in Fremantle on 25 February. Four days later the second phase began with different instruments. The Benthos Boomerang Corer successfully recovered seabed samples, and a RAAF Orion aircraft made sonobuoy and sound propagation runs with a newspaper drop to the ship after completion. At 2 pm, 9 March, *Diamantina* secured to H Berth, Victoria Quay.

From 14 to 24 March a Western Australian Museum party trawled marine invertebrate benthic (bottom dwelling) fauna on the outer continental slope at various sites including Post Office Island in the Abrolhos Group. Several previously unknown species, as well as four more of the shell discovered in 1963 and 1970, and named after the ship, were found. One of the new species, an elongate-ovate shell dredged from fine sand at 119 to 188 metres depth, was named Amoria diamantina. (In the following years two other shells were to carry the ship's name, Muricopsis diamantina and Trigonostoma diamantina.) However, the trip's scientific success was shadowed by concern at the progress of some of the Ordinary Seamen class.

After a CSIRO party replaced the Museum group, and the loop winch was refitted, the ship sailed at 8.30 am, 4 April, to study circulation patterns and vertical distribution of materials in the Southern Ocean and Tasman Sea. The first of a number of samples involving collection to a depth of 1,500 m was made four days later west of Kangaroo Island. The last was taken at sunset on 11 April off Tasmania's south-west tip.

A fire in the main galley next day was extinguished in two minutes, and the otherwise uneventful run to Sydney ended when *Diamantina* berthed on HMAS *Stalwart* at Garden Island in the morning of 14 April. Here, over the next 12 days, eastern states crewmen departed on advance seasonal leave while the remainder carried out self-maintenance - for a change, in the heart of the Navy's main base rather than isolated on the far side of the continent.

The recently completed cruise received some publicity. In *The Australian* of 24 April, an article in the shipping section began by reporting the cruise's findings on the old, slow moving Antarctic water masses impinging on Australia. The article then quoted LCDR Varley as he sketched the importance of oceanography. Then he went further in talking about his ship. After outlining the vessel's first commission highlights, he declared, I *would very much like to see the country preserving her. It would cost a lot of money - you would get no change from half a million dollars, but I really think it should be done...*

The Perth press quoted him further. After referring to the planned replacement of *Diamantina* by *Cook* in 1975, LCDR Varley went on, I *want assurance that the ship will not become razor blades and scrap iron as other ships have become.* He suggested the vessel be preserved in drydock at Melbourne, Sydney, or Western Australia's Garden Island as ...*a fitting memorial to the Navy's part in the War and a heritage for the next generation of Australians.* Official reaction was cool. The Western Australian Tourism Minister stated costs would be "too great." No Navy reaction was reported.

RANRL Trial 3/72 sailed at 9.30 am, 26 April. The five aims were:
1. To test laying a vertical hydrophone array;
2. To test a launcher for Signals, Underwater Sound (SUS);
3. To make acoustic propagation runs;
4. To carry out underwater photography;
5. (If time permits) To carry out radio trials.

The array malfunctioned forcing an evening return to Garden Island. From next morning, the vertical array was laid and recovered, underwater photographs taken, buoys and expendable bathythermographs launched, and SUS tested. All trials were successfully completed in two days. On return to Garden Island, the ship was visited by LCDR D. Davidson, the commanding officer designate.

Two sites were occupied in CSIRO Cruise Dm3/72 which sailed at 10 am, 2 May. In studying the vertical distribution of plankton over 48 hours the first station was occupied from late in the afternoon of sailing day. The next observations were ended off the Queensland coast at 6 pm on 10 May. In between, the bathysonde and a new plankton net were tested, and, on the 7th, the automatic tide gauge at Cato Island was repaired. *Diamantina* tied up at Cairns at 10.30 am, 12 May.

RANRL/CSIRO Cruise Dm4/72 sailed at 8 a.m., 15 May. The researchers investigated the exchange of water through Trinity Opening, upwelling on the edge of the continental shelf, and internal waves and water movement in the Coral Sea.

After laying a deep-sea buoy 30 miles west of Port Moresby, the ship began a port visit on 26 May. On return four days later, a 10-hour search was needed to recover the buoy. A fractured securing pin had set it adrift. Then course was set southward. En route to recover on 1 June, CSIRO current meters laid 16 days earlier on the cruise's first day, measurements were made of water depth, quality, and flow. Further measurements on the run to Sydney detected eddies in the north to south currents. The successful cruise ended at 9 am, 9 June. RANRL stores and equipment including explosives and six miles of cable went ashore.

The return to Fremantle began at 11.40 am, 17 June. En route the new 40/60 gun mounting was successfully tested. Not so successful were the eight to nine hour Bureau of Mineral Resources casts for manganese nodules. These were made on 19, 22 and 23 June. The casts through three miles of water took place 400 miles south of Adelaide, 500 miles south of Eucla, and 250 miles south of Albany. Not a single nodule was recovered - the total catch was a two-ounce golf ball size lump of soft, dark clay. A large crowd greeted the ship when it ended its 12 weeks absence at 10 North Quay on 24 June. Before self-maintenance and leave began the crew was given a security talk.

Sea trials on 17 July preceded Junior Recruit day exercises for the rest of the month. News of the planned fitting of a 60kw Foden diesel generator on the port side in August was welcomed; 70 guests sailed on the Family Day on 21 July. Next day LCDR D.M. Davidson assumed command.

Diamantina sailed at 10.30 am, 14 August, for Christmas Island via the SCOR/UNESCO Reference Station at 32 degrees S, 111 degrees 50' E. Rough weather on the second, third, and fourth nights forced suspension of soundings, smashed the quarterdeck cable reel, and dislodged an air-conditioning unit in the starboard laboratory, allowing water to enter.

From the 20th to the 27th at Christmas Island the ship and shore parties were busy. *Diamantina* tested water characteristics while a ground party at Trig Point RHODA cleared a HIFIX navigation site. On 24th a RAAF Orion made flare and photographic runs that ended with a newspapers drop. Then the ship sailed for Singapore. Six Nansen stations were completed before recurrence of the bad weather made the quarterdeck unsafe and forced the cancellation of two others. When the ship tied up at No. 6 Naval Stores Berth at 9 am, 2 September, 30% of the crew were suffering from Asian 'flu. Over the next 11 days in port the illness, apparently contracted on Christmas Island, ran its course. RANRL personnel changed. At 5.30 am, 4 September, two swimmers from HMAS *Derwent* were apprehended on board. One escaped; the other was delivered to the Dockyard Police.

Back at the island from 16 September to 2 October, work resumed ashore and afloat. Parties set up HIFIX stations at RHODA and next to the police station. *Diamantina* made sounding lines at one-mile intervals to 20 miles east of the island. With the aid of the Christmas Island barges, two main cables and bottom sensors were laid. On 30 September at 3.02 pm, the ship nosed into Garrison Fissure for final, successful tests.

It was not all work. Islanders embarked for a trip to sea on 27 September. On 1 October the crew took part in Territory Day celebrations. The ship's most notable success in the sports was first and third places in the Miracle Mile. The next day, after loading equipment, recovering a wave recorder buoy laid four days before in 800 metres of water north of Rocky Point, and boxing the array, the ship sailed at 7 pm for Cocos Islands to meet a RAAF Orion and a charter aircraft. Anchored at Port

Refuge, *Diamantina* landed nine RANRL researchers and two RAN personnel for return to Australia, and took on four men for Trials 9 and 11/72. One was Captain J. Smith, USN, on exchange to RANRL. A Model 6000 ITT Satellite Navigation System also was installed. Disappointingly, it broke down after operating for just 19 hours.

Propagation runs resumed at Christmas Island on 8 October. Until the 19th the ship laid buoys and fired SUS charges. A buffet on B Deck on 15th entertained 20 islanders. Then, on 19 October, the RANRL shore party was embarked before *Diamantina* sailed at 8.40 pm for Jakarta. Six and a half hours later the log recorded, *0315 commenced firing three minute charges.*

A security address preceded the week in Jakarta from 21 October. On 29th, the day after sailing *Diamantina* made a SUS charge firing run from 9-11 am. Other charges followed at six-minute intervals. After reaching Christmas Island on 30 October, the ship sailed on 4 November. For five days the vessel then made a fruitless search of a 43,000 square miles area east of the island for sea mounts. The three months, 11,000 miles cruise finally ended at No.7 Berth, North Wharf, at 10 am, 13 November.

At 11.10 pm, 18 November, the routine of Junior Recruit day cruises was interrupted. Police boarded in response to a bomb threat. A comprehensive search, including divers inspecting the hull found nothing.

Cruise UDS6/72 (UDS - the Underwater Detection System Group of WRE) investigated 100,000 square miles of the southern Indian Ocean west of Cape Leeuwin from 28 November to 7 December using GEK, Nansen, and XBT. Investigations to the north followed from 11-14 December.

There was one item high on the list of defects to be remedied on the slip. It had been noticed on 13 November when the ship returned from Christmas Island. Old age, rust, and movement through the water were blamed for the port bilge keel's forward nine feet bending back on itself. *Diamantina* was literally cracking up.

1973

On the Fremantle Slipway from 15-19 January, the port bilge keel problem was solved. The bent nine feet (about three metres) was cut off. At the same time an 18-inch (c. half a metre) crack in the starboard keel was welded.

The year's first CSIRO cruise investigated the north to south movement of tropical water over the western rock lobster breeding grounds. From Cape Leeuwin to North-West Cape and to 150 miles out to sea water samples were taken to a maximum depth of 2,000m. These were analysed to record temperature, salinity, and phosphate, nitrate, silicate, and oxygen content.

Before work began on 12 February, *Diamantina* rendezvoused with HMAS *Perth* to transfer mail as the guided missile destroyer left Australian waters for an Indian Ocean cruise. *Diamantina*'s successful cruise, which included a day in Geraldton, ended 11 days later with a return to the slipway. Water was flowing into the forepeak. Overnight the rusted stem was welded, stopping the leak. Between 27 February and 8 March the second CSIRO Cruise was completed without incident.

UDS Cruise 1/73 sailed at 9 am, 20 March after WRE equipment had been loaded. Stations were occupied off the south-west coast to investigate water structure and movement. At one location the ship hove to for 30 hours while bathythermograph readings were taken every 15 minutes to study diurnal effect on the ocean's internal waves. The cruise ended at G/H Berth at 4.15 pm, 11 April.

Junior Recruit day cruises, which had begun on 6, 7, and 8 February resumed on Gage Roads until the vessel sailed on 7 May with 15 tons of RANRL equipment and six scientists on a direct course for Christmas Island. The need to land a seaman with appendicitis forced a diversion to Carnarvon two days out. Then, guided by a Magnavox 702A satellite navigation set the voyage was resumed. After tying up to C Buoy, Flying Fish Cove, at 3.25 pm, 12 May, the crew landed the team and their equipment.

Then it was on to Cocos Island where, four days later a sailor landed to catch the fortnightly Department of Civil Aviation charter aircraft back to the mainland. Six more scientists came aboard while the crew enjoyed a run ashore on Direction Island. *Diamantina* made soundings southeast of the Cocos Islands on the run back before joining the cargo ships lying off Christmas Island at 6 pm on 19 May. Cable laying began on 25 May. A faulty electrical unit meant the cable then had to be recovered, and a return trip made to Cocos from 30 May to 2 June to collect a replacement. The lack of a Christmas Island airstrip was proving costly. On the island it was a different story. Work, including a beach survey, proceeded smoothly. Relations between the ship's company and the island community, already good, became even better. The island's new Administrator set up a Diamantina Club, and 26 officers and sailors became members of the Golf Club.

Offshore there was one further problem. During the cable laying on 3 June, the cable end appeared on deck while the ship was still 300 metres from shore. The captain tersely commented, *In future, RANRL will verify cable length.* Another day was lost while the deficiency was made good and the work completed. At 1.07 pm, 6 June, the ship headed for Singapore with the research programme continuing *satisfactorily* en route. In 10 days from 9 June the RANRL teams changed, and the crew carried out maintenance and enjoyed the port visit. As well, the Satellite Navigation System was repaired.

Back off the island between 22 June and 4 July, the ship deployed and retrieved current meters near the sea floor at depths of 1,000 and 2,000 metres, calibrated *the underwater systems*, and towed an acoustic oscillator at speeds up to 5 knots. At 6 pm, 4 July, passage of Sunda Strait en route to Jakarta began. The now usual security talk *as required by ABR 337* preceded arrival next day. The four days visit was marked by hospitality of *...the same high standard experienced during the ship's visit nine months previously.*

Project Flowerless resumed after the ship cleared Sunda Strait on 12 July. The acoustic oscillator was streamed for 28 hours at 5 knots subjecting the crew to a *...fearful noise throughout the ship especially in the mess decks near the waterline.* In his later report, the captain suggested that future continuous usage be limited to a maximum period of 24 hours at a time.

Divers worked from the 11th to the 15th, protecting the cables while the ship carried out surveys and loaded equipment. A Diamantina Hour of music on the local radio station farewelled the crew from 10 am, 15 July. A fisheries surveillance 10-20 miles off the coast south from the Monte Bellos was the final duty before the cruise ended at 11.45 am, 20 July.

The Annual Inspection went off well, as usual. Not so usual was the arrival of Williamstown Dockyard officers. They inspected the hull to determine the ship's useful life. Their verdict was the hull was in generally good condition, but, in the upcoming refit, the bow contour plating, tank tops under the main boilers, and sections of the tiller flat plating needed renewal.

After a CSIRO Cruise from 22 to 31 August, studied again north-south water movement up to Geraldton, the ship sailed for Hobart at 7 am, 3 September. Two days later *The Daily News* reported *...The Royal Australian Navy's oldest ship has left for a well earned rest after 45,000 hours at sea, and 430,000 sea miles since commissioning in 1945.*

But it was a working trip to the rest. Routine oceanographic observations were made all the way to King's Pier, Hobart, where, on 9 September, CSIRO scientists came aboard. Then, for four days off Hobart and Devonport, three traverses took water and bottom samples to investigate pollution levels.

It was not until 8.30 am, 14 September, that the 'rest' began at Williamstown Naval Dockyard. Three days later the refit began. It was scheduled to take six months. West Australian sailors, in particular, did not relish such a long time away. While the crew settled into the Maribynong Hostel, some shouldered the expense of bringing their families across the continent to join them. In the event the captain was later able to report, ...*By various means, all the married sailors except seven were able to spend the Christmas-New Year period with their families.*

By then the refit was well advanced; 10% of the keel plate had been replaced, and a further 12% reinforced, 75% of the underwater hull had been sandblasted and the hundreds of wasted rivets so revealed made good by replacement or welding.

1974

Until trials began in Port Phillip Bay on 3 April, the ship was at Williamstown Naval Dockyard and the crew at Maribynong Hostel. A persistent knock in the starboard engine was eliminated by 9 April, but the engine had markedly less power than its companion.

Diamantina sailed for Fremantle at 3 pm, 11 April with some work still incomplete. Two WRE and one Flinders University researchers tracked currents and measured temperature and salinity en route. A security talk was delivered to the crew two days before the ship tied up at H Berth at 11 am, 17 April. The absence had stretched to seven and a half months.

Family Day on 2 May also successfully tested the two main engine bearings that had replaced wiped ones. Five days later, after loading three semi-trailer loads of equipment and 12 RANRL researchers, the ship sailed for Christmas Island at 10.30 am. Fisheries surveillance off North-West Cape and a 'creditable' full power trial preceded arrival at the island on 10 May.

The familiar routine of landing scientists and equipment, and laying sensors and cable began. Not so routine was a ship's propeller parting a cable on 16 May. With the ends spliced, the main cable-laying task began on 20 May, when ...*the most distant off-shore sensor yet attempted was laid within five metres of the planned position on the seabed, and the cable run to shore by 1800.* On 21 May, after fuelling, the next 6 km cable was reeled onto the after winch drum. It was pressure tested three days later, and laid on the 26th. Ashore, a new Diamantina Club began operations, and about half the ship's company enjoyed leave each night until 11 pm.

On 1 June the Christmas Island barges assisted in the laying of the third and final cable of RANRL Trial 8/74, Project Flowerless. Three days later *Diamantina* sailed for Singapore. During the 10-day port stay the crew enjoyed leave and carried out self-maintenance. The RANRL team for Trial 10/74 came aboard. LCDR Davidson's Report noted that, with the recent introduction of air services to Christmas Island, future changes of personnel would take place there, and Singapore's only function for his ship would be as a self-maintenance port. The Singapore Naval Dockyard's decline became obvious during this stay. After HMAS *Vendetta* sailed on 10 June, *Diamantina* was the only naval vessel in port until it sailed a week later.

At 5 am, 20 June, *Diamantina* rendezvoused with HMAS *Assail*. After a boat transfer, the frigate deployed a velometer, and proceeded in company with the patrol boat to reach Flying Fish Cove at 6 am, next day. *Assail* was to work with *Diamantina* until 5

July. In less than three hours the technicians were ashore, and the vessels sailed to join *Vendetta* north-east of the island at 11.30 am. The three ships *progressed the aims of Flowerless* by sounding, taking bathymetric readings, and dropping charges until *Vendetta* sailed for the Kangaroo One exercise in the afternoon of 23 June. *Diamantina* and *Assail* continued ...*the lengthy and involved experiments* until they sailed for Darwin via Bali at 5 pm, 1 July.

There was no let up. RANRL Trial 11/74 occupied the next three days. This trial studied ...*the propagation and refraction of radar waves close to the sea surface from transmitting aerials at different heights.* LCDR Davidson reported later it had been ...*a particularly interesting month with its wealth of data collected involving the active involvement of the whole crew, and the rare experience for* Diamantina *of operating in company with other vessels.*

Diamantina tied up at Benoa on Bali's south coast at 8.40 am, 4 July; 10 minutes later *Assail* berthed alongside. The crews appreciated their run ashore in the idyllic, unspoiled little town. The patrol boat sailed the next day to investigate reports of Indonesian fishermen on Australia's remote territory of Ashmore Reef. *Diamantina*'s departure for Darwin was delayed until the following morning. Arrival at Darwin was delayed yet again. At 6.30 pm, 7 July, *Diamantina* rendezvoused with *Assail* to take on an injured sailor. Then the patrol boat headed for Darwin, and the frigate set its new course for Ashmore Reef.

Next morning, over two hours, parties landed on East, Middle, and West Island to investigate Indonesian fishermen's activities. On East Islet the party found fish fillets and bird breasts drying over fires. About seven Indonesian males on a 10m boat moored 100m off shore made no contact with the Australians, but returned to the

Fremantle, August 1974, LCDR D. Davidson and crew. (RAN)

fires when the sailors left. A sailing vessel lay off Middle Island where the four occupants of a hut had dug an eight-foot deep hole to tap a supply of brackish water. Here, and on West Island, tonnes of bird, turtle, and fish meat were drying on extensive racks. All signs, including old graves on East and West Islands, pointed to long-standing Indonesian activity on this Australian Territory. CDRE P.H. Doyle, NOICWA, later commented on the report of this hastily arranged investigation: *As has become the pattern,* Diamantina *continues to meet all her operational commitments, whether pre-planned or unexpected.*

The delayed Darwin port visit was a brief one - from 3 am, 10 July, to 9 am, next day. The RANRL parties changed before the ship sailed for more work on the Study of the Air Sea Interface (SASI) in the Timor Trench area - this time with HMAS *Attack*. Four days later, at 3.20 am, 15 July *Diamantina* tied up at Stokes Hill Wharf.

Two days later the ship sailed from Darwin for a bathymetric survey in the Rowley Shoals area, interrupted on 24 July, by a call at Port Hedland to collect a spare bearing flown from Sydney. Then it was back to the task until it was completed at 8 pm, 29 July. The cruise ended in Fremantle at 11.30 am, 2 August. Annual leave and self-maintenance began. The Annual Inspection was successfully completed on 16 August.

On 3 September LCDR P.G. Brook took over command from LCDR Davidson. A three-day SASI cruise, RANRL Trial 15/74, sailed at 4 pm, 23 September. Working with the patrol boat, HMAS *Acute*, 20 miles west of Rottnest Island, the three researchers carried out radar propagation, scattering, and acoustic experiments. On return to port, self maintenance continued. No score is on record of the Australian Rules game against West Australian Newspapers on 29 September.

Five hours before sailing for Christmas Island on 14 October, four United States Navy personnel boarded. In three hours, the party, under Captain D.M. Jackson, discussed, in the Report of Proceedings' terse words, *a number of projects, including Oolite*. A specific recommendation was that, for greater efficiency, cable be laid over the bow.

En route to Christmas Island the ship kept a lookout for foreign fishing vessels and a satisfactory full power trial was carried out. At 4 pm, 16 October, stores and personnel were taken aboard from HMAS *Moresby*. A swell had closed the port when *Diamantina* reached the island on the 19th, so, for three days the ship idled offshore with four merchant vessels. During the three days drift the crew kept occupied with swimming over the side, target shooting, table tennis, volleyball, and golf on the upper deck. However, work went on ashore with parties landed to set up equipment including the Miniranger Position Fixer. On 19 October, a ship's boat took the Island Harbourmaster, Captain J. McMaster, and Mrs. McMaster ashore from one of the merchant vessels.

Work began when the port opened on 22 October, and ran a generally successful course until 8 November. Acoustic oscillators and charges tested the hydrophone array. The ship also took bathythermograph and wind and wave readings. A RAAF Orion successfully took part in the tests on 6 November. Some of the problems included weather delays to aircraft and water penetration of cable. These were overcome. However, the AO Mk. IV Acoustic Oscillator could not be made to live up to expectations at 60 feet depth. The American recommendation for cable laying over the bow came in for further study on 28 October. The log records, *0923 ship touched vertical cliff at Rhoda Trig. Station. Minor damage only to bow.* Warren Treadgold, who was ashore playing golf at the time, was told that, instead of swinging to pass the cable ashore from the stern, the ship hit the cliff face resulting in *a squashed nose, and slightly bent bow.* The crew aboard went to emergency stations until the damage was assessed as minor.

Christmas Island - joining undersea cable to shore (N. Clarke)

The 'very cordial' relations with the local population were cemented when, two days before sailing, 200 children went to sea on a short trip, and an evening barbecue ashore at the Diamantina Club repaid some of the local hospitality. Equipment came aboard on 9 November. Next day the ship sailed for Fremantle. At 9 am on the 15 November the cruise ended.

The ship settled down for the quiet period of leave and self-maintenance. Early December found *Diamantina* moored alongside the hydrographic ship HMAS *Moresby*, recently assigned to a 10-year survey of the Western Australian coast.

Then came Christmas Day. As news of Cyclone Tracy's devastation of Darwin came in, *Diamantina* was ordered to change status from 24-hours notice for steam to four hours. The holiday became a day of concentrated activity. The ship moved to D Shed, Victoria Quay, and fuelled and stored until 1 am, Boxing Day. Key personnel were recalled from leave in the Eastern States. Local radio broadcasts alerted Perth area crewmembers. By 8.30 am, Boxing Day the fully fuelled and stored ship was back alongside *Moresby*, and ready to sail with 75% of its complement. In the event other ships were ordered to Darwin. But *Diamantina* was held in reserve until she reverted to eight-hours notice for steam on 31 December.

1975

Diamantina's status reverted to 24-hours notice for steam at 1 pm, 2 January. Three days later the ship sailed with one CSIRO researcher embarked. He monitored surface water temperatures as three RANR officers, working towards their Ocean Navigation Certificates, helped navigate the ship eastwards. The destination was, again, Williamstown. Helped by following winds, the ship reached Williamstown at 4.15 pm, 10 January. Three days later, however, it sailed for Jervis Bay.

At 8.40 that night a barely intelligible assistance call had *Diamantina* steaming to rendezvous with the Panamanian-registered *Union Fair* off Eden. Low on water, and with its condenser out of action, the freighter required assistance to reach port. Carrying a harbour chart, the Navigating Officer transferred, and, shortly after midnight, with the ship safely anchored in Twofold Bay, he returned. *Diamantina* then resumed her voyage. On 15 January at Jervis Bay *Diamantina* made eight runs through the sound range before moving to above the hydrophone to record its noise signature. This prelude to operating a new towed array took all day. Then she sailed on the return to Williamstown.

The refit's main purpose was to prepare *Diamantina* to operate the Boolee Towed Array Sonar. So, from 17 January, work concentrated on three main areas - the after winch, forward scientific accommodation, and hull plating. Maribynong's Midway Migrant Hostel again accommodated the crew. Their physical training needs were met with the long awaited arrival of a LSPTI.

Bob Mummery recalled later one unforseen result of the PTI's presence: <u>A Doctor Joins</u>. *On every voyage there are always one or two memorable characters. On this particular voyage the ship was to carry a doctor as was nearly always the case when the ship was to operate outside of Australian waters. The doctors were usually relatively new to the navy and, often as not, new to the practice of medicine. On this particular voyage the doctor joined two days prior to departure from Fremantle and having left a brand new bride in Sydney.*

The ship's company had their first view of Doc as he struggled, in full view of morning quarters, up the gangway resplendent in uniform complete with: camera around neck, tennis racquet under arm and numerous bags in hand. He paused at the top of the gangway, placed all his encumbrances at his feet, saluted with his left hand and marched on board. After this inauspicious start, the Wardroom officers and his Sickbay staff whipped him into seagoing shape so, in due time, he shaped up very well to become a popular member of Ship's Company.

However, it is worth relating that there was quite a contingent on board who were interested in keeping fit. Every afternoon, in the first dog watch, the Muscle Bosun (PTI) would lead a PT Class on the foc'sle and Doc was a regular participant. Sometimes the seaway would make PT a little too difficult to practice and the class would go running instead. For those who are not sure, it takes 24 laps from the bow, around the funnel and return to the bow to run one mile. (You're right, a two mile run is very boring!) On this particular day the sea was up and a few of the brave ones decided a run was in order although PT for the afternoon had been cancelled. After about lap six the sea started to sluice over the port side of the main deck and the runners found the going a little precarious (if not downright dangerous). However, they continued. The sea state continued to deteriorate but this fact was ignored by our health fiends. At about lap 20, the ship was pitching significantly and rolling quite dramatically to port. Now Doc, ungainly at the best of times and seemingly lacking in coordinative skills, is tiring as he hurtled down the port side. Just as he came level with the galley door, in came a wave knocking him off his feet and sweeping him outboard under the guardrail. Fortunately Doc had the presence of mind to grab the guardrail by the left hand as he went out under it. And also with fortune still on the side of the brave, the officer immediately behind Doc had not lost his footing and was able to pull Doc back inboard. Undeterred Doc continued and completed his two-mile run for the day.

A number of other 'happenings' occurred with Doc as the central figure and these all helped with his maturity into the way of the Navy. At the end of the voyage Doc posted out to an eastern states establishment to continue his Naval career, and to take up where he had left off with the new bride!

By April the Boolee winch together with its diesel engine and control hut were in the last stages of installation on the after deck. Attention then turned to extending the accommodation forward, and fitting out the after winch area.

On 24 April, the Fleet Commander, Rear Admiral D.C. Wells, visited the ship. Four days later, nine of the original crew came aboard for the vessel's 30th birthday - coincidentally, the captain's 40th. Ten days after the ship moved to the north side of Dock Pier, a meeting of parties in the Boolee project took place on 12 May. Among those attending was Mr. W. Van Avery, the representative in Australia of the United States Department of Defense Advanced Research Projects Agency. LCDR Brook recorded he ...*appeared disappointed with progress.*

With the ship's company's return on board on 23 May the vessel began to return to life. From 2 to 13 June, Mr. Deward Bruce, a representative of the Boolee winch's manufacturer, Pengo of Fort Worth, Texas, assisted in the work. Mr. Bruce had been the instructor, in Texas, of the ship's POETW J. Sperring, and they had a good working relationship. So there was good progress on all aspects, including the Boolee fairlead and working platform. In basin and three sea trials the ship was taken through its paces and the Boolee winch was tested, with and without a false hub, in laying and recovering cable.

At 9.07 am, 23 June, *Diamantina* sailed on a two part Material Research Laboratory cruise. The first four days of taking water samples to depths of 3,000m off Tasmania's east coast ended in Hobart on the 27 June, the day after the port main generator 'disintegrated'. Here the Fleet Commander inspected the ship.

On 30 June the ship sailed for 46 degrees S, 200 miles to the south. Rough seas, a moderate swell, and westerly winds to 50 knots gave the refit a good test. Except for some minor hull leaks and electrical faults, the ship came through well. The captain rated the main engines as 'excellent.' From 46 degrees S, 148 degrees E, *Diamantina* continued the *reasonably successful* cruise in rough weather northwards past Tasmania's west coast to dock at Williamstown on 3 July. The only casualties of the weather had been the loss of two water-sampling bottles.

Nine days later the voyage westwards began into the teeth of a full gale. At Adelaide, between 14 and 17 July, the Boolee tow cable and array were taken on board. Trials *handling dated explosives* for September seismic experiments in the Timor Sea took place in sheltered St. Vincent Gulf before the ship again faced the gale force headwinds. After rounding Cape Leeuwin a successful day of trials began with the streaming of the Boolee array from 9 am, 23 July. Self-maintenance began soon after docking at Fremantle on 25 July. The battering in the Bight had produced leaking rivets in the forward 4-inch magazine, kit locker, and starboard gland space. Other leaks in No. 10 fuel tank had contaminated the fuel causing the boiler to lose steam. All received attention.

WRE Trial MP3/75 sailed at 9.15 pm, 13 August. From 14-17 August, the Boolee array was streamed continuously at various speeds and depths in ...*generally most successful* acoustic and vessel identification trials. A RAAF Orion aircraft took part in Boolee Trial E on 19, 20, and 21 August. The Satellite Navigation System functioned well.

There were only two blemishes on the cruise. The fuel tank leak manifested itself again. And, shortly after the ship came to anchor in Gage Roads at 8.10 am, 22 August, Customs came aboard to begin a three-hour search for drugs. None were found, but three sailors admitted smoking cannabis during the cruise.

From 23 August a new false core was fitted to the Boolee winch, three replacement rivets went into the fuel tank, and repairs were made to the deep echo sounder. On Tuesday, 26 August, the Boolee Array, tow cable, and electronics van were landed ...*under the assiduous eye of a Russian merchant ship berthed immediately astern*. During the port stay the ship was informed the trials in St. Vincent Gulf had been in vain. The unrest in Timor, site of several monitoring stations, had forced the cancellation of the planned Timor Sea exercise.

A day trip on 8 September proved all repairs successful except for the echo sounder. The next day a new RANRL array cable was wound onto the Boolee winch. After sailing at 7.17 pm, 9 September, the ship used satellite navigation equipment between 12 and 15 September to survey an area to 200 miles west of North-West Cape for RANRL. On 15 September, in a short visit to the United States Navy's Communications Station at North-West Cape, the crew relaxed with a baseball game. Several personnel embarked.

A security talk preceded arrival at Christmas Island at 6.30 pm, 18 September. Until 8 October the only break in work was on 29 and 30 September, when swells closed the port. The morning after arrival the ship's Toyota Land Cruiser was put ashore and immediately began transporting equipment. On board, preparations went ahead to lay a four-element array. Practices culminated in the successful laying of the cable in four and a half hours on 28 September. The shore end was connected at 4.30 pm in pouring rain - the day before a north-westerly swell closed the port and forced the ship to drift offshore for two days.

On 3 October an oceanographic array was successfully laid. But an attempt, next day, to recover 'pingers' from the two arrays was unsuccessful. On 8 October, with the RANRL personnel and the Administrator and Mrs. Webb aboard, the ship sailed for Singapore. Relations ashore had continued at the cordial level of the more recent visits. Almost forgotten was the incident of an earlier year when a stoker had taken an unattended vehicle for a drive. Its owner was the police superintendent. The present incumbent was more favourably inclined to this less light-fingered crew. He himself had spent several years in the RAN. So regular leave to two of the three watches each evening passed without incident.

Territory Day, 1 October, was the ship's social highlight. The crew was represented in all the sporting events except coconut husking, and *Diamantina* men won the 100m, 200m, and mile races. After 'King Neptune' had inducted his new subjects the day before, *Diamantina* secured to HMS *Ajax* in Singapore at 8.33 am, 11 October. During the nine days in port the 10 RANRL researchers changed with 10 others. The return to Christmas Island began at 9.30 am, 20 October. Just out of the harbour the ship hove to and sent a boat back to collect a sailor adrift and a bag of mail. At 3.45 pm the bathymetric run to the island resumed.

From 23 October to 1 November trials went on in constant bad weather. After landing most of the scientific staff, *Diamantina* steamed to 100 miles north of the island for 36 hours of tests *using several acoustic devices*. Charge dropping trials again took place north of the island on 26 October. The next day a RAAF Orion worked with the vessel. The aircraft also performed another important function. It brought and took back mail. On 30 October HMAS *Vendetta* worked with *Diamantina*.

The 10 RANRL scientists and their equipment came aboard and the ship took on fuel on 1 November. The continuing rough weather prevented embarkation of the ship's Land Cruiser. After booking it to return on M.V. *Cape Hawke*, *Diamantina* sailed for Fremantle at 1.20 pm. A fault in the Precision Depth Recorder caused the cancellation of the North-West Cape bathymetric survey. The cruise ended at Fremantle on 6 November.

Four days after the 14 November Annual Inspection, a two days WRE Trial west of Rottnest Island deployed and retrieved a vertically oriented acoustic array. Back in port, the Boolee array was embarked on 28 November, and the ship sailed on 1 December. From the 2 to 9 December, the array was streamed in the area of 31 degrees S, 110 degrees E in very successful trials involving a RAAF Orion.

The year ended at 9 am, 10 December, when *Diamantina* tied up at Victoria Quay to begin the leave and maintenance period.

1976

Trial 1/76 sailed for the Southern Ocean on 27 January. The Monash University team was embarked to search for manganese nodules on the sea floor. With the Boolee array aboard, the smaller oceanographic winch had to perform all oceanographic tasks; 200 miles south of Cape Leeuwin the first dredge was made on 28 January in 4,800m of water. It was unsuccessful. The next attempt, 120 miles further south, resulted in the retrieval of two small nodules, and the loss of a sampler. More dredges to 42 degrees South produced more disappointment. As well, the deep echo sounder was malfunctioning.

After 1 February, the yield improved. Six dredges in 4,500 to 5,000m around 38 degrees S, 103 degrees E brought up more than 600 nodules *resembling black sheep brains*. So, the trip was judged *moderately successful* when the vessel tied up at G Berth, Victoria Quay, at 7.28 pm, 5 February.

Four days later course was shaped north. In a cruise ending on 17 February, two researchers from the University of Sydney, and one from the Bureau of Mineral Resources, dredged and took sea bed cores on the continental shelf to Jurien Bay, and then to 20 degrees S, 101 degrees E.

After repairing the deep echo sounder, fitting a new Precision Depth Recorder, and cleaning the boilers, *Diamantina* sailed on CSIRO Cruise 1/76 on 23 February. The researchers laid buoys, to be tracked by the Nimbus weather satellite, to study the mass movement of water in the southern Indian Ocean. In addition, they took water samples. At month's end the ship was stopped at 37 degrees 08' S, 115 degrees 30' E. taking water samples to a depth of 1,500m. The *very successful* cruise ended at H Berth at 1.30 pm, 4 March.

The crew fired their annual small arms practice at Swanbourne Range on 11 March. Four days later they began a two-day cruise. Three Western Australian Museum researchers made 49 dredges off Fremantle to collect a large variety of seabed fauna, including several previously unknown species. From 19-26 March WRE MP2/76 measured water temperature and currents from Perth to Geraldton.

A decline in morale was the major item in the captain's March Report of Proceedings. LCDR Brook wrote that it was especially evident among some junior sailors, stating four had attempted desertion and seven were listed for discharge, six at their own request. His report went on, *A dozen or so very junior sailors [had] trouble mixing in their mess*. Reasons cited for the problem included bullying and teasing, lack of job satisfaction, and an uninteresting ship's programme. The matter was taken seriously at high level, both out of concern for the sailors' welfare, and, as one Navy Board member noted, because *...Diamantina is frequently engaged on highly classified operations.* In a subsequent Minute the Director of Sailors' Postings addressed the points raised in the captain's report and NOCWA's comment on *...the difficulty of maintaining morale in ships employed on detached and humdrum duties,* and *...the undesirability of posting very young and inexperienced sailors to oceanographic and survey ships.*

The Director reiterated and affirmed the policy of posting *the more experienced ABs to these ships.* But, he went on to point out that, on balance, it was often better for both the person and the service to post a young single sailor with family in Western Australia to make *Diamantina's* long voyages than a married AB from Sydney. In his final paragraph the Director raised another possible cause of the discontent. *It must be remembered that* Diamantina *is a 31-year-old ship...Living spaces are primitive by modern standards and most sailors, whether they be experienced or inexperienced, would react unfavourably to them.* There the matter rested.

During the month in port WRE loaded Boolee equipment. Then, at 9.45 am, 26 April, a seven weeks cruise to Christmas Island began. En route, the large-scale survey of the Fremantle Canyon was continued and passage soundings were made off North-West Cape. 'Hands to bathe' was piped at 4.30 pm on the 30th, after which the array was deployed on the first station south of Christmas Island. So began an interesting cruise. This, and the posting out of four sailors just before sailing, were given the credit for a marked improvement in the ship's morale. Another possible contribution came from the second place in the Inaugural Beer Can Regatta of the ship's entry, 'Tintania', and the ship's team's win in the mini-Olympics against HMAS *Leeuwin*, and USS *Oklahoma City*.

On 1 May, at 12 degrees 20' S, 105 degrees 40' E - 110 miles directly south of Christmas Island - *Diamantina* deployed the Boolee array. Alternating with *other trials*, the ship maintained minimum heading of about one and a half knots while successfully monitoring charges dropped by a United States Navy Orion aircraft in areas between Perth-Christmas Island-Cocos Island-Broome until recovering the array at 7 pm, 5 May. After only a day in Flying Fish Cove to refuel *Diamantina* sailed at 7 am, 7 May, to then deploy the Boolee array 60 miles east of the island. Over the next four days US Navy and RAAF aircraft joined the trials. On the last day the RAAF aircraft dropped two canisters in the sea to be recovered by swimmers in 10 minutes.

On 12 May, at Christmas Island, the ship received and sent mail before sailing again at 5 am next day, this time to the north-west of the island. There, three more days' work with USN and RAAF aircraft ended when the array was recovered at 4 pm on 15 May, and course was set for Singapore.

During the week to 26 May, a lecture on hydrology to Singapore Navy midshipmen was one variation from the usual port visit activities. Another, reported by the captain, was a *disastrous Rugby game against the New Zealand Army battalion in which a hundred Australian Rules players were no match for 500 large Maoris.* The captain seemed unaware that a Rugby side is limited to 15 players. Perhaps he was referring obliquely to meetings between the Anzacs at other venues like the bar in Sembawang where, when Electrician Glenn Ridgewell replied to a New Zealand inquiry if there were any Aussies there, he received a swift 'knuckle sandwich.'

In four hours at Flying Fish Cove on 29 May, the ship refuelled before sailing to the south-east at 11 am. During this brief stop, as on the other two, divers repaired damage to the RANRL cables at Garrison Fissure. At 7 am, 1 June, *Diamantina* anchored off North-West Cape. Later that day a WRE scientist transferred to the ship by boat from the US Navy's Harold E. Holt Communications Station at the Cape.

Equipment, too, came aboard. The ship then put to sea and deployed the Boolee array. For a week the ship conducted Boolee tests from 75 miles north-west of Point Murat on the Cape to 250 miles west. With the array deployed at depths to 400m, *Diamantina* worked with the patrol boat HMAS *Adroit*, and the submarine HMAS *Ovens*. Both these vessels provided noise sources, including underwater charges.

The cruise ended at 11 North Wharf at 2 pm, 11 June. The captain reported that the trials were successful, but the prolonged periods of slow speed made them *dull and boring* for ship's company. As the Boolee material was landed, and 20 tons of equipment and 7 RANRL researchers came aboard for Langwith Trials, half the crew went on leave. On 4 July, three ship's divers flew to Sydney to join two Clearance Diving Team I members and RANRL personnel on a RAAF flight to Christmas Island. There they would repair storm damage to the arrays. Two days later the ship sailed for the island, making continuous soundings en route. When *Diamantina* tied up at Flying Fish Cove at 8 am, 11 July the major arrays were already repaired.

Until sailing for Singapore on 4 August, *Diamantina* stood on and off the island conducting a variety of tests. In the week from 18 July detection exercises involved working again with the submarine, HMAS *Ovens*. Five days into the tests the vessels rendezvoused to transfer a sailor with a hernia to the ship and *Diamantina's* doctor to the submarine. A rubber dinghy, on loan from the Special Air Service Regiment, made short work of the trips. Next evening, at 8 pm, the dinghy recovered from *Ovens* a scientist as well as the doctor. He had seen 15 crewmembers preparatory to the submarine sailing for Pearl Harbor.

The next trials, from 26-30 July, involved deploying noise sources about 125 miles north of the island. In choppy seas and windy weather sailors launched and recovered, over 100 times, devices weighing from 200-500 pounds (90-240 kgs). The Mk. 4 Acoustic Oscillator was streamed from the starboard forward derrick, while the 'Jester' device worked off the oceanography winch, and the C.R.C. 'Yellow Submarine' from the quarterdeck minesweeping davit. There were short breaks. On 25 July the cricket team played an island team. Six days later 60 schoolchildren enjoyed a short cruise that included a small arms and Bofors shoot.

A fault in the Satellite Navigation System threatened the bathymetric work north of the island on 2 August. Hourly charges were fired to fix positions and successfully conclude the work. From noon the next day the RANRL researchers disembarked at Flying Fish Cove. *Diamantina* sailed for self-maintenance in Singapore at noon on 4 August. 'King Neptune' initiated his new subjects from 4.05 to 5.25 pm, two days later. During the week in port the Satellite Navigation System's fault was rectified, and the portable air compressor, embarked at Fremantle, serviced. It had performed well, allowing the boilers to be shut down in port, providing air for the C.R.C. noise source, and powering 'windy hammers' for rust removal.

On 17 August the new RANRL researchers and a seven-man Clearance Diving Team embarked at Flying Fish Cove. Three days later the ship recovered the inoperative Q Oceanographic Sensor Array with the help of two island barges. However, an hour later, the cable broke and fell into deep water. A cocktail party that evening preceded the 9 pm sailing north for acoustic trials. On 21 August, the ship deployed three noisemakers at seven different stations, and took bathymetric readings. Three days later course was set for Fremantle, and the cruise ended at G Shed, Victoria Quay at 9 am, 29 August.

RANRL material was replaced by equipment for WRE's Vertical Line Array tests. On 10 September the Annual Inspection passed uneventfully. Three days later the VLA, less its electronics, was successfully deployed off Rottnest Island to 3,782m, and recovered. A week later, *Diamantina* returned to port where, at 11.30 am, Father Rolfe christened Tammy Cherie, daughter of ABQMC K. Simmonds, in the ship's bell.

After sailing the previous day, the ship began further comprehensive tests using sound projectors and sonobuoys at 8 am, 21 September. With a RAAF Orion surveying shipping and monitoring ambient sea noise, work was proceeding well when, at 4.10 pm, a signal ordered the ship to steam to the assistance of injured Japanese fishermen. As the array was being recovered, a float and gear were lost at 6.15 pm; 45 minutes later they were aboard and *Diamantina* set off on a course of 210 degrees to intercept the fishing vessel. But the Japanese had changed course and it was not until 4.10 next morning that the doctor boarded *Kaishin Maru*. As he treated one seaman for a stab wound to the abdomen and another with a deep head cut preparatory to transfer to the ship, *Diamantina* was not idle and took water samples. By 5.35 am, the boat had been recovered and the return to Fremantle began; 40 miles west of Rottnest Island HMAS *Acute* met *Diamantina*. The patients were transferred as tests resumed. In fact, the array was streamed 25 minutes before the patrol boat detached.

At 10.30 am, 25 September, a pleasant weekend in Geraldton began. However, the captain's report did comment on *Diamantina*'s recurring problem with using commercial wharves, ...*the ship was made to feel almost at home in Fremantle on Sunday morning when it was necessary to shift berth to allow another ship to berth.*

A neighbouring vessel at Geraldton wharf caught LCDR Brook's eye. The Vertical Line Array tests were not going well. He partially attributed this to competition with the Boolee System causing the programme to be rushed. However, he also pointed to another factor; Diamantina *is not a satisfactory ship to deploy the array in its present layout.* He went on to note the oil rig service vessel, *Lady Vera*, with its A frame aft, bow thruster, protected propellers, small crew, and charter rate of $3,000 per day was ...*a far more satisfactory vessel for the task.*

Diamantina sailed at 6 pm, 27 September, for 250 miles west of North-West Cape. Here, after deploying the Vertical Line Array, the ship would steam several miles away to continue the tests. On 1 and 3 October a RAAF Orion assisted by surveying ships and monitoring ambient noise. In an added service, on the second visit, a low pass delivered the Saturday newspaper. A fault in the array brought an early return. But the drawback of using commercial berths manifested itself again. With a full port, *Diamantina* had to anchor in Gage Roads, and then tie up at Kwinana before G/H Berth was free at 10.15 am, 9 October.

This was the year's last cruise, and the annual refit began. On 15 and 19 October the outer and inner funnel shells were removed. On 21 October, the ship went on the Fremantle Slipway. With work on the galley part of the major refit, HMAS *Moresby* fed the crew. On 15 December, LCDR GLEX P.J. Cooke-Russell took command.

The refit's aim was, pending the delivery of her ordered replacement, to prepare the 31-year-old ship for a further five years of service. As it happened, *Diamantina*'s age, and place in history, had been put in the spotlight by an August letter to the *Sydney Morning Herald*. Writing in response to a report in the 18 August issue on the retirement from the New Zealand Navy of the Australian-built corvettes, *Inverell*, and *Kiama*, CDR (Ret.) M.G. Rose corrected an error of fact. The reporter had stated the corvettes had been the last ships in Western navies powered by reciprocating steam engines. *Diamantina*'s commissioning commanding officer pointed to his ship's continuing service powered by just such engines.

Two former crewmembers provided some fascinating insights into operating these vintage engines. First, Bob Mummery: <u>Circular Motion</u>: *Circular motion, or so the story* goes, can occur when conditions are made just right. In this instance conditions that bought about circular motion lay in the weather, the seaway, the time and a mechanical phenomenon. Let's deal with the mechanical phenomenon first.

Diamantina's main engines; quadruple cylinder, double acting, triple expansion steam reciprocating engines, are directly coupled to their respective propeller shafts i.e. a Port Main Engine and a Starboard Main Engine directly driving the Port propeller and the Starboard propeller respectively. Steam is admitted to the engine via a manoeuvring valve and, in the normal cylinder valve configuration, the main engines will operate, or rotate, in the 'Ahead' mode. To go 'Astern' the cylinder valve configuration has to be altered to 'reverse' the engine's rotation. To effect this the engine throttle operator admits steam to a piston assembly which causes the 'reversing quadrant' to alter the cylinder valve configuration to the 'Astern' mode. It was normal practice that when Special Sea Dutymen were closed-up, or whenever the ship was about to enter a period, eg manoeuvring, that the master steam valve to the reversing quadrant was opened. Thus, when required to go astern, the steam actuating valve lever, when actuated, admits steam to the piston driving the reversing quadrant and an immediate shift to the astern mode could thus be achieved. Under normal steaming practice, steam to the reversing quadrant was isolated to prevent any accidental operation of the system.

The main engines are an open crankcase design. That is one can look in to the piston rods and crankshaft, eccentric sheaves and valve rods and watch the operation of all. Splash guards are fitted to prevent soogee (lubricating medium of soluble oil and water) being thrown out when the engines pick up speed. In the 'Ahead' mode with both main engines running at the same speed, particularly at 126 rpm, engine-room vibration is minimal and both main engines are turning (rotating) outboard. Now; picture the Middle Watch (0001 to 0400) associated with a warm balmy night, a following sea and a small swell. The ship was 'on passage' and had been steaming nearly all week at 126 revolutions. When Special Sea Dutymen had fallen out nearly a week earlier the isolation of steam to the reversing quadrant on the port main engine had not occurred. The ship was proceeding as it had for a number of days, conditions in the engine-room were cosy with a slight regular roll port to starboard and back as she ran before the sea. The Artificer of the Watch and his Third Hand had decided that it was coffee time and were engaged in idle chatter not paying any real attention to the job at hand when, much to the Tiffy's surprise, the Captain called down from the bridge demanding to know why the ship was going round in circles!

In essence the steam having been left on the reversing quadrant, coupled with years of minor wear on both the steam piston actuating valve and the quadrant mechanism, had allowed a small steam pressure to build behind the reversing quadrant piston. The slow build up of steam pressure, the loose mechanism and the roll of the ship all combined with the right moment and suddenly the Port Main Engine had gone from 126 rpm ahead to 126 rpm astern - without missing a beat. No unusual vibrations had been felt but as soon as the Captain called the On Watch Tiffy noticed both main engines rotating in the same direction and he knew immediately what had happened! Circular Motion - QED.

Warren Treadgold provides some additional insights into the vagaries of reciprocating steam engines: Flashing up the boilers during these times was fairly laid back even though starting off was hard work if we were away from Fremantle. No one was too worried about the copious amounts of black smoke which would billow out of the stack to begin with but as people became more environmentally aware and others were upset with their washing being covered with black soot, it was obvious we had to change. Even after the boiler had been flashed up for some time, the Engineer, who used to live in the Tingira Flats overlooking the harbour, would sometimes ring the ship from his home if he saw we were making a bit of smoke and tell the Officer of the Day to pass the message on to stop making smoke. So we flashed up while it was still dark, easy fixed. Flashing up while alongside in Fremantle was one thing but elsewhere, well that was another story. While in Fremantle, we had the use of an air compressor which we would connect up to the reciprocating fuel pump. This would provide sufficient air to kick over the pump just enough to provide fuel to the sprayer and get a fire going in the boiler. Once we had about 60/70 psi in the boiler, we would change over to steam and hopefully, with the aid of a few curses and a spanner, it would pump fuel normally. Away from Fremantle, we didn't have the luxury of the compressor so it was the hand-raulic pump. This was a pump which had to be turned by hand which meant we had to have three or four stokers down the boiler room to begin with to operate this pump. It was hard work, particularly up north in the tropics. We might have even tried to change over to steam at 50 psi in those conditions.

We were burning black oil or Furnace Fuel Oil (FFO) at this time also which added another dimension to flashing up. Because we were burning FFO which had a fairly high flash point (about 170 degrees F as I recall), it meant we had to have some way of heating the oil to make it burn albeit not very cleanly. Someone well before my time invented what became known as the 'coffee pot' which was a steel pot which fitted around the sprayer (the device fitted at the end of the fuel line which sprayed the fuel into the boiler furnace). It was the size of a large coffee tin and made of heavy steel so it wouldn't buckle and was open at each end. Rags were soaked in diesel fuel and placed into the 'coffee pot' and then set on fire; this would heat up the sprayer and raise the temperature of the oil as it passed through the sprayer. Of course, at the same time, the boiler room was slowly filling with smoke which was another incentive to change over to steam as soon as we could or, on occasions, as soon as the pumps would go. And people complain these days of passive smoking.

In the early 70's, it was decided to change a couple of tanks over to diesel fuel which had a couple of advantages. The first one was that it was a cleaner flash up; secondly the fuel didn't need to be preheated because it had a lower flash point and of course the fuel was easier to pump. Later again, during the 1974 refit I think it was, all of the fuel tanks were converted to take diesel fuel. And even later still, the ship would carry its own compressor on the upper deck. Strike me lucky, how easy can it be.

Prior to 1974, when the ship carried FFO, the fuel would leak from the tanks through the rivets. When we were working in the southern oceans, it was not so noticeable because the fuel being cold, it didn't flow so quickly but when we moved into warmer waters it would seep out much quicker which meant we were regularly wiping the bulkheads in an attempt to keep the spaces (boiler rooms and engine room) clean. In order to prevent this happening with the more refined diesel fuel, all of the tanks were cleaned (which was an enormous job) and steel plates were welded over the rows and rows of rivets....

Usually on the way back to Fremantle, the boys down the 'hole' (the boiler room) would try and squeeze as much out of the boilers as possible without lifting the safety valves and over in the engine room, the tiffies would try to get as much speed out of the engines as they could without it being too obvious. It was not unusual for the Navigator, when he was taking his fix, to mutter some obscenities about bloody stokers because he would realise he was way out on his previous estimations.

One of the stokers onboard, Cliff Walsh, was a mad fisherman and he would constantly harass the skipper about calling into the Abrolhos on the way home to do a spot of fishing if we were ahead of time. Usually Cliff would win because on many occasions, on the afternoon/early evening of the eve of sailing into Fremantle Harbour we would drop the 'pick' (the anchor) at the Abrolhos and there he would be pulling in some big ones...

The refit went on with the rebricking of both boilers. On New Year's Eve the funnel was replaced. The last bluewater vessel in Western navies powered by reciprocating steam engines was preparing for her most distant deployment ever.

1977

The WRE researchers and the Boolee array arrived on 10 January, and all were embarked by the 14th. Sea trials and compass adjustment disclosed faults in steam stop valves, safety valves, engine bearings, steering, and the gyrocompass. All repairs, except the steering telemotor's were completed by 24 January. At 1.30 pm, 24 January, *Diamantina* hove to at 32 degrees 02.2' S, 115 degrees 42' E. There the ashes of Miss Elizabeth DeVries, sister of POCK J.H. DeVries of the ship were scattered on the sea.

Two days later, after sailing at 9 am, for Operation Bearing Stake, the ship paused at the same position to commit the ashes of LCDR R.A. Ruttle, MBE, RANR (Ret.) in the presence of his widow and daughter. After the mourners had landed, course was then set for Colombo via Exercise Area R139 where, by 1.20 pm, a 40/60 and small arms shoot had been completed. Work proceeded on the steering repairs, and they were completed in early February.

With the Precision Depth Recorder registering inaccurate readings at depths greater than 2,000 fathoms, the ship anchored in Port Refuge, Cocos Islands, at 11.54 am, 31 January. Here divers tightened the instrument's dome while the ship entertained the Administrator and Resident Medical Officer and their families on board. The voyage resumed at 6.25 am, next day.

While the ship refuelled at Colombo on 6 February five WRE researchers embarked. On sailing for Karachi at 10.42 am, next day, *Diamantina* came under the control of the Commander of Task Group 73.8. Project Bearing Stake's Site 3 was reached at 10 am, 11 February. Here the Long Acoustic Towed Array (LATA) was streamed . Two days later the ship recovered the array, and continued for Karachi. After tying up at No.24 Berth, West Wharf at 9.42 am, 15 February, the ship departed next day for Bearing Stake's Site 1B.

On site at 9.50 am, 18 February, the ship again streamed LATA. It stayed deployed for four days. During this time *Diamantina* made visual contact with the United States research ships, USNS *Kingsport, Wilkes*, and *Albert J. Meyer. Jane's Fighting Ships* 1979 described these ships. In summary it said: *Kingsport* (ex-*Kingsport Victory*), 10,680 tons laden, had become, in 1962, the world's first satellite communications' ship. In 1966 the vessel was reassigned to hydrographic research. *Wilkes*, 2,580 tons fully laden, was completed in 1971. Designed specifically for surveying she had a bow propulsion unit for precise manoeuvring, and could carry 30 scientists. *Albert J. Meyer*, 7,810 tons fully laden, was a 'Neptune' class cable repair ship. She carried electric cable handling equipment, and precision navigation instruments.

All three ships were operated by Military Sealift Command. The Americans were not the only vessels to join *Diamantina*. Shadowing the three were the Soviet Union T58 Class minesweepers, MSF 836 and 847. During the trials the Russians stayed in close company. Flag greetings and naval salutes were exchanged.

Bob Mummery recalls more: *A Russian Escort. Throughout the 1970's Diamantina conducted many passive defence equipment trials. This era, being the height of the Cold War between the Eastern Bloc countries and the Western World, found the ship under regular surveillance from units either belonging to or associated with the Navy of the USSR.*

On one particular deployment the ship was required to steam into the sea making little or no headway for 14 days at a time whilst some passive equipment was deployed, at depth, and towed astern of the ship. At this time a Russian Minesweeper became our constant companion. As one can imagine, being at sea and going nowhere, life was a bit predictable, i.e. sunrise would see clear skies, calm seas, moderate temperature and a Russian Minesweeper as escort. Evening, in much the same global position, would see a setting sun, calm seas, moderate temperature and a Russian Minesweeper as escort. Morning ... Etc. Evening ... etc.

As it was perfectly obvious that the ship was going nowhere but WAS doing something - the Russian captain set about entertaining both Diamantina *and his own ship's crews. He did this in a number of ways that always ended up with the minesweeper steaming past and saluting* Diamantina. *Under international protocol* Diamantina, *having the senior by rank of the two captains, was the senior ship and the senior ship should always be saluted when it is passing or being passed. The manner of the Russian prior to saluting varied from having the ship's company, in full dress uniform, line the ship to holding a sports day on the ship's sweep deck. Interesting to say the least.*

Of course, like all good 'spy' ships, it was up to the Russians to attempt to find out just what Diamantina *was up to! In those days ships used to dump garbage (gash) and other waste into the sea and there it would settle and eventually sink to the ocean floor (Oh well that was the theory). The Russians, forever inquisitive, would haul as much of* Diamantina's *rubbish onto their own deck and sift through it before once more consigning it to the deep. As things stood we were also monitoring ocean temperatures by way of bathythermographs. This was achieved by dropping a bomb shaped device that streamed a copper wire, into the sea and, as the device went to the ocean floor through various water layers of differing temperature, the temperature was recorded, via the copper wire, on a special graph recorder. These bomb devices, colloquially known as Bathy Bombs and about the size of two coca-cola cans end to end, came in lots of one dozen in specially fashioned polystyrene boxes.*

Noting the Russian penchant for sifting through rubbish, we decided to lift the Russians' spirit. A Bathy Box was hollowed out, loaded with girlie magazines (Penthouse, Playboy etc), a bottle of Johnny Walker Scotch whiskey and a bottle of Bundaberg rum, sealed watertight and floated out with the day's rubbish. The Russians duly recovered the box. Next day, following her formal steam-past, the Russian dropped the box over her side ahead of Diamantina *indicating that it should be recovered. Recovered and opened, the contents revealed some good quality vodka, but no girlie magazines.*

If any moral can be gained from this story it is one that indicates sailors are brothers and that it is not they who start wars, rather the sailor is one who must from time to time do the bidding of his master!

On 21 February, *Diamantina* floated four boxes to *Wilkes*. Then LATA was recovered, and, in the afternoon, course was set for Bahrain. *Diamantina's* log entries for this leg include: *21[Feb.] 1615 USSR T58 Class minesweeper, side number 836, passed at one cable along port side 22[F] 1230 Flown over by Iranian Lockheed P3c Orion aircraft, Flt. No. 58705. DR [Dead Reckoning] Position 25 degrees 01N, 57 degrees 41.2E [In the Gulf of Oman]. 23[F] 1103 overflown by Iranian Lockheed P3c Orion side number 58702 in position 26 degrees 23.1N, 54 degrees 22.1E [At the western end of the Strait of Hormuz].*

Diamantina was receiving a lot of close attention - close enough to read an aircraft's number.

There was an engineering problem on the run up The Gulf. Bob Mummery has the story: *From Fremantle to Bahrain, including 'weeks' on station trialling some passive defence prototype equipment, was a long haul by any stretch of the imagination and not to have had a main engine bearing give a bit of a knock or two was quite something. However, an eccentric sheave bearing (of 22 inches internal diameter and about 6 inches wide with a 1 inch wide stepped locating ring) said that it had had enough of our silly games and decided to 'wipe' itself the day before arrival in Bahrain. Fortunately the Tiffy on watch had caught the problem, and although a little loose on the sheave, we managed to keep the engine fully operational until arrival. (An eccentric sheave is in fact a cam lobe (one per valve) on the main engine crankshaft* and is the mechanism where-by the valves are appropriately positioned, as the crankshaft rotates, to allow the steam to either enter or exhaust from the cylinders. This failure was probably due to the fact that we were low on lubricating oil (soodgee) and had been supplementing the sump with tried and true mixtures of soap, tallow, castor oil, kerosene and other 'old salt's' remedies. See further on for another anecdote on Soodgee).

Wiping of eccentric sheaves is a relatively infrequent occurrence and, in company with Murphy, no spare was held on board. Similarly Diamantina, having not roamed the world for a very long time, had neither forge, nor materials, nor the equipment on board to conduct a new bearing pour and the associated machining necessary to complete a repair. URDEF signals sent ahead were met with replies indicating no spare in Australia and no repair workshop available in Bahrain. Expertise on board for white metal bearing repair resided in the Engineer and the Chief Engine-room Artificer only.

During the run into Bahrain, under the instruction of the Engineer and the CERA, the Engineering Department set about fashioning a forge and a pouring bench from spare boiler bricks and other handy materials. The oceanographic winch on the starboard side of the main deck, and our largest diameter winch, was prepared for transformation into a lathe. Fortunately, upon arrival in Bahrain, we were to find that Qantas had delivered a spare that had been miraculously discovered in the old Randwick stores depot in Sydney. Pity about the skills of the Engineer and the CERA, they were never tested!

At 9.58 am, 24 February, the last line was secured to berth the vessel starboard side to the three-year-old, 4,000 tons Knox class frigate, USS *Pharis* at Bahrain. The captain made his calls on local dignitaries, the Commander of Middle East Force, United States Navy, and the captains of *Pharis*, and the flagship, *La Salle*. The 14,000 tons command ship, a converted Amphibious Transport Dock, was painted white to reflect the Gulf heat.

The crew enjoyed the unusual leave port. Just as welcome was the first mail in a month - five separate deliveries. Bob Mummery amplifies the official report with some details: *Port Visit – Bahrain. Somewhat of a memorable visit. From Fremantle to Bahrain, including 'weeks' on station testing some passive defence prototype equipment in a tri-nation exercise, was a long haul by any stretch of the imagination and the troops were fit for a 'run ashore'. We moored outboard of USS La Salle, then the flagship for the Commander, Middle East Forces. Our 2,000 tons against her 15,000 tons must have looked odd indeed.*

As usual for the first night in a foreign port, the Wardroom officers held a cocktail party and a Beat the Retreat ceremony for local dignitaries including the Admiral from USS La Salle. Two other usuals for first nighters also followed the official cocktail party and ceremony. A Wardroom party for selected guests raged most of the night and the Ship's Company, who were not members of the Duty Watch, stepped ashore. By all accounts everyone had a great time; USS La Salle was amazed at the numbers of PYT's (Pretty Young Things - mainly expatriate air hostesses from Gulf Air) who kept on arriving all through the night looking for the Wardroom party. However, the Admiral was not pleased to be jeered at and have sticks and other objects thrown at his car when he refused to give some Diamantina sailors a lift back to the ship (naughty boys!) No doubt the latter of these two incidents was the reason the Captain was required to call on the Admiral, complete with sword and medals, the following morning. As to the remaining high jinks, around breakfast time two Senior Chief Petty officers of USS La Salle were leaning on the ship's guard rail looking down on Diamantina and one was heard to say to the other, "I wonder what she will be when she grows up!.

The city of Bahrain was quite some distance from the dockside, and to that end the dockside was a long way from the wharf gates hence the trouble with the Admiral, and taxis were common place ferrying officers and Ship's Company to and fro. It came to be known that the majority of the trips into Bahrain were to visit the expatriate airhostesses who lived in an apartment complex adjacent to the Bahrain Pepsi-Cola bottling plant. The area, being so frequently visited by our guys who spoke no Arabic and the taxi drivers conversant only in broken English, soon became known as the Pepsi Flats. And thus it ended up that as soon as an Australian got into a taxi, the taxi driver always asked, "Pepsi Flats?"

Course was set for Operation Bearing Stake's Site 4 at 10.03 am, 2 March. There were some incidents on the way, however. One day out the ship stopped and a diver went over the side to repair a blocked toilet valve. What conclusions were drawn by the two Iranian P3c s that overflew on that day is not known. Then, with coldroom and freezer temperatures rising alarmingly, the ship anchored at Minah Al Fahal at 7.30 am on 4 March. The Engineer and Supply Officer took a boat ashore to arrange repairs. A second task was to find a supply of the rare lubrication oil needed by *Diamantina's* antique engines. Bob again fills in the details: _The Soodgee Story_ (and here we question spelling of soodgee). *Because of the amount of condensed steam and other free water entering the open sumps of these engines soodgee, a mixture of soluble oil and water, is the basic lubricant of the steam reciprocating engine types used in the ships of* Diamantina's *vintage. During World War II and for sometime thereafter, when there were many of these types of engines afloat, soluble oil (OM something or other) was readily available worldwide, however, the ship was now very much 'one off' worldwide and soluble oil was not now so plentiful.*

The oil refineries in Bahrain were unable to mix the requirement for us inside the length of our stay but indicated that an oil refinery in Oman would be able to mix and have it available as the ship made passage south out of the Persian Gulf. It would mean a short stopover of about two hours in Masqat (Muscat), the capital of Oman. Boy, what a lifesaver!

However, things did not go according to Hoyle! We arrived off Masqat but could not get port clearance to enter. In fact we could make no radio contact at all. The Captain, always eagle-eyed, spied a wharf on the coastline and a sizeable number of buildings nearby. By quick command, the Engineer and the Supply Officer found themselves in a 'rubber duckie' (inflatable boat) speeding to the wharf with instructions to find a telephone and contact some authorities. Easy as pie they thought, but, on reaching the wharf it was easy to understand why the Captain had discovered it for it stood over 30 feet (9 m) above the water and was exceedingly long. At least there was a ladder to climb so the two intrepid officers made there way up to the top and proceeded towards the shoreline. The local policeman, having been warned of a foreign warship lurking on the horizon, and Oman being at war with Yemen, came marching towards them with pistol drawn. In broken English he refused all requests for assistance and demanded the officers return from whence they came, as they were illegal immigrants. The Supply Bob decided to argue the case. The policeman cocked his weapon and immediately looked very, very threatening. The two officers beat a hasty retreat. On return to the ship they found that the ship had made radio contact ashore and had been granted permission to proceed to the harbour. It takes all types!

The Main Refrigeration System. *(No! We did not lurch from crisis to crisis, it just seemed like we did!) It was an overnight steam from Bahrain to Oman and in that time the main refrigeration rooms were getting alarmingly warm. An investigation revealed that the only condenser had failed and allowed seawater to enter the evaporator (room cooling coils) and freeze therein. How did such a thing happen? Suffice to say that, at some previous maintenance period, an unauthorised modification to the main refrigeration had been carried out. Notwithstanding that the person responsible for the modification had conducted the change with the best of intentions, his design was fundamentally flawed and now placed the ship's program in jeopardy.*

Fortunately the self-styled Australian Agent General in Oman, one expatriate Aussie going by the name of Don Diaper (alias Nappy) was able to put us in touch with some American air-conditioning experts who came to our assistance.

Our stay in Masqat was extended by a few days. The Oman Army loaned mobile refrigeration vans and our refrigerators were de-stored to them. Cooling coils were stripped by the ship's staff, frozen seawater removed, expansion valves cleaned, and the remaining refrigeration gas pipe-work and compressors cleaned and surveyed. Concomitantly our American friends produced a satisfactory design of replacement piping and condensers to give us an extra condenser and safeguard our system from perils similar to that which we had just experienced. Our program, being now in somewhat of disarray, was reworked and we recovered by missing a port call to Djbouti and catching up with our tri-nation team for more time on task.

There was an irony in *Diamantina's* departure from the Gulf. By sailing time only 36 of the ordered 90 tons of fuel had been delivered. So, at 6 pm on Monday 7 March, the ship cast off with only 86% of capacity fuel embarked. As this meant she would arrive in her next port, Mombassa, with 21% fuel remaining, less than the regulation 25%, special permission had to be obtained before the ship left the world's greatest oil exporting region - short of oil.

The preliminary Long Acoustic Towed Array streaming began at 8.40 am, 11 March. By 8 pm, the 80 minutes recovery operation was completed. After adjustments, the process was repeated next day. Tests at Site 4 ran from noon 13 March to 5 pm, 20 March. *Diamantina's* log for this period records two more close encounters with a Soviet vessel: *13. 1900 Russian white hulled Akademik Krilov class research ship named* Admiral Vladimirsky *closed on course 320 degrees Sp 17.4 [kts.] to pass 2.5 cables up port side. 14.* Admiral Vladimirsky *passed starboard side 1.5 cables 1121.*

At 9 pm, 20 March the ship turned for Mombassa, and it tied up at No. 3 Wharf Port Kilindini at 12.37 pm, four days later. Amid the usual calls, visits, and cocktail party, WRE personnel joined the ship. The correspondent on the ship reported to *Navy News* that the captain also eagerly awaited the arrival of parts for the intermittently malfunctioning Precision Depth Recorder and radar.

On 4 April the American ships *Kingsport, Albert J Meyer*, and *Mizar* put to sea. Next day *Diamantina* sailed for Site 5. There, north-west of the Maldive Islands, around 9 degrees 20' N, 68 degrees 20' E, LATA was streamed near the surface and at depth until 5 pm, 17 April. *(Jane's Fighting Ships* listed *Mizar* as an oceanographic research ship transferred to the technical control of Naval Electronics Command on 1 July 1975. The ship was ...*equipped with a centre well for lowering oceanographic equipment including towed sensor platforms.)*

Three days later *Diamantina* was alongside Queen Elizabeth Wharf, Colombo. The captain dined next evening at the Australian High Commissioner's Residence with the Prime Minister of Sri Lanka and the High Commissioners of Australia, Great Britain, and Canada to celebrate the Queen's Silver Jubilee.

Another anniversary was celebrated aboard the day after sailing for Bearing Stake's last tasks. On the 24 April, the crew enjoyed a buffet lunch on the upper deck to celebrate *Diamantina's* 32nd birthday. CPOETP3 W. Swan, born 19 days before the ship's commissioning, assisted the captain to cut the cake.

Site 2's location was at Position DP2B, around 10 degrees 59' N, 61 degrees 47' E [south-east of the Seychelles]. Streaming and recovering the array ran from 1 pm, 27 April to 3 pm, 1 May, when *Diamantina's* involvement in Bearing Stake ended. In a variation, it was Soviet merchant ships rather than dedicated surveillance vessels that made close passes here.

Diamantina was back in Colombo from 6 to 8 May. LCDR Cooke-Russell's April Report of Proceedings stated, *...approximately half the spares ordered for the radar have arrived and been fitted and radar reliability has been restored.* The Precision Depth Recorder was another story. *Spares ordered for the PDR became entangled in the Kenyan Customs and the latest advice from Nairobi indicates that the PDR spares were inadvertently exported from Kenya. The PDR remains unserviceable.*

During four days in Singapore from 14 May, the Small Ships' Chaplain, Rev. A. Rosier transferred from *Vendetta*, and stayed aboard to Fremantle. The deployment ended there in gale force winds and rain on 25 May.

In her furthermost voyage from the Australian coast, *Diamantina* had been away for four months and steamed 18,677 miles. In his covering letter to the May, Report of Proceedings NOCWA, Commodore N.A. Boase, gave his opinion of the ship's achievement: *I consider that* Diamantina*'s performance during her deployment from 26th January to 25th May, 1977 has been most creditable.*

The maintenance period had two highlights - the order, 'Splice the Mainbrace' was cheerfully obeyed at 12.30 pm, 10 June, while NOCWA's inspection from 11-15 July was followed by a ship's company photograph.

The Department of Natural Resources, Monash University, and the Western Australian Museum had researchers on board the cruise from 25 July to 2 August. They took samples from the shallow bottom off Cape Leeuwin on 26 July, and then moved to dredge specimens and manganese nodules from an average depth of 4,500m. The dredging continued in deteriorating sea conditions. Then, at 12.20 pm, 1 August, all work stopped and the ship raced for Fremantle. Omar (Peter) Amjah, the Petty Officer Meteorologist takes up the story: *Bill Hay [Stores Petty Officer] was involved in a serious accident at sea. I happened to be in the messdeck at the time. We had been*

Diamantina's crew, July 1977. (RAN)

working on mapping out the mineral field in the Southern Ocean south of Cape Leeuwin. I was the Meteorologist [and Safety Equipment Officer, ship's barber, and fishing organiser] and I had reported to the captain that we were in for a rough time and that we would not have time to complete our work.

The seas began to rise so the ship was secured for rough seas. Typical of the Southern Ocean, the weather was upon us before we could be fully prepared. To cut a long story short we really took a pounding and we had water coming in. I had reported swells higher than the highest point onboard, as, when we were in a trough, the peak could be seen above us. Bill was in the messdeck wedged between the small two-seater table we had and the bulkhead, trying to read. To his right was our hot water urn which was about one third to a half full, and easily managing to contain its contents. An exceptionally large swell hit the side of the ship and caused it to screw around. Then another hit from the opposite side and jarred the ship heavily. It was enough to tear the urn from the wall, and it dumped its contents on Bill. There was enough warning for Bill to raise his head, but that's all. As it was very cold he was wearing heavy warm clothing which acted like a sponge and soaked up all the boiling water. Bill literally had the front of his body steamed from his neck to his feet where the hot water pocketed in his boots and heavy socks before we could get his clothing off and get him into the shower.

We managed to get him into the sick bay where his underwear had to be cut away from his burnt skin. The Sickbay Attendant, named Daylight, did his best to settle Bill down. From then on, it was burn treatment and painkillers until we could get Bill to Fremantle. The course to Fremantle meant turning the ship in very heavy seas, as we were riding it out before the accident. That is another story, but it all happened. The ship sustained a lot of damage, but Bill made it, and, after many months, fully recovered, although badly scarred. Out of 20 years, I have calculated 14 of them on ships in some heavy seas, but that event, I believe, exposed me to the heaviest seas I have encountered. It may have been due to the size of Diamantina, but I believe, as a meteorologist, they were simply exceptionally big.

Bill was not the only casualty of the mountainous seas; 10 dredgings were unsuccessful. As well, two survival packs were lost overboard, four others, three life rafts, and a ladder were damaged. Inspection in Fremantle after tying up the day after the accident revealed the Edo echo sounder dome had been torn from the hull.

Another disturbing incident was the theft of Self Loading Rifle 6709762 from the Gunner's Store on 11 August. It was recovered next day. The Board of Inquiry completed its investigation the day before Diamantina sailed for Adelaide at 9 am, 19 August.

More extremely rough weather battered the ship for the first three days. Then, at 3.15 am on 22 August, a deep dredge was made for the Department of National Resources at 38 degrees 01' S, 127 degrees 04' E. In five days at Adelaide from the 24th, the Boolee equipment was loaded. Two hours after sailing, the ashes of retired L/Cpl. E.W. Neal, Royal Marines, were scattered in St. Vincent Gulf at 34 degrees 58.3' S, 138 degrees 19.2' E at 11 am on 29 August.

For the first time, Diamantina was bound for New Zealand. On passage the ship dropped expendable bathythermograph (XBT) probes every two hours after crossing the 300m line. As well, deep and shallow probes were made. While the crew enjoyed Auckland from 5-8 September, the captain made his calls and attended briefings. The Boolee Array sea tests in the South Fiji Basin and Coral Sea would involve the submarine, HMAS Onslow, RAAF and RNZAF Orion aircraft, and the RNZN oceanographic ship, HMNZS Tui. Diamantina had worked with Tui before. Then she had been USNS Charles H. Davis. On loan from the United States, she had been commissioned into the RNZN on 11 September. Jane's Fighting Ships, 1979-80 notes, Operates for NZ Defence Research Establishment on acoustic research.

At Site A on 9 September, *Diamantina* streamed Boolee to make repairs. An 8 am, rendezvous with *Tui* next day saw the first task begin when the array reached its 300m working depth at 9.05 pm, that night. On 12 September, a noise-maker was added to the array at 100 feet depth while a RNZAF Orion carried out a shipping survey. *Tui* detached for Noumea at 10.30 next evening. *Diamantina*, after completing zigzag and sea noise tests, recovered the array at 5.32 pm, 14 September, and followed. After three days in port, *Diamantina* cast off for Site B in the Coral Sea on the 20th.

From 2.45 a.m., 24 September to 1.57 p.m, 27 September, Boolee was streamed at depths to 300m and recovered while *Diamantina*, *Tui*, and *Onslow* made runs. A RAAF Orion dropped pattern charges around the site, and surveyed shipping. Orders on 27 September, to go to the aid of the sinking fishing boat, M.V. *Chiffong*, 470 miles to the east had *Diamantina* recover the array, flash up its second boiler, and steam into a 33-knot headwind. At 1.15 pm next day news came of the crew's rescue. Heading was then altered to Brisbane. *Diamantina* and *Tui* tied up at New Farm late on 30 September. The New Zealand ship hosted the cocktail party.

Both ships slipped early in the morning of 3 October for Site C. Approaching the area, both made XBT runs to determine the position of the Tasman Eddy. On site, east of Noumea, at 34 degrees 12.2' S, 154 degrees 43.3' E, *Diamantina* streamed Boolee to operational depth at 5.25 pm, 5 October. Then the minesweeper, HMAS *Ibis*, made passes towing a noise projector. Poor weather hindered Tasks J and D with an Orion from 6-8 October. The weather did moderate on 8th, when the aircraft made a shipping survey. Next day *Tui* detached for Sydney. *Diamantina* recovered the array from 1.55 to 3.10 pm, and then followed. For most of the time between 9 and 17 September, *Tui* was outboard of *Diamantina* at Garden Island.

At 10.15 am, 17 October, *Diamantina* sailed for Adelaide. Two hours later she carried out a two-hour anti-aircraft firing exercise. In Adelaide from 20-21 October, the ship fuelled, unloaded the Boolee equipment, and set up the Vertical Long Array.

South of Kangaroo Island at 4.05 pm, 21 October, three days of successful tests of the new VLA design began. Back in Adelaide on 25th, 10 sea cadets, two instructors, the WRE researchers, and their equipment were all offloaded in three and a half hours. Then the ship sailed at 11.43 am for home.

A deep dredge south of Albany at 38 degrees 25' S, 118 degrees 07' E at 8.05 am, 28 October, brought up sea urchins and manganese nodules from 5,300m. Two days later, at 1.30 pm, *Diamantina* berthed at No.1, North Quay. The samples went to DNR, Canberra, the crew began the long leave and maintenance period. On 30 October the successful year of far-ranging cruises into the Indian and Pacific Ocean was over.

1978

In a sombre prelude to the cruise season, the captain and crew -members, on 10 February, attended the funeral of ABMTP C.J. Swayn. Swayn's body had been found floating astern of the ship at 6 pm, 6 February. He had been absent since 1 February. Police investigations found no suspicious circumstances. At 9.06 am, 15 February, AB Swayn's ashes were scattered from the ship into Gage Roads in the presence of the ship's company and his family. As the bereaved family went ashore in a HMAS *Leeuwin* boat, *Diamantina* proceeded to sea on final sea trials. These included a 40/60 shoot which destroyed a 44 gallon drum. Course was then set to work up at Albany. From 16 February the crew exercised from Frenchman's Bay. At 7.59 am, 20 February, the ship sailed to take a core in the Fremantle Canyon. A thirteen and a half hour operation produced only one core. The vessel was tied up at No.3 North Quay at 9.02 am, 22 February.

Three days later the year's bad start continued when two sailors were seriously injured in a motorcycle accident.

Five Material Research Laboratory staff were aboard when *Diamantina* sailed at 8.30 am, 28 February. MRL Cruise 1/78's aim was to examine, to a depth of 4,000m, metals, nutrients, and dissolved oxygen, to as far north as the waters of the Java Trench area. The study involved 11 stations over 14 days in a racetrack pattern with its northern extremity 95 miles north north-west of Christmas Island.

Stations took an average time of four hours daily between 1 and 11 March. Water depths sampled ranged from 1,000 to 4,000m. As well as the water collected in Nansen bottles, a Phleger Corer took samples on stations 9, 10, and 11. The result on the first was not good. Better cores resulted on the other two when a squash ball was adapted to act as a core catcher. On the way home, the full power trial produced a speed of 19.5 knots. The successful cruise ended at A Berth, Victoria Quay, at 11.26 am, 12 March.

In the days following the Family Day on 21 March, five RANRL and three MRL researchers boarded with their equipment. Then the ship sailed at 10 am, 28 March, for Adelaide. En route, in a first for the area, the RANRL team measured volume reverberation and propagation while the MRL scientists collected information on marine life, water density, and salinity variations. The acoustic work involved the ship stopping every evening for six hours around sunset to fire small explosive charges. Excellent Phleger cores were obtained at 5,000m depth using a *Diamantina* manufactured brass core catcher to supersede the squash ball. The crew's ingenuity would soon be needed in another field. The Satellite Navigation Unit was soon to be transferred to HMAS *Flinders*, with an obvious effect on location accuracy.

South-east of Port Lincoln, at 36 degrees 14' S, 134 degrees 31' E, a RAAF Orion co-operated with the RANRL team on 2 April in acoustic propagation measurements. After a final water sample and core, the ship tied up at Outer Port Adelaide at 8 am, next day.

Here equipment for Project Taniwha (named for a mythical Maori water monster) came aboard. As the Vertical Line Array was loaded, hydraulic rams were fitted to the quarterdeck A frames. When all was aboard, *Diamantina* sailed for Sydney at 6 pm, 6 April. Twice on the way the ship tested launching and recovering the VLA. At Garden Island's Fitting Out Wharf from 10 April, more equipment, including a Horizontal

GOR 266 leaving Sydney in 1978. The single Bofors forward of the enclosed bridge is above the scientists' accommodation. The white Boolee container laboratory is aft of the funnel sporting its 'Western Australian Navy' black swan. (RAN)

Planar Array (HPA) came aboard. Three American scientists from Silver Springs also embarked. [Silver Springs, Maryland, is home for the United States National Oceanographic and Atmospheric Administration (NOAA)].

LCDR Cooke-Russell invited another visitor aboard. CDR M.G. Rose, RANR (Ret.), *Diamantina*'s first Commanding Officer, relived his memories of the ship. The current captain had another link with his visitor - he had served on HMAS *Warramunga* with CDR Rose's son Dennis.

The ship sailed at 1.30 pm, 14 April for the first leg of Project Taniwha. A 40/60 anti-aircraft firing was completed on the way to Site A at 39 degrees S, 154 degrees E (SE of Cape Howe). Here, in deteriorating sea conditions, measurements were carried out with a United States Orion aircraft. The worsening sea conditions then forced the ship to the sheltered waters in and around Jervis Bay to continue the HPA sea-handling trials. *Diamantina* began her return to Site A at 2 pm, 18 April. At 3.48 am, next day, *Diamantina* rendezvoused with HMNZS *Tui* on site. The continuing bad weather prevented launching of the arrays, and forced the ships to proceed north to a new Site B east of Brisbane at 27 degrees S, 154 degrees 40' E. On passage, *Diamantina* trailed a large helium balloon (Kitoon) at 900 feet (c. 300m) supporting an aerial for the HPA.

On 21 April, from 3.10 am to 8 pm, the ships continued the trials programme with the frigate launching and recovering the VLA and HPA. The next morning both tied up at No. 1 Berth, New Farm for a busy four days. The usual calls were made on the Lord Mayor and Governor. The latter had more than the usual interest. Sir James Ramsay had had *Diamantina* under his charge when he had been NOCWA. Anzac Day was the high point of the visit with 65 of the ship's company taking part in the march. *Tui* also participated.

The day before, 15 members of the Queensland Maritime Museum had visited the ship. LCDR Cooke-Russell later reported, ...*The Museum is interested in acquiring* Diamantina *after she pays off and laying her up in the South Brisbane Dock.* He went on,

Tasman Sea - Underwater acoustic propagation studies. (RAN)

This would be an appropriate end to a ship that started her active life in Queensland waters 33 years ago.

At 4 pm, 26 April, the ships sailed for Site B. Work with the HPA and VLA began with the launching of the former at 6.44 am, next day. The array's performance was monitored over the following two days. Late on 29 April, ABTMP Drummond's wedding ring caught in an upper deck fitting, injuring his finger. Work was suspended, and the ship steamed to rendezvous with the pilot vessel, *Matthew Flinders*, off Mooloolaba and transfer the injured sailor for treatment ashore. Then the trials ships turned for Site C.

Here, far out in the Coral Sea, east of Townsville, at 18 degrees 30' S, 154 degrees E, the tests went on. In poor weather, from 6 am, 1 May, to 8 a.m, on the 4th, the ships worked with the HPA and VLA arrays, sonobuoys, and the JPI projector. Then, after taking seawater samples and a bottom core, *Diamantina* headed for Auckland. It wasn't a rushed trip. In a drift over Three Kings' Bank the ship's fishermen hauled enough aboard to provide two meals for the entire ship's company.

At E Berth, Calliope Wharf, Devonport, from 9 am, 10 May, all the HPA equipment was unloaded for Silver Springs, and SUS charges transferred to *Tui* for Taniwha's second stage. *Diamantina* followed its companion to sea at 2 pm, 17 May. At Site D, south-east of Norfolk Island, at 30 degrees 30' S, 176 degrees E, from 19-24 May, the VLA was twice laid and recovered. The acoustic experiments included firing three rounds from a self- loading rifle into the sea at 7.01 pm on 21 May. An appendicitis case on *Tui* forced the cancellation of Site E while both ships sped for Karerarera Bay in the Bay of Islands.

Work resumed at Site F, east of Kermadec Island, at 32 degrees 15' S, 174 degrees E, at 12.47 pm, 28 May. Here, in periods when quiet was essential, all machinery was shut down. The VLA was recovered at 8.28 am, 29 May. Then *Diamantina* joined *Tui* in searching for a lost United States autobuoy (a free-floating submersible array). *Diamantina* found the $US700,000 buoy after three hours, and it was safely re-stowed on *Tui*. Deteriorating weather ended Taniwha at 3 pm, next day. The ship tied up in Auckland at 4.51 pm, 31 May.

Diamantina sailed for Hobart at 8.58 am, 3 June. In three days there from the 8th, the ship refuelled and the crew enjoyed leave. Then it was south around Tasmania to reach Adelaide at 6.52 am, 14 June. In less than five hours the VLA equipment was unloaded and the ship sailed for Fremantle. The cruise ended at 10.57 am, 18 June. After the Annual Inspection between 20-23 June, the mid winter leave period began on 26th.

Garden Island Destroyer Wharf was the ship's location in the log entry for 26 July. But it wasn't in Sydney. *Diamantina* was the first ship at the new base on Cockburn Sound, south of Fremantle. The ship's company was happy to move there. Home porting in the busy commercial harbour at Fremantle had meant many changes of berth. HMAS *Stirling*'s commissioning from 10.15 am, 28 July, had *Diamantina* playing a prominent role. The ship, dressed overall, with the crew manning the port side, was the backdrop of the ceremony - the Navy's oldest ship opening its newest base.

The veteran had a visitor that month. Murray McFarlane of Naracoorte, South Australia, one of only thirty 1945 commissioning crewmembers to serve aboard throughout that commission, returned to his old ship. In *the proudest day of my life*, the former 18-year-old radar operator and Mrs. McFarlane were piped aboard for lunch with the captain in his cabin.

The ship sailed from its new base at 9 am, 31 July for a 12-weeks scientific cruise to the Tasman Sea and South Fiji Basin. From 7-11 August preparations for RANRL

Experiment 28/78 went on in Sydney. Among the equipment loaded was the Satellite Navigation System, returned from HMAS *Flinders*. Depth recording runs between Norah Head and Sydney revealed a fault in the EDO echo sounder. In five hours at Garden Island on 12 July, this was fixed. Back at the Fitting Out Wharf three days later, microbubble measuring equipment, and the radiolocation fixing aid, Raydist, were installed. In the afternoon of the 18th, the microbubble and some scientists were landed at Watson's Bay. The ship then proceeded to sea where tests showed Satnav, Raydist, and EDO to be performing well. The Precision Depth Recorder needed further adjustments.

At Garden Island from 25 August the ship loaded equipment for the Joint Australian and New Zealand Sea Test, and the USA Heat Capacity Mapping Mission (USAHCMM). It was not all work. On 3 September at 3 pm, Amanda Marie Walkley was christened on board.

USAHCMM, WRE, and RANRL scientists were on board when *Diamantina* sailed at 9 am, 4 September. There was another supernumerary aboard - LCDR R.J. Burns, GM, RAN, the commanding officer designate. The planned anti-aircraft practice shoot in Exercise Area R 47 9 was cancelled when the aircraft did not arrive at the appointed time. The ship then turned south-east to begin USAHCMM en route to Auckland. A Geomagnetic Electro Kinetograph (GEK) was streamed throughout the passage, and water temperature and salinity were continuously monitored. Until 1.30 am, 8 September, the ship launched Expendable Bathythermographs (XBTs) hourly, and when else needed to locate the boundary between the warm northern and cool southern water masses.

In Auckland from 10 September, to prepare for a study of the acoustic properties of the Coral Sea the ship met up again with *Tui*. As well, it loaded a variety of stores needed for a survey of Funafuti atoll, Tuvalu (formerly the Ellice Islands). The New Zealand Hydrographer provided much appreciated copies of USS *Pathfinder's* 1943 survey. With sinkers for channel buoys unable to be located, the crew used a cement mixer to make 20 on the wharf. These performed every bit as well as the small number of conventional ones located and delivered just five minutes before sailing.

LCDR Burns left on 13 September, before the ship sailed for Site X-Ray north-east of Lord Howe Island at 30 degrees S, 163 degrees E. Here *Diamantina* towed a noise projector for a RAAF Orion. After a break to transfer stores and mail to *Tui* on the 16th, the work continued until shortly before arrival at Suva on the 22nd. At King's Wharf the ship refuelled. A survey party, which had flown to Fiji to join the ship, consisting of former commanding officer, LCDR P.G. Brook and a Petty Officer Surveyor came aboard with a Motorola MRS3 Mini Ranger, and a Ratheon 719 Portable Echo Sounder. In a stroke of luck, the Commander of the Royal Fijian Maritime Force, CDR S.B. Brown, MBE, who had detailed local knowledge of Funafuti, accepted an invitation to join the survey.

From 25 to 30 September the ship assisted the specialists in carrying out a sketch survey of Funafuti Lagoon prior to the arrival of larger warships for the Tuvalu Independence Celebrations. It was not all work. Calls were made on the 25th, and, next evening, the crew enjoyed the dress rehearsal of the independence celebrations.

The survey parties worked from two boats from early Monday morning, 25 September, to the evening of the next day marking channels and shoals. *Pathfinder's* wartime work was found to be quite accurate, and a number of World War II bases secured the moorings and guys of the three red and one green leading marks, and seven red, four green, and one yellow buoys laid. On 27 and 28 September *Diamantina* replenished the Fijian minesweepers, *Kula*, and *Kiro* in Funafuti anchorage. Time was also found for community aid projects. Crewmembers rebuilt a 40 h.p. outboard motor and removed half a sunken freighter from the approach to Funafuti's barge landing. (The other half was left for HMAS *Perth*) But what was most immediately appreciated was the double feature film show the ship staged for a crowd of 600 in the open-air cinema.

At 8.03 am on 29 September, *Diamantina* sailed to meet USS *Benjamin Stoddert* and HMAS *Perth*. Commander Brown joined the American vessel, and LCDR Brook the Australian. With both safely in the anchorage, LCDR Brook returned aboard, and, at 10.20 am, course was set for Suva.

So ended, in her second last year of active life, an episode with echoes of the ship's first year. Tuvalu, which celebrated its independence two days after *Diamantina* left, had been, when the ship had visited Tarawa in the Gilbert Islands in 1945, part of the colony of the Gilbert and Ellice Islands.

Engine failure on *Tui* ended an expensive and disappointing test series. After four days in Suva, *Diamantina* sailed for Lautoka on 4 October. There, before sailing next afternoon, the ship took all Australian equipment from her New Zealand consort. Five scientists and their equipment landed in Melbourne between 12-15 October. On the 16th, in Adelaide the Defence Research Centre material went ashore in two hours. The cruise ended at A Berth, Victoria Quay, at 9.15 am, 21 October.

Five days later, at 11.59 pm on 26 October, LCDR R. J. Burns, GM, RAN, assumed command. Burns, a highly qualified naval diver, from August 1967 to February 1968 had commanded Clearance Diving Team 3 in Viet Nam. He had earned his George Medal on 3 June 1969. The citation reads: *Robert James Burns was a Lieutenant in the RAN, stationed aboard HMAS* Melbourne. *During the morning of 3.6.1969, Lt. Burns was on a RAN vessel, the aircraft carrier HMAS* Melbourne, *in the South China Sea, some 240 odd miles East South East of Saigon, involved in an exercise with the USN destroyer, USS* Frank E. Evans, *when the two vessels were involved in a collision.*

The call to emergency stations was sounded at 0315 hours, and Lt. Burns proceeded to his appointed station on the quarterdeck. There he saw an injured American sailor struggling and floundering in the ocean, desperately calling for help. He was in immediate danger of drowning. With complete disregard for his own safety, and while HMAS Melbourne *was still moving, and without knowledge of the rescue attempts being organised, Lt. Burns unhesitatingly dived over the side of the aircraft carrier and swam to the now exhausted sailor and rendered assistance to him keeping him afloat and towing him to a nearby life raft which had been released by HMAS* Melbourne. *After hauling the sailor into the life raft, Lt. Burns then tended to the man's injuries.*

Lt. Burns then dived back into the water and swam some 200 yards to the assistance of a second American sailor who was also injured, and was again successful in towing this man to the safety of another life raft where he once more rendered essential first aid. Then hearing more cries for help coming in from the darkness, he left the life raft and swam out to sea, endeavouring to locate the person calling for assistance, and making sure that no one was missed and left behind in the water. This time he was unsuccessful in locating any further persons.

On the Public Works Slipway from 7-27 November, a full hull survey reported *ship in good condition.* The day before unslipping, Danielle Peta, daughter of LSMTP Miller was christened on board.

So, the year that began sombrely with a funeral, ended with the celebration of a new life. In between, the ship had made contact with its past, and assisted in the birth of both a new Navy base, and a new nation. On balance, it had been a satisfying year.

1979

The annual musketry practice on 15 January preceded the resumption of full naval routine 11 days later. The next day, 27 January, saw two events that were not routine. LCDR Burns was called to treat a civilian male suffering from the 'bends'. The more disturbing event was an abnormal rise in water level in the ship's bilges necessitating a visit by a civilian septic truck to pump them out.

Trials on the last two days of January and the first two of February included testing the Precision Depth Recorder, and gun function. All were successful. From 5-9 February 'infiltrators' from Clearance Diving Team 4 enlivened the midnight watches. All were apprehended, except for the last group whose only trace logged was *wet footprints seen*. To hands with a sense of history it stirred memories of the World War II Z Force raid on the ship in Maryborough. Clearance Diver Burns commented on the incursions, *Both sides learned a lot from the exercises*. He went on to comment cryptically, *...they resulted in one simple solution to the problem of unauthorised entry*.

On 12 February, *Diamantina* sailed for Adelaide. There, from the 16th, Defence Research Centre personnel and their equipment came aboard. The media - at least six local newspapers and four TV channels - paid particular attention to one scientist - Mrs. S. Ball. The first woman scientist to sail on the ship was also celebrating her birthday. This presented an irresistible temptation to some unknown press officer. A press release informed the media *Diamantina* had baked a cake for the occasion. When the reporters descended on the ship on Monday morning to see the cake, a previously unaware LCDR Burns had to do some hasty improvisation. (Murray McFarlane of the commissioning crew disputed the press's assertion that Mrs. Ball was the first woman given permission to sleep aboard a RAN ship. He recalled *Diamantina* had carried the Solomon Islands wife of a New Ireland soldier when his platoon took passage for leave in November 1945. The crew decorated the after gun shelter with palm leaves and chalked 'Honeymoon Cottage' on it. Native drums and Snowy Kilburn's saxophone serenaded the couple)

Mrs. Ball and the other three less newsworthy DRC team members sailed at 11.18, Monday morning, 19 February. Weapons Scientific Research Laboratory Trial 1/79 measured currents and temperatures from 38 degrees South until arrival in Sydney. From one minute after midnight, 22 February, until the final readings were taken 100 miles north-east of Sydney on 1 March, the researchers worked with expendable bathythermographic probes (XBTs) and the Geomagnetic Electrokinetograph (GEK) from 150 to 158 degrees E, and between 38 and 34 degrees S. A RAAF Orion P3 aircraft also took part.

During the first night the Orion made two low runs on *Diamantina* in which it suddenly illuminated the ship in its powerful searchlight. Burns then directed it to surprise the nearby HMAS *Ibis*. He had been her Executive Officer in 1965. The aircraft found a radar contact and 'sneaked up' to suddenly flood the minesweeper with light. The RAAF crew's embarrassment was matched by the shock of the watchkeepers on the Japanese merchantman suddenly transfixed in the glare, while little *Ibis* sailed on in the dark nearby.

A meeting next morning with the freighter *Lake Eildon* while *Diamantina* was carrying out a 'man overboard' exercise had the merchantman cheekily signal the veteran warship, "You're a picture straight out of Victory at Sea" [A popular TV series on the World War II naval war]. When heavy fog closed in at 10.10 am, the two ships sailed in company until it cleared three hours later. Then *Diamantina* trumped the cocky freighter. The old frigate used her state-of-the-art Satellite Navigation System to find their precise position, and passed it to *Lake Eildon* before sailing off - another victory at sea.

The WSRL equipment and researchers landed in Sydney after the ship docked at 9.33 am, 1 March. The captain's report on the presence of the *lady scientist* included, *...the only noticeable change...[was]...a definite toning down of bad language*. He concluded, *I see no problems if females are embarked for future cruises*.

With SUS charges and hydrophones embarked, the ship sailed on RANRL Trial 9/79 at 9.15 am, 5 March. The captain reported next day that the cruise, plagued by bad weather and equipment malfunctions, was of *little value*.

With WSRL equipment re-embarked, there was time for a Family Day and bubble gear trials on 7 March, before *Diamantina* sailed next day to carry out WSRL Trial 2/79 en route to Adelaide. A leak in an air-conditioner sea tube forced a return to No. 2 Woolloomooloo. On 12 March, Clearance Diving Team 1 members attempted unsuccessfully to stop the inflow. The ship's divers then went down. In three hours the Commanding Officer and Executive Officer completed the repairs. The ship resumed its voyage at 2.30 pm, next day.

In three days in Adelaide from 7.48 am, Friday, 16 March, the Boolee array was loaded. The ship then sailed for home at 12.56 pm, 19 March. It was a day earlier than planned. *A major drop in morale* was the reason for the captain's haste. The causes included problems with a senior sailor, rumours of the ship's uncertain future and its replacement's possible Eastern States home- port. But the major unsettling factor was the anxiety of crewmembers who lived in the Rockingham Married Quarters. Their wives were disturbed by two recent murders nearby, and the activities of a prowler. Burns ended his March Report of Proceedings, *I consider that unless the prowler is caught and a definite statement is made on the ship's future before mid-April, there will be a major welfare and morale problem during the April to August deployment*. The ship arrived at the Submarine Wharf at 6.30 pm, 23 March, and four weeks of maintenance and leave began.

When *Diamantina* sailed on 26 April on the four-month deployment, morale was no longer a problem. Although the prowler had not been caught, he was no longer active. As well, a number of compassionate postings had been completed. The price of some key billets being filled by new personnel, or even not at all, was accepted. Scientists from CSIRO, RANRL, and WSRL were aboard along with the Boolee array and CSIRO equipment for the First Garp Global Experiment (FGGE). The captain wrote: *Scientific equipment for the FGGE Cruise was fitted and set to work during the period 21st to 25th. Some CSIRO gear was embarked and placed in the large shipping container on the starboard side. A second, smaller container full of RANRL equipment was loaded onto the port side of the iron deck, aft of the Boolee generator. Other RANRL gear was set up in the laboratory and on the Boolee platform. The meteorological office was fitted with a number of special instruments for the FGGE experiment. The meteorological instruments were provided by the World Meteorological Organisation and came as a complete package, even down to deck chairs and card tables! As sailing time approached the upper deck of the ship closely resembled the upper deck of a coastal trader. On the starboard side was a large yellow sea container and on the port side a smaller container in Army green. 71 cylinders of helium were lashed around convenient parts of the upper deck and 'elephant hut' while on the iron deck twenty drums of lubricating oil were lashed where ever space allowed. The gun deck was home to an ozone sampling machine and two CSIRO drifting sea buoys. The quarterdeck was covered in water sampling devices, current meters, microbubble frames, hydrophones, and miles of electrical cable on an assortment of drums and reels; none of which could be fitted into the already overcrowded laboratory or full shipping containers.*

(*Diamantina* regularly embarked containers. The Weapons Research Establishment had one painted white, air-conditioned, and equipped as a laboratory. It was secured on *Diamantina*'s upper deck for the WRE's *...underwater acoustic research programmes...aimed at gathering a better understanding of the phenomena affecting undersea sound propagation over great distances*)

Diamantina's 34th birthday was celebrated next day on the FGGE's first station west of Geraldton at 28 degrees 36.5' S, 113 degrees 29' E, during microbubble and current observations. After a diversion to Port Hedland to embark a replacement for a CPOMTP3 posted off just before sailing, month's end found the ship drifting for 12 hours on a FGGE station near Rowley Shoals at 18 degrees 28' S, 120 degrees E. With no fuel available at either Christmas Island or Jakarta, *Diamantina* refuelled at Singapore. During the two days port stay, an Australian National University scientist and an RANRL researcher joined the ship.

After sailing on 9 May, RANRL 1/79 and FGGE Leg 2 took measurements from the upper atmosphere to the ocean depths. The ship ranged as far as 5 degrees N, 92 degrees E (off northern Sumatra) before returning to Singapore on Monday, 21 May. In this four-day stay five CSIRO researchers replaced those from the RANRL and ANU. As well, damage from a minor engine room switchboard fire was repaired, and the captain addressed the crew *on security and alcohol problems*

FGGE Leg 3, *a very thorough and professional cruise* began on 28 May. Before it ended at 10 am, 5 June, the five CSIRO researchers had taken current and water quality readings over an ocean area west of central and northern Sumatra from 4 degrees 30' S, 92 degrees E to 5 degrees N, 95 degrees E. Every 30 miles the ship stopped to make Nansen and Niskin Current Meter casts. As well, every 15 miles, expendable bathythermographs (XBTs) went over the side. *Stations of interest* were probed with expendable salinity bathythermographs (XSBTs). During this busy time, maintenance went on. Readjustment of restriction tubes improved boiler fuel combustion. And completely stripping and descaling the evaporator increased daily output from 18 to 25 tons.

LCDR Burns, in his May Report of Proceedings, added his voice to previous captains, *The ship's company is taking a keen interest in the disposal of the ship after decommissioning. At least three organisations are known to be interested in acquiring* Diamantina*...I believe it would gain great public support and goodwill for the Navy if the ship was handed over to one of these organisations as opposed to being used as a weapons target or being sold for scrap.*

Back in Singapore on 8 June, *Diamantina* tied up at No. 6 Berth, Sembawang, to USS *Robinson* at 9.01 am. USS *Safeguard*, a 2,000 tons salvage ship, was nearby; 10 days later the ship sailed with Dr. J. Bye of Flinders University aboard to take surface samples and XBT readings en route to Darwin. On 25 June, with *Diamantina* in Darwin this time beside *Safeguard*, the CSIRO team disembarked. Boolee and 10 WSRL researchers took their places. The captain, after making his calls, flew to conferences in Sydney and Canberra on the ship's decommissioning. The Minister for Defence, Mr. D.J. Killen, had made the long awaited announcement on 11 June. *Diamantina* would decommission at Garden Island, Sydney, on a day to be fixed in December.

The ship sailed for Boolee Trials at 10 am, 2 July. Next day at Site P, east of Timor at 9 degrees 58.6' S, 126 degrees 19.7' E the array was streamed for tests involving a P3 aircraft. Two days later, with Boolee at 300m, HMAS *Aware* towed a 'Banjo' sound source and dropped charges while the P3 joined in with other charges. On 6 July, the ship began Task H - array motion studies. With Boolee initially at 300m depth, the ship set the array *sinuating between 070T and 090T at different depths*. There was an unforeseen result from this test. When the array was recovered on 9 July, teeth were found embedded in its tail, from what the captain identified as *…now a 'gummy shark'*.

Early that evening the ship increased speed when CPO O'Callaghan suffered a suspected angina attack. An ambulance met the ship early next morning to take him to hospital. Two days later *Diamantina* sailed for Cairns. It was an eventful cruise.

At 5.30 am, Saturday, 14 July, as he later reported, the captain was awakened by *a brew in the face*. A sailor enjoying a hot drink in the wheelhouse moved his chair. When a leg broke through a wasted section of deck, both sailor and brew were upended. The hot cocoa cascaded through the hole onto the face of the captain, asleep in his bunk below. It was an 'in your face' reminder of the ship's age and wear.

Defects in the gyrocompass and radar forced the ship to spend that Saturday and Sunday nights anchored off Cairncross and Stanley Islands near the tip of Cape York. The WSRL technicians joined the ship's electrical staff in working overnight to restore the radar by 6 am, Monday, 16 July. The ship reached Cairns at 9 that evening, 11 hours late. Next day, now only one hour late, *Diamantina* sailed for Boolee Site Q far to the east of Mackay at 19 degrees 30' S, 155 degrees 10' E. Here, on 18 July, investigation of flooding found a corrosion hole and a keel crack between Frames 99 and 100. The trial was aborted, and the ship made for Brisbane.

Diving inspection began at 7 pm, Friday, 20 July, with the ship at anchor in Moreton Bay. Three hours later the Fleet Shipwright Officer, a naval architect, and HMAS *Moreton*'s Engineering Officer joined. From 8.15 to 11 next morning the ship's divers and the RANR diving team continued the assessment. HMAS *Moreton*'s LT A.J. Jacobs, investigating with his diving knife, made another hole in the keel between Frames 98 and 99. The ship then moved to Dalgety's Wharf for urgent docking. From 7.30 pm, Monday 23 July, to 8 pm, next day repairs were carried out in Cairncross Dock. Trials began at 8.30 am the next day.

On 26 July at 8.40 am, Boolee was again streamed at Site Q east of Rockhampton at 23 degrees S, 154 degrees 30' E. A P3 aircraft dropped SUS charges and monitored passing ships, while HMAS *Kimbla*, another product of Walkers Shipyard powered by a steam reciprocating engine, towed a sound source. The trials provided *very useful information*. There was one more addition to the voyage's misfortunes. At 8 am, 30 July, eight hours before Boolee was recovered, the vessel was pooped with resulting damage and flooding. Next morning the ship anchored in Watson's Bay at 11.21.

At Site R on 1 August, *Diamantina* deployed the two and a half mile long Boolee array in surface and deep streams, and straight and sinuating runs. Until this successful exercise ended at 11.22 am, 5 August, *Kimbla* again towed its noise source, while the submarine, HMAS *Onslow*, monitored ships, and made submerged runs across the array.

In three hours off Sydney on 6 August, *Diamantina* demonstrated Boolee to 14 senior scientists from Canberra, the Royal Australian Navy Research Laboratory, and the Weapons Scientific Research Laboratory. Then, at 2.10 next afternoon she sailed for Adelaide. There, in three days from the 10th Boolee was landed. The cruise ended at HMAS *Stirling*'s Submarine Wharf at 9 am, 13 August.

While the ship lay at the wharf throughout the month, two notable events took place ashore. On 15 August, the captain presented the Fremantle Golf Club's major trophy to its 1979 winner. Donated by the ship's company in 1964, the Diamantina Cup is still contested annually. Then, on 28 August, over 300 persons attended *Diamantina*'s Decommissioning Ball.

CHAPTER 9

DIAMANTINA COMES HOME

In Sydney in late August Garden Island's Acting General Manager called for comments on a proposal to preserve *Diamantina* in a dry berth at Garden Island. On 4 September the Superintending Naval Architect submitted an outline of necessary work. It was in vain for in the event the ship returned to Queensland. HMAS *Stirling*'s ship's company lined the wharf and cheered ship as *Diamantina* sailed for Fremantle at 8.58 am, 1 October. Today *Stirling*'s main wharf bears *Diamantina*'s name. Sailing from Fremantle, her old home-port, on the last Family Day next morning, the veteran ship attracted a lot of press and TV attention. Not so successful were the last public inspections. In three hours on the afternoons of 6/7 October, only 45 and 133 visitors came aboard.

But, in spite of poor weather on 9 October, the final farewell was a rousing one. NOCWA (Commodore R.H. Percy) and the Premier of Western Australia (Sir Charles Court) both visited the ship and remained on the wharf for the sailing. For Sir Charles it was the end of an association that dated from well before *Diamantina* had arrived in the West over 20 years before. As a young Army officer in Bougainville he had seen the frigate many times in 1945. But to most West Australians it was *Diamantina*'s 20 years as the Navy's presence in their state, so remote from the centres of population and power in the East, that had endeared 'The Grey Ghost of the West Coast' to them. The ship had another title - 'The West Australian Navy'. For decades she had, against strict Navy regulations, proudly flaunted this status with black swans on her funnel. In this Western Australian festive year the WAY 79 logo had replaced them.

The Navy's last World War II survivor's paying off pennant had to be a compromise. Its length, if calculated by the correct formula, would have made it a hazard not only to other ships, but also to low- flying aircraft. So it was limited to 100m supported by two helium balloons. To the strains of the Fifth Field Force's pipes and drums playing the Evita hit adapted to 'Don't Cry For Me, Diamantina' and 'Auld Lang Syne,' the 105-man crew took their ship out of the Swan River for the last time.

Heavy following seas and gales sped *Diamantina* across the Bight in an uneventful passage. A steering motor failure with 20 degrees of starboard wheel on approaching Bradley's Head in Sydney Harbour at 8.49 am, on Tuesday 16 October, meant the ship had to be steered by engines to No.3 Buoy for deammunitioning. At Garden Island the ship prepared for RANRL Trial 16A/79. The veteran had other duties as well. On the weekends of 19, 20, and 26, 27 October she was, as the only vessel capable of putting to sea, duty ship.

RANRL Trial 16A/79 to measure seasonal variations in volume reverberation in Eddy J (33 degrees 30' S, 153 degrees 30' E) was successfully carried out from 22-27 October. The captain did comment, however, on a particularly awkward 450 kg, 2x1.5 metres Canadian cone hydrophone. The 'witch's hat' proved prone to failure, but did make a good sea anchor. Two female RANRL researchers and a female naval architect sailed on the cruise. Miss Shapcott, the naval architect, took turns at the wheel. On return to Garden Island, lower deck was cleared at 8.17 am, Saturday the 27th, for the presentation of her 'Helmsperson Certificate.'

A helium balloon supports the paying off pennant as *Diamantina* departs Fremantle for the last time. The Western Australia anniversary flag flies from the starboard yard. Between the whip antennas and the 'elephant hut' the Boolee control cabin looms over its reel. (RAN)

RANRL Trial 13/79, after a practice on the last day of October, laid two cables with hydrophones on 8 November from two miles east of Sydney Heads to Lady Bay. The preludes to decommissioning went on among the work. On 17 October the 40/60 gun had gone ashore. On the evening of 8 November, the Diamantina Shield, keenly contested by the messes on many tedious voyages, was presented to Senator John Knight representing the Diamantina Scout Troop at Kalleen High School, Canberra.

Between 12-19 November, the Boolee winch, control hut, drum, and after platform were removed. Then, from 19-23 November, *Diamantina* successfully carried out its last research task. In RANRL 14A/79 the ship worked at sea and in Broken Bay with M.V. *Sieglinde* in propagation trials using XBTs, charges, and hydrophones.

At 5.30 am, Friday, 23 November, *Diamantina* weighed anchor in Broken Bay for Sydney. In the Harbour, near Number 2 Buoy, 130 guests came aboard for the final Harbour cruise. They ranged from the first commanding officer, CDR M.G. Rose, RANR (Ret.), through members of historical societies to leaders, cubs, and scouts from the Diamantina Scout Group. CDR Rose spent much of the time on the bridge in the same captain's chair Walkers had made to his specifications in Maryborough 35 years before.

The first and the last. In the chair Walkers built to his specifications Maurice Rose chats to LCDR Robert Burns during *Diamantina's* farewell Sydney Harbour cruise. (RAN)

The paying off pennant, supported by six helium filled meteorological balloons, had to be dipped when passing under the Harbour Bridge and turning near Goat Island. Other ocean going vessels, ferries, and even a train crossing the bridge, sounded their sirens in farewell salutes. The cruise ended when the ship secured, bows north, at Garden Island's North-east Cruiser Wharf at 10.32 am.

That evening LCDR Burns hosted a cocktail party and buffet supper for *Diamantina's* former captains. All, except the second, LCDR PJ Sullivan, had been located. Of the 13 invited, seven attended, and their wives represented two others. CDR Rose was accompanied by his daughter. She had first visited the brand new ship as a seven-year-old in 1945.

Three days later a laconic log entry recorded, *1600 all personnel cleared of messdecks. Duty watch only accommodation on board.* While the ship remained at Garden Island, most of the ship's company dispersed to leave and postings. By month's end most stores had followed them, and pumping had reduced fuel stocks to 39%.

In his November Report of Proceedings LCDR Burns's feelings for *Diamantina* came through. Under the heading 'Engineering and Electrical he wrote, *All main and auxiliary machinery continues to function in a most satisfactory manner. Proof of the robustness and reliability of steam reciprocating machinery.* In the 'Decommissioning' section he noted, *The ship's excellent stability characteristics were found to be a nuisance on Thursday 1st [Dec.] when it became necessary to heel the ship to caulk a small oil leak from a join in the shell plating. 26 tons of portable weights were embarked and stowed outboard on the upperdeck before the ship acquired the required three and a half degrees list.*

On 19 December, the colours were half-masted for the funeral of ABCK J.L.Pardon. He had been shot in Adelaide at 12.30 am, the day before. LCDR Burns relinquished command to LT R.A. Diciunas on 14 January 1980. On Leap Year Day, 29 February 1980, *Diamantina* was decommissioned. Transferred to Active Reserve in the custody of the Commanding Officer Reserve Ships, the ship moved to Athol Bight across the Harbour. There the ship, *too bloody good for razor blades* with engines, in the words of former commander, James Buchanan, and Norman Rivett, *fine and rare working examples of a design which was the pinnacle of 160 years of development of steam engines at sea*, awaited its fate.

In early August 1980, the Officer in Charge, Fleet Maintenance Party, was ordered to assess whether preparing the ship to steam to the Queensland Maritime Museum in Brisbane was practically and financially possible. The order passed down the chain of command to lodge in the hands of Warrant Officer Engineer, Jack Cox. Years later, in retirement, he recalled, *It is probably fair to say I may have been somewhat biased in the decision, as I had served on* Barcoo, *a sister ship, during the war.* Jack Cox's answer was the already very busy Fleet Maintenance Party would accept the challenge to get the ship, already on 'Rotten Row' (the scrap line), and stripped of some machinery, ready for sea. There was no shortage of volunteers for the onerous task.

So, on 27 August, 1980, the Prime Minister, Mr. Malcolm Fraser, announced the gift of *Diamantina* to the Queensland Maritime Museum Association. The Queensland built ship, named after the Queensland river bearing the name of the wife of the State's first Governor, was going home.

On Wednesday, 1 October, 1980, while the Navy Band played, the Museum's President, Dr. G. R. McLeod, presented the ship's last Naval Ensign to the Commander, Support Command, RADM A.J. Robertson. Then, flying the Red Ensign and the flags of Queensland and the Museum, the ship cast off from Garden Island for the last time. The mixed RAN and Museum crew and the venerable steam engines smoothly brought the ship into Moreton Bay on Saturday, 4 October. There CDR Rose joined for a triumphant progress up the Brisbane River. Six months later the caisson of the South Brisbane Dry Dock closed behind the ship. *Diamantina* settled on the blocks in her final home.

Less than 20 years later the dock caisson (gate) failed. The river flooded in and *Diamantina* was once again afloat. The ship rose and fell with the tides as Museum officials negotiated with authorities. In 2004 the Queensland Government announced a grant to reseal the dock. By the end of 2005, the 60th anniversary year of *Diamantina*'s commissioning, the ship will be resited on blocks in the restored dry dock. The world's last River class frigate and Australia's largest World War II veteran will continue to educate and inspire her visitors and honour her builders and crews.

Anzac Day, Brisbane, 1995 (E. Valler)

APPENDIX 1

HMAS *DIAMANTINA* - LIST OF COMMANDING OFFICERS

LCDR Maurice George ROSE, RANVR	27.4.1945	22.11.1945
LCDR Philip Jack SULLIVAN, RANR (S)	22.11.1945	17.7.1946
LCDR Bruce Dudley GORDON, RAN	22.6.1959	16.3.1960
LCDR George McCallum JUDE, RAN	16.3.1960	7.9.1961
LCDR John Gostwyck YULE, RAN	7.9.1961	7.6.1963
LCDR Richard Bradford NUNN, RAN	7.6.1963	18.1.1964
LCDR Peter Edwin Mansfield HOLLOWAY, RAN	18.1.1964	8.6.1965
LCDR Peter George DUNCAN, RAN	8.6.1965	28.12.1966
LCDR Murray WARD, RAN	28.12.1966	6.1.1969
LCDR James Ellis BUCHANAN, RAN	6.1.1969	16.11.1970
LCDR Michael William VARLEY, RAN	16.11.1970	22.7.1972
LCDR Donald Montgomerie DAVIDSON, RAN	22.7.1972	3.9.1974
LCDR Philip Graham BROOK, RAN	3.9.1974	14.12.1976
LCDR Peter John COOKE-RUSSELL, RAN	14.12.1976	27.10.1978
LCDR Robert James BURNS, GM, RAN	27.10.1978	14.1.1980
LEUT Rimaudas Adolfas DICIUNAS, RAN	14.1.1980	29.2.1980

APPENDIX 2

HMAS *DIAMANTINA* - COMMISSIONING CREW, 27 April 1945

Key

A	Able-bodied Seaman	L	Leading Seaman	O	Ordinary Seaman	S	Stoker
E	Engine Room Artificer	L S	Leading Stoker	P	Petty Officer		

Surname	Given Name	Rating/rank	Surname	Given Name	Rating/rank
Adams	Desmond	A	Bunney	Archibald	S
Anderson	John	O	Burgess	Ronald	Lieutenant
Ash	Arnold	S	Butler	Colin	A
Baillie	William	L S	Campbell	Stanislaus	O
Barrie	John	A	Cannell	Alfred	L
Beard	Edward	Telegraphist	Carter	Sydney	O
Blackadder	Joseph	L S	Carty	Michael	S
Bleakley	Edward	Cook	Cathierwood	Trevor	P
Boxhall	Derwent	O	Church	Geoffrey	A
Brayshaw	James	Chief S	Church	John	Lieutenant
Brown	Hugh	A	Coles	Colin	Coder
Bulfin	Raymond	A	Collins	William	A
Bull	Kenneth	Engineer Lieutenant Commander	Cooper	Donald	A
			Corr	Rex	A

Surname	Given Name	Rating/rank	Surname	Given Name	Rating/rank
Crawford	Fred	Chief P	May	Jack	P
Crowe	Geoffrey	L Sick Berth Attendant	Mearns	Jack	A
Cuckette	Edward	A	Miller	John	A
Currie	Frederick	S	Mitchell	Brian	Signaller
Daly	Thomas	O	Mowatt	Reginald	A
Dickens	Brian	A	Munro	Donald	L Signaller
Doran	Bruce	A	Murray	Francis	S
Elmer	John	E	O'Sullivan	John	L
Ey	Stanley	S	Parkin	Ian	Sub-Lieutenant
Farrell	John	A	Patterson	George	A
Fettes	Rupert	Sick Berth Attendant	Payne	James	A
Fitzgerald	Leonard	S P	Powell	Aeneas	S P
Franklin	Frederick	E	Quinn	Ronald	O
Frost	Thomas	A	Quirke	John	O
Fryer	Alfred	O	Rabbage	Robert	A
Graham	Gerard	S	Reid	William	Lieutenant
Grevell	Arthur	O	Reinke	Cyril	Motor Mechanic
Grimmer	Alan	A	Robinson	James	L Cook
Growther	Colin	A	Robb	James	A
Hains	Ronald	A	Rodwell	Keith	A
Hall	Alfred	S	Romeo	Francis	A
Harold	Laurence	Signaller	Rose	Maurice	Lieutenant Commander
Herd	Ronald	A	Ryland	Keith	A
Hewitt	Albert	A	Sanderson	Charles	S P
Higgins	Douglas	A	Silver	Kenneth	A
Hilbig	Ronald	A	Smith	Gordon	L S
Homann	Harold	A	Spotswood	James	A
Howe	Charles	A	Staple	Eric	A
Hudson	Henry	E	Stewart	Robert	S
Hulford	Neville	A	Stolzenhein	Robert	A
Hull	John	S	Strother	John	A
Hynds	Edward	Chief E	Suters	John	A
Kilburn	Leslie (Snowy)	L S	Taylor	Alan	A
Kirk	George	E	Taylor	Cyril	A
Knight	John	Signaller	Taylor	Daniel	Coder
Kolher	Keith	A	Taylor	Douglas	Cook
Kruger	Edward	Signaller	Taylor	John	O
Lane	Stanley	Telegraphist	Theakstone	Norman	O
Larking	Benjamin	L S	Tugwell	Douglas	A
Lawrie	Robert	A	Valler	Eric	Telegraphist
Layton	Frederick	S P	Vincent	Robert	O
Lewis	Glen	P	Wackwitz	John	L Sick Berth Attendant
Lloyd	Frederick	Chief P	Wade	William	Sick Berth Attendant
Loane	Sydney	A	Waller	John	O
Locke	Reginald	L S	Wallis	David	A
Lythall	Phillip	A	Ward	Denzill	A
McDonald	William D	Cook	Watson	James	L S
McDonald	William E	S	Webb	Jeffrey	S
McFarlane	Roderick (Murray)	O	Webb	Ronald	A
McKendrick	William	Lieutenant	Weinheimer	Stanley	Mechanician
McNab	Colin	S	Weston	Joseph	Wireman
McNee	Robert	A	Whittington	Murray	S
McWhinnie	Kenneth	O	Wicks	Eric	S P
Mace	Kenneth	Steward	Wills	Perry	O
Maher	Kevin	S	Wildman	Douglas	S
Malcolmson	John	Telegraphist	Wilson	John	A
Malone	Ronald	A	Wilson	Leslie	Steward
Mangnall	William	L	Young	Crawford	Telegraphist
Martin	Raymond	A	Younger	Charles	Lieutenant
Mascord	Ronald	P	Zubrenick	Leslie	A

CHRISTENINGS IN HMAS *DIAMANTINA'S* BELL

Mark Overell Tagg ARUNDEL, 26 Jan 1963.
Lisa Michelle BAINBRIDGE-FULLER, 22 Feb 1976
Tania Leanne BAINBRIDGE-FULLER, 22 Feb 1976
Erica Jane BARTLETT, 29 June 1963
Alexandra May BROOK, 23 Dec 1975
Anthony Phillip CLARE, 31 Aug 1975
Timothy Mansfield HOLLOWAY, 8 Nov 1964
Greta McKAY, 22 Feb 1976
Marcus McKAY, 22 Feb 1976

Tammie Cherie SIMMONDS, 12 Sep 1976
Matthew James SULMAN, 1 May 1966
Frayne Ashley SUMMERS, 29 June 1963
Deborah Jane TERRY, 10 April 1960
Alister Charles Ferguson WATSON, 19 Aug 1973
Tiffany Isobel WATSON, 13 Aug 1972
Gareth Andrew WILSON, 11 July 1965
Johanna Hardy YULE, 15 July 1962

Seen from the Queensland Martime Museum's welcoming party's launch, *Diamantina II* approaches the Brisbane River for the first time - December 2002 (W. Rigall)

THE NAME LIVES ON

HMAS *Diamantina II* was commissioned into the Royal Australian Navy on 4 May 2002 at HMAS *Waterhen* on Sydney harbour. Mrs. Maureen Bryden, daughter of CDR Maurice Rose, *Diamantina I's* first commanding officer was the commissioning lady.

Diamantina II was the fifth of six Huon class minehunters to join the fleet. Displacing 720 tons and 52.5m in length the ship is about half the size of its namesake. Six officers, six senior sailors and 27 junior sailors are the normal crew for a vessel that is a world leader in minehunting technology.

Representatives of the Queensland Maritime Museum and of the crew of *Diamantina I* attended the commissioning.

Diamantina II has already had deployments as far afield as South-East Asia and the Solomons. On calls at Brisbane the crew has maintained links with the Queensland Maritime Museum, home of *Diamantina I*, and western Queensland's Diamantina Shire.

Yet it was in Canberra that a prized part of *Diamantina I* was recovered. At a ceremony in the nation's capital scouting official Mr. Peter Burrows (exRN) handed over to the ship's company the Diamantina Shield. He had found the treasured inter-mess trophy, presented on de-commissioning to the Diamantina scout troop in 1979, in a back storeroom. It was soon back in use. In the first new competition the senior sailors edged out the juniors by one stroke in a golf tournament at Jervis Bay.

HMAS Diamantina - Commissioning Ship's Company

LCDR	M. J. Rothwell RAN		LS	A. P. Crowe		AB	S. J. Bennett
			LS	A. Down		AB	J. D. Case
LCDR	D. S. Griffiths RAN		LS	L. P. Dunn		AB	A. Collin
LEUT	N. A. Carn RAN		LS	T. M. Eather		AB	R. E. Corney
LEUT	P. C. Sedgman RAN		LS	S. Ellis		AB	G. M. L. Devitt
SBLT	B. D. Brown RAN		LS	B. W. Kendall		AB	B. C. Fish
SBLT	J. C. Taylor RAN		LS	S. Mantovani		AB	R. K. Free
			LS	J. A. Maynard		AB	D. Hubbard
WO	B. R. D. Wardrop CSM		LS	L. N. Patterson		AB	S. D. Mawer
			LS	C. Premanan		AB	C. J. Reaney
CPO	D. G. Cooke		LS	G. J. Sherrin		AB	S. K. Roberts
CPO	P. T. Coy		LS	J. J. Streeter		AB	P. M. Tori
CPO	M. I. Hurley					AB	C. E. White
CPO	P. C. Morris		AB	K. Amery			
			AB	T. B. Austin			
PO	B. J. Rieusset		AB	C. Baird			
PO	S. Warne		AB	K. Beard			
PO	D. A. Jenner						

(W. Rigall)

Amjah, PO O; 138-9
Andrews, LCdr AA; 56
August Moon; 86
Austin, Lt JS; 49
Australian Army units
    II Corps; 23
    11 Brigade; 36
    23 Brigade; 24
    31/51 Battalion; 44
    Z Special Unit; 17-8, 146
    Special Air Service Regt: 55-6, 62-3, 70
    42 Landing Craft Coy; 44
    ANGAU; 52
Ball, Mrs S; 146-7
Bartlett, Erica; 75
Bartlett, CPO R; 95
Batavia; 109-10
Belcher, RAdm OH; 81
Bird, Flt Lt; 17
Bird, LCdr; 70
Bissett, JA; 36, 45
Blackwell, LAirman BS; 81
Blue, Lt RS; 70
Boase, Cdre NA; 138
Bott, Mr; 45
Bougainville; 22-9
Bowen, Lady Diamantina; 12-13
Bowerbird; 99
Boyd, OD M; 95
Bridgland, JR; 92
Bromley, AB W; 53
Brook, LCdr PG; 122,125, 127, 130,
    144, 154
Brown, Cdr SB; 144
Bruce, D; 125
Bryden, Mrs M; 157
Buchanan, LCdr J; 98, 108, 154
Bull, LCdr K; 17-8, 48
Burgess, Lt R; 49
Burns, LCdr RJ; 144-9, 152, 154
Bye, Dr JA; 92, 98
Cape Hawke; 127
Cardno, Cdr P; 86
Chan, K; 71
Chesterman, Lt H; 16
Chetwynd, Rev CW; 62, 75
Chiffong; 140
Chittleborough, Dr; 75-7
Church, Lt J; 49
Clarke, N; 110-1
Cleodora; 31, 41
Collins, OD P; 84, 88

Cooke-Russell, LCdr PJ; 130, 138,
    142-3, 154
Corkhill, PO; 89
Court, Sir C; 150
Cowper, R; 95
Cox, WO J; 153
Crawford, LCdr R; 103
CSIRO; 54, 56, 58-9, 61, 64-6, 69-71,
    77, 80-4, 90, 92, 95-6, 103, 112,
    116-20, 148
Cude, Mr; 45-6
Dales, OD P; 92-4
Davidson, LCdr DM; 116-7, 120-2, 154
Davis, Fl-Lt B; 33
Day, ABWMG R; 112
De Vries, E; 133
de Vries, POCK JH; 133
Diamantina Deep; 60-1, 65-6, 83
Diaper, D; 137
Diciunas, Lt RA; 152, 154
Dillon, Cdr HW; 78
Donald, T; 97
Dowling, AL; 31
Doyle, H; 61
Doyle, Cdre PH; 115, 122
Drummond, AB; 143
Dunlop, Lt D; 109
Duncan LCdr PG; 81, 86, 88-9, 154
Edwards, POQMG J; 93
Ellis, Sir A; 36-7, 40, 44-46
Evans Deakin; 30, 43
Everingham, IB; 89
Ewing, Dr M; 91
Fields, Gracie; 29
Finlay-Jones, Surg-Lt LR; 24
Fish, Capt WW; 41, 44, 46
Fisher, Prof R; 65
Folkhard, A; 97
Forbes, A/ERA G; 95
Fosse, Capt R; 99
Fowler, Cdr A; 24, 27, 31, 33
Fox-Strangways, Col V; 34, 36, 39
Franklin, Lt W; 49
Georgeff, Dr G; 74
Gibbins, J; 109
Gibson, ABQMG; 93
Gibsone, ABUC KR; 108
Gloucester, HRH Duke of; 24
Gordon, LCdr BD; 54, 57, 61-2, 154
Grettons, Cdr P; 16
Hagmier, Dr E; 68
Hale, FE; 86

Halverson, G; 67
Hamilton, Adm Sir L; 52
Hamon, B; 70, 96
Hann, LS AV; 82
Harper, W; 85
Harrington, SurgLt; 67
Harris, RAdm DH; 54
Hawkins, Prof LV; 91, 102
Hay, PO W; 138-9
Hennion, J; 61
HMAS *Acute*; 130
HMAS *Adroit*; 129
HMAS *Anzac*; 61, 74
HMAS *Arunta*; 52
HMAS *Assail*; 120-1
HMAS *Attack*; 122
HMAS *Aware*; 148
HMAS *Balmain*; 12
HMAS *Barcoo*; 12, 53
HMAS *Barwon*; 12
HMAS *Bass*; 81-2
HMAS *Bataan*; 50
HMAS *Bowen*; 14
HMAS *Bunbury*; 41, 43
HMAS *Burdekin*; 9, 12, 14, 17, 53-4
HMAS *Cairns*; 14
HMAS *Cerberus*; 92, 108
HMAS *Colac*; 23, 29
HMAS *Condamine*; 12
HMAS *Cook*; 115
HMAS *Cowra*; 41, 50
HMAS *Culgoa*; 12, 90
HMAS *Derwent*; 117
HMAS *Diamantina*; 1945 9-49; 1946 50-3;
    1947 53; 1959 54-60; 1960 60-5;
    1961 65-68; 1962 69-72; 1963 72-7;
    1964 77-9; 1965 79-82; 1966 82-9;
    1967 89-94; 1968 94-8; 1969 98-103;
    1970, 104-8; 1971 108-15; 1972
    115-8; 1973 118-20; 1974 120-3;
    1975 124-7; 1976 127-32; 1977,
    133-40; 1978, 140-5; 1979, 146
    1980 152-3; badge -13, 57-8;
    construction, 9-10; launching - 10-1;
    fitout & commissioning -17-9; Bougainville
    campaign - 23-9; Japanese surrenders -
    30-41; recommissioning - 54;
    oceanographic research - 54-149;
    decommissioning - 148-9
HMAS *Diamantina II*; 157
HMAS *Dubbo*; 23, 27, 41
HMAS *Flinders*; 141, 144

HMAS Fremantle; 54
HMAS Gascoyne; 9, 12, 58, 71, 81
HMAS Gladstone; 9, 14
HMAS Hawkesbury; 12
HMAS Ibis; 140, 146
HMAS Kanimbla; 41
HMAS Kiama; 23, 27
HMAS Kimbla; 14, 149
HMAS Lachlan; 9, 12
HMAS Leeuwin; 66, 77, 83, 89, 98, 108, 128, 140
HMAS Lithgow; 23, 26-9, 33
HMAS Lusair; 24, 31, 41
HMAS Macquarie; 12
HMAS Manoora; 41
HMAS Maryborough; 14, 50
HMAS Melbourne; 29, 145
HMAS Melville; 62
HMAS Moresby; 81, 122-3, 130
HMAS Moreton; 149
HMAS Murchison; 12
HMAS Parramatta; 86
HMAS Perth; 118, 145
HMAS Onslow; 139-40, 149
HMAS Otway; 99, 100
HMAS Ovens; 129
HMAS Quality; 50
HMAS Queenborough; 43, 58, 98
HMAS Quiberon; 51-2
HMAS Quickmatch; 58
HMAS Rockhampton; 14
HMAS Rushcutter; 15, 17, 53
HMAS Samarai; 97, 107
HMAS San Michele; 27
HMAS Shoalhaven; 12, 17, 53
HMAS Stalwart; 107, 116
HMAS Stirling; 143, 150
HMAS Sydney; 64, 78
HMAS Tamworth; 14
HMAS Tarangau; 97, 107
HMAS Tingira; 64, 66
HMAS Toowoomba; 14
HMAS Torrens; 68
HMAS Vendetta; 30, 91, 120-1, 126, 138
HMAS Vampire; 85
HMAS Voyager; 77
HMAS Westralia; 42
HMAS Williamstown; 12
HMNZS Inverell; 130
HMNZS Kiama; 130
HMNZS Otago; 97
HMNZS Tui; 139-40, 143, 145
HMS Alisma; 15-6, 42
HMS Ajax; 126
HMS Andrew; 85, 88
HMS Apollo; 41
HMS Britannia; 74
HMS Brown Ranger; 85, 86, 88
HMS Buttermere; 15
HMS Cassandra; 71
HMS Centaur; 60

HMS Dampier; 63, 85-6, 88, 91
HMS Delight; 86
HMS Duke of York; 28
HMS Erica; 15
HMS Fal; 16-7, 20, 42
HMS Firedrake; 15
HMS Formidable; 41
HMS Guardian; 22
HMS Kia Kia; 34, 37, 40
HMS Rother; 12
HMS Snowflake; 16
HMS Taciturn; 72
HMS Tay; 16
HMS Tidepool; 86
HMS Verulam; 85, 88
Holloway, LCdr PE; 77, 79, 81, 154
Holloway, T; 79
Horace Lamb Institute; 95, 99, 103
Hughes, OS GA; 77
Humphrey, G; 58, 109
Hunt, Brig GP; 74, 80
Hunter, Dr WF; 99
Idemitsu Maru; 98
Ikegama, Cdr; 31
Jackson, Capt DM; 122
Jacobs, Lt AJ; 149
Jesson, E; 61
Jitts, H; 54, 59-63, 71-2, 84, 91, 96, 109
Jones, B; 105
Jude, LCdr G; 61-2, 154
Kaishin Maru; 130
Kanda, Lt-Gen M; 31-3, 45
Kaye, E; 112
Kelly, Lt-Col J; 34, 38
Kelly, T; 82
Kidd, SurgLt AL; 66
Kilburn, LStkr L; 26, 49
Kiro; 144
Kishimoto, LCdr; 34
Komata; 44
Komet; 41, 44
Krollig, LS B; 93
Kula; 144
Lady Vera; 130
Lake Eildon; 146
Lamb, R; 65
Lane, S; 22
Laughton, CPO JA; 75
Leitl, SgnLt S; 102
Lennard, Capt; 17
Lever, Lt L; 38
Lloyd, CPO F; 47, 49, 51-2
Ludwig, Dr W; 102
Lumanauw, Lt AL; 67
Lyons, Chap F; 103
Maria Augustina Bank; 76, 112, 114
Makata, Maj-Gen; 31
Marks, Cdre WBM; 70, 74, 80-3
Marquis, PO LS; 38
Marshall, Sub-Lt; 33
Matthew Flinders; 143

Maureen; 40
Mauritz, SubLt; 60
May, A; 94
May, PO J; 48
McCreddie, J; 109
McDonald, Capt N; 75
McFarlane, M; 20-1, 28, 143, 146
McGowan, Lt KH; 98
McIntyre, Dr J; 67
McKendrick, Lt J; 49
McLeod, Dr GR; 153
McMaster, Capt J; 122
McNally, Fl-Lt; 33
McVeigh, J; 93
Miller, DP; 145
Miller, LSMTP; 145
Mills, J; 105
Milton, J; 85
Morling, A/SubLt A; 95-8
Morris, Maj-Gen B; 51
Morrow, Cdre JC; 55-6
Mulholland, SurgLt; 57
Mummery, R; 124-5, 130-1, 133-7
Naruto; 52
Nauru; 34-8, 41, 44-5
Neal, L/Cpl EW; 139
Nethertons, LtCdr WJ; 20
Newell, B; 69, 70
Ngurah Raj; 76
Norling, POM (E) DJ; 74
Norman, B; 94
Nunn, LCdr RB; 75, 154
O'Callaghan, CPO; 149
Oceanography; 58-60
Orion; 41, 44
Pacific Pride; 109
Pardon, ABCK JL; 152
Parkin, Lt I; 17, 20, 49
Patamsing, Lt N; 78
Percy, Cdre RH; 150
Phipps, Cdr P; 36, 43, 45
Porter, ME1; 73
Potts, Brig AW; 24
Queensland Maritime Museum; 12, 142-3, 153, 157
Rabasch, U; 68
Ramsay, CdreSir J; 94-5, 106, 142
Read, Lt W; 49
Renwick, Capt G; 36
Rhoades, Cdre R; 65
Rice, W; 106
Ridgeway, M; 34, 44-6
Ridgewell, G; 128
River Glenelg; 34, 38, 43-45
River Burdekin; 31, 34, 38-46
River class frigates; 11-12
Rivett, N; 153
Robertson, RAdm AJ; 153
Robertson, PO; 17
Robinson, Capt; 17
Rochford, DJ; 54, 64-5, 70, 80, 92

Rogers, OD B; 86
Rolfe, Fr; 130
Rose, Cdr MG; 15-26, 28-42, 48, 130, 142, 151-4, 157
Rosier, Rev. A; 138
Rowe, Capt R; 80
Rule, LdgAirman; 66
Russian vessels; 133-4
    Admiral Vladimirsky; 137
    Novoaltaisk; 108
    Vedyansk; 63
    Vityaz; 72
Ruttle, LCdr RA; 133
Ryan, T; 24
Samejima, VAdm; 31, 33
Savige, Lt-Gen SG; 23-4, 29, 32-3, 45-6
Scott, R; 105
Scully-Power, P; 114
Seymour, PO CGF; 57
Shand, Maj; 52
Shapcott, Miss; 150
Shinkawa, LtCdr; 31
Simmonds, ABQMC K; 130
Simmonds, TC; 130
Sizeland, LCdr M; 86
Smethurst, Lt N; 55
Smith, D; 47
Smith, Capt J, USN; 118
Soeda, Capt H; 36-7
Sperring, J; 125
Sporer, A/LSCD EC; 94
Sprenger, Maj LB; 63
Stanifort, J; 54
Stephens, F; 107-9, 113-5
Stevenson, Brig JR; 34, 36, 39
Stevenson, Cmdr; 90
Stewart, Capt; 50, 52
Sturdee, Lt-Gen VAH; 24
Sue, Sgt J; 17

Sullivan, LCdr PJ; 42, 47-8, 53, 152, 154
Summers, Lt A; 76
Summers, Frayne; 75
Suzuki, LCdr N; 40
Swan, CPO W; 137
Swayn, AB CJ; 140
Sweeney, N; 109
Takenada, Capt; 33
Terry, Deborah; 62
Terry, Lt; 62
Theakstone, N; 28
Tranter, D; 66-7
Treadgold, PO W; 94-5, 105, 122, 131-2
Trienza; 37
TS *Bedford*; 55
TS *Cresswell*; 55
TS *Cunningham*; 55
TS *Endeavour*; 96
TS *Vancouver*; 54
Tyson, Russ; 24
Uksi, Lt V; 77
US Vessels
    Albert J Meyer; 133, 137
    Argo; 65
    Bartlett; 114
    Baya; 99-102
    Benjamin Stoddert; 145
    Charles H Davis; 99, 102, 139
    Edward Sinclair; 29
    Kingsport; 130, 137
    La Salle; 135
    Mizar; 137
    Monticello; 108-9
    Nautilus; 59
    Oriskany; 86
    Oklahoma City; 128
    Pathfinder; 144
    Pharis; 135
    Robinson; 148

    Safeguard; 148
    Vema; 60-1, 75, 85, 91, 93, 96
    Wilkes; 130
Union Fair; 124
Utting, J; 67
Van Avery, W; 125
Varley, LCdr MW; 85, 88, 115-6, 154
Von de Boch, Dr C; 90
Walkers Ltd; 9, 13-15, 48, 50, 53, 151
Walkley, AM; 144
Walsh, C; 131
Ward, Capt; 27
Ward, LCdr M; 89, 91, 98, 154
Waring, R; 97-8
Watts, LCdr D; 86
Watson, Lt A; 56
Wauthy, B; 71
Weir, G; 107
Weir, ID; 62
Wells, RAdm DC; 125
White, Comd NHS; 57
White, Cdr W; 99
Whitemore, Cdr ER; 97
Wilga; 81
Wilkinson, AA; 113
Wilkinson. Lt JL; 55
Wilson, SubLt S; 78
Wilson, LCdr W; 70
Winter-Irving, WCdr; 18
Wojcik, ORDWM R; 94
Wong, Sgt P; 17
Wood, AB K; 79
Woodman, J; 26
Woolstencroft, ME2 DM; 57
Wright, Capt; 60
Wyber, R; 86
Younger, Lt C; 48
Yule, LtCdr JG; 68, 71, 75, 154
Yule, JH; 70